SCOTTISH RECORD SOCIETY
NEW SERIES
VOLUME 48

THE WORK JOURNALS OF
WILLIAM DICKSON
Wright at Cockenzie (1717-1745)

SCOTTISH RECORD SOCIETY

Since its foundation in 1897 the Scottish Record Society has published numerous volumes of calendars and indices of public records and private muniments relating to Scotland. A list of the Society's publications and membership forms are available on request from the Honorary Secretary or online at www.scottishrecordsociety.org.uk.

Membership of the Society is open to all persons and institutions interested in its work.

President
George MacKenzie

Chairman
Dr Tristram Clarke

Secretary
Samantha Smart
c/o National Records of Scotland,
H.M. General Register House,
2 Princes Street,
Edinburgh, EH1 3YY

Treasurer
Tessa Spencer

Editor
Victoria Arrowsmith-Brown

THE WORK JOURNALS OF WILLIAM DICKSON
Wright at Cockenzie (1717-1745)

The Man who Helped Build Scotland's First Railway

Edited by

The 1722 Waggonway Heritage Group

SCOTTISH RECORD SOCIETY
EDINBURGH
2022

With contributions from the 1722 Waggonway Heritage Group:

Ed Bethune, Aaron Allen, Annie Rayner and Gary Donaldson

Alan Braby, Gillian Hart, Tim Rayner, Gareth Jones, Sheila Ritchie, Penny Forbes, Bryan Hickman, Malcolm Priestley

©Scottish Record Society 2022
Introduction and group photograph on the jacket©The 1722 Waggonway Heritage Group 2022
The images of William Dickson's Journals are reproduced by kind permission of the National Records of Scotland, RH9/1/212
Appendix 1 Crown copyright. National Records of Scotland, CS133/421
Appendix 5 Crown copyright. National Records of Scotland, CC8/8/95
Figures 2 and 3©Alan Braby
Detail of William Forrest's map of Haddingtonshire 1802 reproduced by permission of the National Library of Scotland, https://maps.nls.uk/index.html
Detail of C18:14/1, J. Adair, c.1686 'A mapp of the parioch of Tranent with the port of Seaton belonging to the Right Honorable the Earl of Wintoun' reproduced by permission of the Centre for Research Collections, Edinburgh University Library

All rights reserved. No part of this publication may be reproduced, stored in a retrieval system or transmitted in any form by any means, electrical, mechanical or otherwise, without first seeking and obtaining the written consent of the copyright owners.

British Library Cataloguing-in Publication Data:
A catalogue record for this book is available from the British Library

ISSN 01439448; ISBN 978-0-902054-73-8

Typeset by Victoria Arrowsmith-Brown
Printed by 4Word Ltd, Page & Print Production

CONTENTS

Preface vii

Introduction xi

Bibliography xliv

Transcription
    Book 1 (1717-1732) 1
    Book 2 (1728-1745) 157

Appendices 227

Glossary 239

Indices 251

PREFACE

This book arises from the work of the 1722 Waggonway Heritage Group, and the 'Waggonway Project' which was started by Ed Bethune to explore the history of Scotland's first railway. This wooden waggonway[1] ran from the coal mines of Tranent to the harbour and salt pans of Cockenzie and Port Seton, and is one of the most important aspects of the heritage in the local area. As such, many of the residents have taken an interest in the history, and contribute to the archaeological, historical and cultural endeavours of the museum formed by the 1722 Waggonway Heritage Group. One such endeavour was to explore what records were held relating to the Waggonway.

In 2018, as part of exploratory research looking for source material relating to the 1722 Waggonway, Bethune discovered a description of the 'Journals of William Dickson' in the National Records of Scotland (NRS) digital catalogue. It described a document containing 'extensive references to the Tranent-Cockenzie Waggonway', which proved to be absolutely correct. Together with archaeologist Alan Braby, Bethune visited the NRS and viewed the journals for the first time. Whilst on that occasion, on account of the challenging handwriting and spelling, it was a struggle to fully get to grips with the full significance of the text, they were able to read enough to know that these documents would provide a wealth of information relating to the areas of research in which the 1722 Waggonway Heritage Group was concerned.

Photographs of the pages were purchased from the NRS, and members began meeting to work on transcribing the text. When the transcription was finished, a smaller team of members who had training in palaeography began the checking phase while the transcription project was proposed to the Scottish Record

---

[1] Canmore Id: 55012.

Society. As it was known the 300th anniversary was coming in 2022, time was of the essence, but thanks to the hard work and collaboration of the 1722 Waggonway Heritage Group and the Scottish Record Society, the work journals that Dickson wrote are now published – three hundred years after he began work on Scotland's first railway.

We would like to thank several people for their help on this project. First of all, thanks are given to the staff of the archives which made this project possible. The staff of the National Records of Scotland not only gave access to the Dickson journals and appended material, but also helped with photography and expert advice. The map images of the National Library of Scotland's world-class digital collection of maps enabled us to understand *where* Dickson was working, and we are also grateful for their permission to use the detail from the Forrest map. Likewise, we are thankful for the expert help with research queries offered by the staff of the National Mining Museum and the John Gray Centre. One cannot help but be struck by how richly endowed Scotland is in terms of its archival provision, and we are grateful for all the help we received.

We would also like to thank Dr Alex Murdoch and Dr Darren Layne for their help in identifying Andrew Fletcher's signature in the manuscript transcribed in the first appendix. We are grateful to Sally Blackledge who first pointed us in the direction of the Fife place name 'Pickletillim', not to mention the many others who helped us puzzle this out. Professor Chris Whatley, Dr Joanna Hambly, Dr Iain Flett, Dr Simon Taylor, Catherine Smith, David Orr, Professor David Worthington, and Matthew Jarron, and many more people on Twitter, all helped us find our way to one of Robert Gordon's seventeenth-century maps which finally made the place name make sense.

A number of people gave us advice on specific industries or technologies. Dr Coralie Mills and Dr Hamish Darrah helped us with enquiries about timber, while Dr Jill Turnbull advised on glass-related matters. Dr Anthony L. Dawson not only advised on railway history and jargon, but also helped with the 2021 excavations which revealed multiple phases of wooden waggonways. George Haggarty helped us with ceramic queries, including the mysterious 'pot house' reference, while the Traditional Sail Worldwide Facebook Group helped with some of the more obscure shipbuilding terminology. Still others helped with the editing phase, including the insightful contributions (and superior spelling) of Mrs Christine Bethune and Mrs Joanna Allen.

Last, but certainly not least, we offer our sincere thanks to all those who have been involved with the 1722 Waggonway Heritage Project. They have supported us through the many archaeological, cultural and social endeavours which fed into this transcription project. Their contributions to the excavations, to the work in the museum, to the lecture series, and to the journal club have all informed our understanding of Dickson's journals. To those who helped to transcribe and to those who helped bring our understanding forward, we are grateful.

Ed Bethune, Aaron Allen, Annie Rayner and Gary Donaldson, writing for the rest of the 1722 Waggonway Heritage Group who worked so hard on this edition.

1st April 2022

INTRODUCTION

The transcription in this volume contains the work journals of the Cockenzie wright, William Dickson, who was not only a carpenter and a joiner, but also a shipwright, a cooper, a wheelwright, and a roofer. Most importantly, he was one of the men who built Scotland's first railway, the 1722 Tranent-Cockenzie Waggonway.[2] As such, he played a key role in a crucial chapter of Scotland's industrial history, and the details in the transcription below are indispensable for reconstructing this early phase of Scotland's industrialisation.[3]

Dickson left two separate work journals, which, due to some unknown court process, ended up with the various household, legal and business accounts presented to the Edinburgh Commissary Court. They ended up in the care of the National Records of Scotland (NRS).[4] The first of these volumes (B1) consists of 53 folios including covers and the endpapers, and covers the period 1717 to 1732. Volume 2 (B2) contains 45 folios, with some additional material pinned between folios 24 and 25, with a few folios torn out. Sewn into the back cover are a range of folios which appear to have been scrap paper used for stiffening the back cover. Writing practice, ecclesiastical notes and a copy of Psalm 23 are visible, but inaccessible due to the sewing. For clarity these two work journals will be referred to throughout as Books One and Two ('B1' and 'B2' – see Figure 1). Additional materials which were pertinent to Dickson's work and community have also been added as appendices at the back of the volume.

---

[2] Canmore ID: 55012.
[3] A note on the conventions used in the transcription process will be found at the end of this introductory essay.
[4] NRS, RH9/1/212, 1720-1745.

While it is clear that Dickson was the main author from the many instances of his practising the writing of his name, there is at least one other hand visible in sections of the manuscripts. At one point a man named 'Robeart' appears to have signed his name as well, so it is possible that Dickson occasionally had one of his workers take notes in the work journals.[5] It also might have been Dickson's wife helping out in the family business, though this can only be conjecture. What is more certain is that Dickson himself was not an accomplished writer. Instead his writing was functional and often minimalistic, suggesting someone who was *just* literate, and certainly not proficient in spelling or grammar.

It would appear that the purpose of the work journals was quite simply to act as memoranda for Dickson. They were to help him remember. As such, notes of how many days he worked figure heavily, as do accounts of materials and labour. Occasionally, costs and prices are noted, as with the shilling Dickson apparently charged for 'making a trap and a board and a barrow' in August of 1733.[6] It is clear that these books functioned as Dickson's accounts, and entries can be seen which demonstrate their use on reckoning days when the accounts were cleared and the money was paid: 'Desember 1722 cownted and cleard with John Gowen of all precidens'.[7] But they were more than just accounts. Dickson also wrote down personal information he wanted to remember, like the date of his anniversary, or the death of his mother.[8] Indeed, the very first entry is the well-known mnemonic rhyme, 'Thirty Days Hath

---

[5] B2, f42r. This is likely to be Robert Kinllie. See B2, f16v.
[6] B2, f5r.
[7] B1, f8v. See also B2, f23v, f24r, and f28v.
[8] B1, f42r and f51v.

September', which no doubt helped with both business and social engagements.⁹

Figure 1: *Dickson's work journals. B1 (left), B2 (right). NRS, RH9/1/212.*

While clearly intended by Dickson as a form of memory, later generations have found the journals helpful for reconstructing Scotland's industrial past. Jill Turnbull, one of Scotland's foremost experts on glass, used Dickson's journals for her PhD thesis, which was later published as a Society of Antiquaries of Scotland monograph.[10] Similarly, Dickson's writing has informed the archaeological excavations by the 1722 Waggonway Heritage Group of the Waggonway he helped to build. Indeed, if a published edition had been available earlier,

---

[9] B1, Endpaper.
[10] J. Turnbull, *The Scottish Glass Industry, 1610-1750: 'To Serve the Whole Nation with Glass'* (Edinburgh: Society of Antiquaries of Scotland, 2001), Chapter 11, esp. page 252.

other important works on the history of the Waggonway, on the coal and salt industries, or even on the York Buildings Company, might have been able to include material from Dickson's writing.[11] Through this critical edition, future generations will now have greater access.[12]

While Dickson's writings have not been used as often as they might have been, this is not to say that the area's rich industrial history has not been well covered in the literature. The industrial endeavours in the Tranent and Cockenzie area are known to go back to at least the twelfth century, and several historians have sought to explore the socio-economic, ecclesiastical and political aspects of the region's past. Both M'Neill and Worling included chapters on the medieval industry of the area.[13] Frustratingly, our understanding of the medieval industry suffers

---

[11] For examples regarding the Waggonway: M. J. T. Lewis, *Early Wooden Railways* (London: Routledge & Kegan Paul, 1974), 133, and M. J. Worling, *Early Railways of the Lothians* (Dalkeith: Midlothian District Libraries, 1991) Chapter 1. For the coal and salt industries in the area: National Coal Board, Scottish Division, *A Short History of the Scottish Coal-Mining Industry* (Edinburgh: NCB, Scottish Division, 1958), 34 and 53, and C. A. Whatley, 'A Saltwork and the Community: The Case of Winton, 1716-1719', in *TELAFNS*, 18 (1984), 45-59. For works on the YBC: A. J. G. Cummings, 'The York Buildings Company: A Case Study in Eighteenth Century Corporation Mismanagement', 2 vols (unpublished PhD Thesis, University of Strathclyde, 1980), and A. J. G. Cummings, 'Industry and Investment in the Eighteenth Century Highlands: The York Buildings Company of London', in A. J. G. Cummings and T. M. Devine (eds), *Industry, Business and Society in Scotland Since 1700: Essays Presented to Professor John Butt* (Edinburgh: John Donald Publishers Ltd, 1994), 24-42.
[12] For a similar type of publication, see David Rowand (ed.), *The Jobbing Book of Mr Waterston, A Paisley Glazier 1736-1744* (Gourock: Renfrewshire Family History Society, 2016).
[13] P. M'Neill, *Tranent and its Surroundings: Historical, Ecclesiastical, & Traditional* (Edinburgh: John Menzies & Co., 1884), Chapter 1, and Worling, *Early Railways of the Lothians*, Chapter 1.

from the traditional problem of finding source materials, though the potential for archaeology in the area is vast.[14]

From an unlikely source, we know that there were old coal workings below what would become Port Seton, as several houses related to the eighteenth-century Port Seton Glasshouse, or 'the Pavilion', fell into a coal sink in 1731 with the loss of at least two glassmakers.[15] While the Pavilion survived (see Figure 3), much damage was done, as 'The ground below is all wrought coal.'[16] A 'Cole heugh' was certainly labelled on Adair's c.1686 map of Tranent Parish.[17] While little is known about these early workings, what is clear is that there was early exploitation of the coal nearer the shore of the Firth of Forth.

By the sixteenth century there were attempts by the Setons to exploit the natural resources in the region. Harbour developments at Cockenzie in the 1590s facilitated the shipping of coal, while we are told by one family history that George Seton, tenth Lord Seton and third Earl of Winton (1584-1650) not only built a newer harbour at Port Seton, but also twelve salt

---

[14] For example, much work might be done comparing 'the Heugh' on the west of Tranent with the mine workings on the south-east of the Maiden Brig to the north of Newbattle Abbey. J. C. Carrick, *The Abbey of S. Mary Newbottle* (Edinburgh: John Menzies & Co., 1908), 87-94.

[15] Turnbull, *Scottish Glass Industry*, 258-9. A London newspaper also carried a notice: '*Edinburgh*. Three men fell into a Coal pit at *Port Seton*, and were kill'd. –At *Cockeny* some of the houses belonging to the Glass works, suddenly sunk down, and the water rushing up, several of the servants perished.' *The Gentleman's Magazine: Or, Monthly Intelligencer. For the Year 1731.*, Vol. I (London: F. Jefferies, 1731), 269.

[16] This quote, reproduced by Turnbull, comes from a 1938 history of Jacobite glass which quoted a now untraceable source, the '*Daily Post*'. See footnote 52 in Turnbull, *Scottish Glass Industry*, 258.

[17] University of Edinburgh Library, Special Collections, C18:14/1: J. Adair, c.1686, 'A mapp of the parioch of Tranent with the port of Seaton belonging to the Right Honorable the Earl of Wintoun'.

pans at Cockenzie.[18] While the larger coal was shipped to markets domestic and foreign, a profit was salvaged from the smaller waste coal, or 'panwood', by using it to evaporate sea water into marketable salt.[19] Indeed, such economic developments are a key context to the Waggonway which was later built by Dickson, as we see in them the nascent industrial complex which brought about Scotland's first railway.

The importance of these developments was not lost on contemporaries. The dedication to the fourth Earl of Winton in George Sinclair's 1669 book, *Satan's Invisible World Discovered*, gives praise for the coal and salt works, with interesting detail of mine, pan and harbour, mentioning, *inter alia*, pillars within the labyrinths and levels, and mechanical engines for drainage.[20] He also mentions the defence of the salt pans against waves from the north east, which is tempting to read as the curved gable ends still visible in the extant archaeology.[21]

By the eighteenth century the twelve salt pans and two coal heughs on the Winton estate formed the heart of a developing industrial community with such rich resources that it soon attracted the investment of the London-based York Buildings

---

[18] G. Seton, *A History of the Family of Seton During Eight Centuries*, Vol. 2 (Edinburgh: T. & A. Constable, 1896), 857-8, and Sir Richard Maitland of Lethington, *The History of the House of Seytoun to the Year M.D.LIX* (Glasgow: Maitland Club, 1829), 33, 75 and 89.

[19] T. C. Smout (ed.), 'Journal of Henry Kalmeter's Travels in Scotland, 1719-1720', in *Scottish Industrial History: A Miscellany* (Edinburgh: Scottish History Society, 1978), 16; Whatley, 'A Saltwork and the Community', 46; and M'Neill, *Tranent and its Surroundings*, 30 and 174-5.

[20] For the text, see the quotation in the 'Notes' of Sir Richard Maitland of Lethington, *The History of the House of Seytoun to the Year M.D.LIX* (Glasgow: Maitland Club, 1829), 111. For more on engines for drainage, such as the 'Egyptian Wheel' used at Culross in the earlier seventeenth century, see D. Adamson, 'A Coal Mine in the Sea: Culross and the Moat Pit', in *Scottish Archaeological Journal*, 30:1/2 (2008), 172-4.

[21] Take, for example, the Auld Kirk panhouse at Cockenzie.

Company (YBC).[22] But this investment was not into the coffers of the Seton family, as the Earl of Winton lost his estates and nearly his life in support of the Jacobite cause. After the 1715 Jacobite rebellion, the Winton estate was forfeit, and after being sold in 1719 to Robert Hackett and John Wicker for £50,300 sterling, the estate was transferred to the YBC on 6th April 1720.[23] Thus began half a century of mismanagement and financial scandal. Despite efforts to offload the estate, it would not be disposed of until the 1770s.[24]

While the overall management of the estate left much to be desired, component parts of the endeavour might be considered more successful, as the estate consisted of different ventures and was run by a series of lessees who paid rent to the York Buildings Company.[25] For example, at one point in the early eighteenth century, Cockenzie was Scotland's largest saltworks,

---

[22] Turnbull, *Scottish Glass Industry*, 239; Cummings, 'The York Buildings Company', Vol. 2, 309-11; and Worling, *Early Railways of the Lothians*, Chapter 2.

[23] Turnbull, *Scottish Glass Industry*, 239.

[24] Turnbull, *Scottish Glass Industry*, 238-9 and 265; Cummings, 'The York Buildings Company'; and M'Neill, *Tranent and its Surroundings*, 202-3.

[25] For example, 'gin' mechanisms had already been in use for lifting coal out of the mines, but the YBC appear to have built a Steam Engine at the Elphinstone pit on the Tranent estate. D. Murray, *The York Buildings Company, A Chapter in Scotch History Read Before the Institutes of Bankers and Chartered Accountants, Glasgow 19th February 1883* (Glasgow: James Maclehose & Sons, 1883), 65. Whilst Murray is cautious, note that both Cummings and Turnbull accept the engine as having actually been used at Tranent. Cummings, 'The York Buildings Company', Vol. 2, 310, and Turnbull, *Scottish Glass Industry*, 241-2. One lease holder, the architect William Adam, was also described as being 'salt grieve', or oversman of the salt pans, at Cockenzie. For more on the role of the grieve, see Whatley, 'A Saltwork and the Community', 45-59.

producing and selling about 20,000 bushels of salt a year, or just above 8 per cent of the national output.[26]

Looking just at the lessees of the coal and salt works, there does not seem to have been longevity in the endeavours. Thomas Mathie, merchant, and John Horsely, agent for the YBC, leased first the barony of Tranent from 11th November 1721 and then the coal works from 15th May 1722.[27] From 1727 new tenants took over. YBC agents George Buchan and the celebrated architect and industrialist, William Adam, took over the estate first, but added a lease of the coal and salt works at Martinmas 1728. Next came a series of lessees from 1736, of which the particulars are not wholly clear. Included were Adam's brother-in-law, Archibald Robertson, and Francis Grant, the brother of Sir Archibald Grant of Monymusk, demonstrating a disconcertingly high turnover in the first two decades of the Waggonway's working life. Indeed, in 1778, just before the YBC finally managed to sell the Winton estate, it was pointed out that the yield of the estate was down to £300 per annum, though in 1719 it had been over £1,000 per annum.[28]

While the management left much to be desired, the continued use of the Waggonway long after the YBC was gone is a testament to the technological successes of the wider operation. Subsequent owners converted the railway to iron rails in 1815,

---

[26] C. A. Whatley, *The Scottish Salt Industry: An Economic and Social History 1570-1850* (Aberdeen: Aberdeen University Press, 1988), 13 and 39, and Whatley, 'A Saltwork and the Community', 45, 55 and 57. We are grateful to Professor Whatley for sharing his research and data with us.
[27] Turnbull, *Scottish Glass Industry*, 242, 248.
[28] NRS, CS133/421 (see Appendix 1); Turnbull, *Scottish Glass Industry*, 265; and M'Neill, *Tranent and its Surroundings*, 5-10 and 202-3. For valuable details of the sale of the estate from 1778 to 1779, see Seton, *History of the Family of Seton*, Vol. 2, 1009-18. For an assessment of Adam's success as salt grieve, see Whatley, 'A Saltwork and the Community', 55-6.

and it continued to carry coal from mine to harbour through much of the nineteenth century. Coal and salt continued to be extracted into the twentieth century. While the business dealings of individual owners or lessees might not have been successful, the industrial enterprise itself has a long and important history.[29]

Much of the work noted in the journals is what would generally be expected of a wright. Throughout the books we see Dickson and his men putting up partition walls, making window frames, sorting out doors and laying flooring. Other aspects of Dickson's work were more specialised. One might not expect to find entries for the making of furniture, such as 'winged tables', or the repair of wheels, let alone coopering work, but Dickson undertook all of these specialised tasks.[30] He was very much a 'Jack of all trades', but this versatility made him indispensable in the industrial setting in which he lived and worked. Because he was able to do a range of woodworking tasks, he was able to undertake work in many different areas.

Most important was Dickson's work on the Waggonway, as it was Scotland's first railway. The Tranent to Cockenzie Waggonway has long been noted as being constructed in 1722,

---

[29] It should be pointed out that Dickson's Waggonway sits in a wider context of proto-industrialisation. There were attempts from at least 1606 to devise a waggonway system in Scotland (*RPC*, 1604-1607, 278-9), though it appears this was never built. There were certainly impressive coal mining operations in the sixteenth- and seventeenth-centuries up and down the Firth of Forth, including the moat pit and Egyptian wheel at Culross, the other waggonways built at places such as Pittenweem, or Sir John Erskine of Alva's canal works. D. Adamson, 'A Coal Mine in the Sea: Culross and the Moat Pit', in *Scottish Archaeological Journal*, Vol. 30 (1–2), 161–199; Whatley, *Scottish Salt Industry*, 24; R. A. Lodge, 'Kellie Lodging, 23 High Street, Pittenweem, Fife: A Reappraisal of its Origins and History', in *PSAS*, 150 (2021), 70 (John Sime's map); B. F. Duckham, *A History of the Scottish Coal Industry, Vol. 1 1700-1815: A Social and Industrial History* (Newton Abbot: David & Charles, 1970), 220.

[30] B1, f7r, f16r, f36r and f15r.

with a wide variety of texts through the years stating that the date of construction was in that year. However, evidence or source material relating to these claims has always been elusive, with David Murray's 1883 publication of selected material relating to the business dealings of the York Buildings Company being as close as one can get to a reliable, but still unsubstantiated, source.[31]

The journals of William Dickson change everything. Dickson's extensive descriptions of his work around Cockenzie, Port Seton and Prestonpans not only throw a bright and unexpected spotlight onto the details of the coal, salt, glass and brewing industries, but finally provide a chance to elucidate the inception, timescales and technicalities of the construction and maintenance of Scotland's earliest railway. His descriptions of what was involved in constructing waggons are detailed enough to show us that although coal waggons of this period were predominantly constructed from wood, they did require iron work for certain fittings, such as the coal doors.[32] Similarly, he provides superb detail relating to the volume of work required for maintaining and replacing the perishable parts of waggons, with extensive entries detailing the manufacture of 'wagen wheals'.[33]

Additionally, entries relating to 'sawen realls for the ows of the wagenway' confirm that Dickson was indeed engaged in the construction of the track components.[34] His role in facilitating this industry was detailed and fully engaged. But it is Dickson's entries relating to the construction of the Waggonway itself which give the most intriguing insight into not just this Waggonway, but potentially early wooden railways across the

---

[31] Murray, *York Buildings Company*.
[32] B1, f23v.
[33] E.g.: B1, f3v.
[34] B2, f28v.

British Isles. From his first recorded construction of rails on 7th May 1722, there follow over a busy twenty-two-year period, three distinct groups of entries relating to work on the construction and maintenance of the Waggonway. The first is 1722-5, the second 1728-30, and the third 1743-4 (see Figure 2).

These three phases of work include all the jobs expected, from 'maken at the realle' and 'sawen wagen wheals', typical tasks for constructing a wooden railway, to more general references of longer spells of work, with months at a time devoted to 'worken at the wagenway'.[35] Further insight into the logistics of the construction of an infrastructure project on this scale in the eighteenth century can be found in Dickson's building of a 'leatren' (latrine).[36] Built immediately prior to the commencement of the works in 1722, this was an essential facility for the many workers required.

However, the three distinct phases, with little or no activity directly relating to this particular industry falling in between these timeframes, are intriguing, and the question of what their significance might be is something which has driven the Waggonway Project's research. But in September 2021 archaeology and historical research dovetailed neatly together, for during the Waggonway Project's excavations on the route of the original Waggonway, a unique discovery would change our understanding. The archaeological evidence showed that rather than one wooden Waggonway being constructed, there had in fact been three wooden railways, each one laid on top of the last. When comparing the phasing in the ground with Dickson's journal records, it soon became clear that the timeline of his work matched the archaeology.

Adding to this developing clarity, the industrialists who held the 'tack' on the coal and salt works, and therefore the

---

[35] B1, f7v, f15v, f22r, f23r; B2, f3r, respectively.
[36] B1, f11r.

Waggonway, during each phase are known. The standout name is William Adam, the celebrated Scottish architect, who was tacksman during phase two (1728-30), but 'Thomas Mathe', another of the tacksmen, features heavily in these journals providing yet more compelling linkage between this text and the archaeological record.[37] When we examine Adam's phase two, Dickson's entries show an intense and systematic construction period, indicating well scheduled and organised work which corresponds well with the second and best constructed of the three waggonways discovered. It has the hallmarks of sound engineering, and an architectural touch, with a neatly packed, cobbled walking surface for the horses between the rails of four-foot gauge wooden track.

Another fascinating feature of the three waggonway phases is that the first phase takes Dickson far longer than the second and third. The descriptors used for the work in phase 1 include 'mendin the wagenway', a frequent reference to the fact that he has need to repair it. This terminology does not appear in the second and third phases, building up the impression that during the first phase, the entire operation from design and scheduling to construction was being undertaken by people who may not have done this before; after all, this was the first railway in Scotland and building waggonways had not been done here before. The picture is completed by Dickson's order and efficiency for phases two and three, both being completed in around eighteen to twenty-four months, despite being no less of a feat of engineering.

---

[37] For more on Thomas Mathie, see Turnbull, *Scottish Glass Industry*, 195 and 242-3; K. Zickermann, 'Scottish Merchant Families in the Early Modern Period', in *Northern Studies*, 45 (2013), 106-7; Peter M'Neill, *Prestonpans and Vicinity: Historical, Ecclesiastical, and Traditional* (Tranent: P. M'Neill, 1902), 155 and 162; and appendices 2, 4 and 5 of this volume.

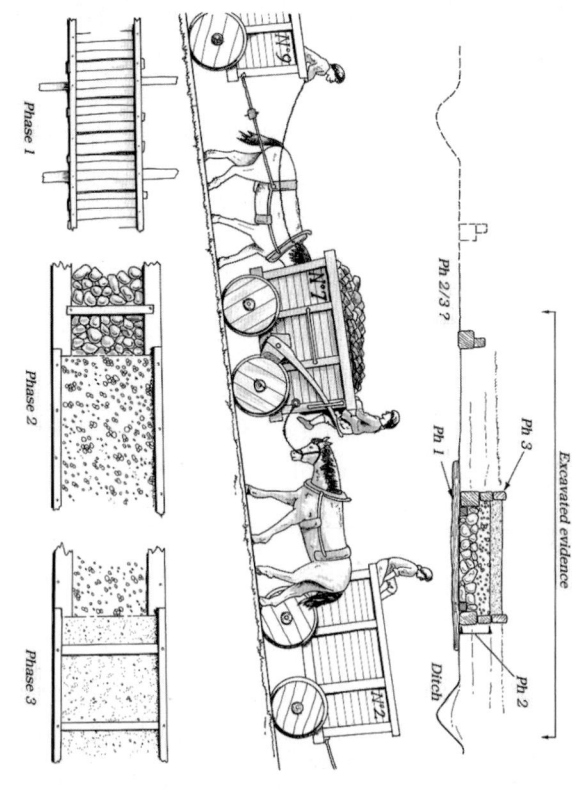

Figure 2: Reconstruction of the phases of the Waggonway based on archaeological excavations, September 2021. Created by Alan Braby.

Dickson's journals provide a new clarity to the history of early railways. They provide contemporary, documentary evidence to illuminate our understanding of how, and how quickly, these waggonways were constructed. As such, the importance of what was written in these pages cannot be understated.

Another area of Dickson's work, which can offer unparalleled insights into the industries of eighteenth-century Cockenzie, includes the frequent and copious work he undertakes at the town's salt pans. At the time he was working, the Cockenzie salt works, made up of at least 12 salt pan buildings, was responsible for around 8 per cent of the total national output of this industry and the regularity of Dickson's activity here is evidence of this. Indeed, Professor Whatley's paper on the Winton (Cockenzie) Salt Works provides excellent insight into the many ancillary industries which were required to support the size of works being operated here.[38] Dickson's activity adds to and complements this research, with the great variety of specific terminology contained in these journals providing a unique insight into the industry.

We understand from Whatley that although salt pans would boil constantly, with production close to continuous, there were also extensive periods of 'down time', as the corrosive nature of salt production and the coastal location meant equipment and infrastructure needed frequent repair.[39] Dickson's work supports this analysis, with many references to repairs to pan roofs, 'panstands' (supports), 'panwands' (long poles for raising water with a bucket), 'spoutes' (channels for running brine into the pans), 'sallt cart wheals' (salt cart wheels), wheelbarrows, and 'pump and tap trie' mechanisms (water pumps).[40] This wealth of

---

[38] Whatley, 'A Saltwork and the Community', 45-59.
[39] Ibid., 47-9.
[40] B1, f18v; f9v; f29r; f9v; f16r; f10r and f23v respectively.

information confirms our understanding of the equipment required for the salt-making process, from collecting seawater in the 'bucket pots' (rock-cut seawater collection ponds),[41] to the assemblage of tools and infrastructure required for the transport and boiling of the brine.

Our understanding of the Cockenzie salt works is not only improved by better understanding of the paraphernalia mentioned in these journals; we also see the human and geographical elements, with the names of salters being attributed to the bucket pots which Dickson was working on, such as, 'Robeart Donelson bucket patt'. We also learn of a Fife salt-panning site which was previously unknown. The forgotten place name of 'Pickeltillem pan' is therefore a particular highlight, referring to a salt-panning operation swallowed up by Kirkcaldy, Fife, sometime in the mid-eighteenth century.[42]

Alongside the larger scale and well recognised coal mining and salt production, which were the backbone of the industrial landscape in the lands of the former Winton Estate, there were also other industrial processes in the area. The pottery produced at Prestonpans is a prime example. However, a short-lived glassworks appears to have been in operation at Port Seton at just the time when Dickson was engaged in this area. There are references to constructing boxes for packing glass.[43] Also of note is his use of the term 'gllearis', or glaziers. After all, glass making was a specialist industry and was new to the area in the early part of the 18th century, as Jill Turnbull's seminal text alludes to.[44] Indeed, records for this glass works are so scarce,

---

[41] E.g.: B1, f29r.
[42] B1, f16v. Several people helped us to identify this, and they are named and thanked in the Preface.
[43] E.g.: 'maken 6 bockess for paken glleas at Port Seaton and puten up a boord for the glleaeris thear' (B1, f29r).
[44] Turnbull, *Scottish Glass Industry*, Chapter 11.

that Dickson's handful of references are some of the best evidence which can help pin down the dates of its operation.

Importantly, Dickson also uses the term 'Pavilion' when describing the glassworks,[45] terminology which has been used relatively recently to refer to the final remaining glassworks building, also known as the 'Inkbottle House' (see Figure 3).[46] This unusually shaped building has long intrigued locals and historians alike, yet the use of it to describe the glassworks in 1728 provides crystal-clear evidence that the building which survived until the mid-twentieth century was indeed the 'Glasshouse' or 'Pavilion', with the name living on within the community and consequently being recorded on Ordnance Survey maps.[47]

Figure 3: *Postcard of the 'Pavilion', or the 'Inkbottle'. Note the later association with Johnnie Cope. Collections of the 1722 Waggonway Heritage Centre, Cockenzie.*

---

[45] E.g.: 'worken at the Glleashous rueff or Pavellen ruff' (B1, f30v).
[46] Canmore ID: 368962. See also Appendix 3.
[47] NLS, OS, 25 Inch, Haddingtonshire IX.2, 1892 (1894), and Canmore ID: 368962.

Dickson did a great deal of work on various kinds of boats and ships. Some were specified as barques or sloops, while others were noted as being a 'meal ship' or a 'malt ship'.[48] Others came from abroad, as with the 'Danish' ships, or were specified as belonging to various named masters, highlighting the shipping networks and the brisk trade of the ports around Cockenzie, Port Seton and Prestonpans. While some ships were dedicated to particular cargoes, many carried whatever cargo was commissioned, whether boxes of indigo or barrels of gingerbread.[49] As such, the usage of space in the hold varied from voyage to voyage. In order to ensure stability of the cargo or the ballast in rough seas, partitions called 'bulkheads' had to be erected before each voyage.[50] Dickson spent a lot of his time working on these.[51] It would appear that these bulkheads were temporary and movable, as one entry notes how Dickson and his man spent half a day taking one down and putting it up again.[52]

Aside from securing the cargo, they also needed to protect it, and much effort went into lining the holds of ships with planks called 'bukdellen'.[53] In 1725 he laid a bukdellen, 'in the sleoup calead the Beatte', while in 1733 he laid, 'a bugkdailin in the meal shipe'.[54] The frequency of such entries is important, as it suggests regular damage from water. Indeed, another entry relating to a sloop mentions 'putting up the pomp wall and laying

---

[48] For examples: B1, f2r; B1, f38r; B2, f5r and B2, f22v respectively.
[49] Ian Hustwick, *The George of Port Seton* (Caithness: Whittles, 2000), 39, 56-9, and 65-73.
[50] Ibid., 44.
[51] For just two examples, see his work on the ships of John Mathie or Stephan Jolly. B1, f2v and f38r.
[52] B1, f15v.
[53] See DSL/DOST: 'Buk-denning'.
[54] B1, f18v and B2, f5r.

down some of the wiring in the hould'.⁵⁵ Such entries suggest repairs to the infrastructure for managing leaking water.⁵⁶

While it does not appear that he built any ships from scratch, Dickson regularly repaired ships. Ian Hustwick, in his meticulous examination of a late-seventeenth-century ship, *The George of Port Seton*, discusses why maintenance was essential after nearly every voyage: ships were made of wood, which was prone to expansion and shrinking, not to mention rotting, so maintenance was necessary whenever a ship reached port.⁵⁷ Dickson's journals bear testament to this labour-intensive aspect of the shipping industry.

He worked on the frames of ships, as with his work on keels and keel-ribs. After laying a bukdellen in a ship belonging to 'Sepkaar Cheapllean' he then spent two days 'menden the kellrebs and the cudell abuf the kiell'.⁵⁸ Another 1721 entry was, 'for puten in the bates in the kiell and the cheans and the bead for the kiell'.⁵⁹ While it is not always clear what some of the nautical jargon means, in the context of working on a ship at the harbour, the words like 'keel' make clear that his work often dealt with the very structure of ships and not just with refitting their holds. Indeed, in 1741 he was called to Musselburgh to help the harbour master with a shipwreck. A sloop had apparently been 'cast on the rocks' on the east side of the harbour, and Dickson was able to help fix the damage and set up new bulkheads.⁶⁰

Other ship-work was more auxiliary in nature. He spent three days working on the cabin of Andrew Yonge's ship, while

---

⁵⁵ B1, f38r.
⁵⁶ For more on pump technology in ships of the period, see Hustwick, *George of Port Seton*, 11-13.
⁵⁷ Hustwick, *George of Port Seton*, 12 and 43-4.
⁵⁸ B1, f33r.
⁵⁹ B1, f2r.
⁶⁰ B2, f22v.

another time he mended 'the skeapers bead for Mr Mathe use'.[61] He also made a sea chest for Thomas Mathie, younger, demonstrating that many, if not all, of the needs of a ship's crew might be dealt with by the local craftsmen. Some ship-related tasks were more obscure, however, as with the putting up of 'steallen' or the making of 'coines'.[62] Were these references to stealers and quoins? While we may not be completely certain about these terms, the point here is that Dickson knew, emphasising the breadth of his technical knowledge.

As ale and beer were of critical importance to the diet of all men, women and children, it is little surprise that Dickson was frequently employed in the brewing and malting industries. He often noted down working at breweries and brewhouses in both Cockenzie and Prestonpans. In one case, he made a trellis for a brewhouse, presumably to allow airflow while excluding animals, while another time he noted down making a 'crib' for the copper used to boil the water and a 'false bottom' for a brewing vat, which was a form of filtration system used to remove the mashed grain from the liquid 'wort'.[63] He also recorded altering and sealing the 'coolers', which were trays for quickly lowering the temperature of the wort during the brewing process.[64]

Aside from the infrastructure, Dickson also repaired brewing 'lowems', or tools, and even fabricated new ones, as with the two new 'mask-ruthers', which were the distinctive paddle-like implements for stirring the mash.[65] He made larger tools, such

---

[61] B1, f5v and f37r respectively.
[62] See for examples B1, f34r and f37v.
[63] B1, f6r and f15r.
[64] B1, f36v. A surviving cooler can be seen at the brewery at Lacock Abbey. See also, S. Peachey, *Food and Cookery in Elizabethan and Early Stuart England, Volume 18: Brewing and Malting Equipment and Ingredients* (Bristol: Stuart Press, 2019), 38 and 43-4.
[65] B2, f24r and B1, f7r, respectively.

as sleds for moving the casks, and even did coopering work, 'girding' tuns and vats.[66] While the versatility of his woodworking skills was clearly useful, he was also paid for related tasks, as when he went to Edinburgh to source the copper, and then worked with the coppersmith to install it at Prestonpans.[67] At one point he even moved, or 'flit', an entire brewery from Prestonpans to Cockenzie.[68]

Similarly, his wright skills were crucial for the local malting industry which kept the breweries running. Malt kilns, barns and lofts are all mentioned. In one entry, he made a funnel for a malt loft.[69] At one point we find him 'maken the couch for the mallt', whilst another entry records the timber needed for the roof of the malt barn.[70] While work was also done on malt lofts, more of Dickson's attention went to the building and upkeep of malt kilns, which were used in roasting malted bere to stop the germination process.[71] He made cooms, or wooden frameworks, for the use of masons building undisclosed parts of a kiln, and he also did a great deal of work making doors, windows and floors for the kilns.[72] One was a 'lifting door in the floor', whilst another was a door at the stair head of the kiln 'buste', or fire chamber, giving intriguing clues about the fabric of these lost buildings.[73] One of the more common tasks involved the regular repair of kiln 'ribs', which according to DSL/DOST were strips

---

[66] B2, f10v; B1, f36r; and B1, f15r respectively.
[67] B1, f36r.
[68] B2, f13v.
[69] B2, f14v.
[70] B2, f10v and f42r, respectively.
[71] Several excellent examples can still be seen today, as with the renovated, but intact, kiln at Preston Mill near East Linton (Canmore ID: 347489), or the ruined kiln to the north of Haddington's Court Street (Canmore ID: 367716).
[72] B1, f1r; B1, f45v; and B1, f43r.
[73] B1, f43r and f45v, respectively.

of wood laid across support beams to make a lattice-work floor for the kiln's drying chamber.[74] The frequency of such work speaks volumes about the labour-market needs just to keep the brewing industry operating.

Many other forms of work also appear, from working at a 'pot house', to building a horse stall, or 'triffice', and a manger at Cockenzie House.[75] Some work was more agricultural in focus, as when he enclosed hay fields in Seton park, or worked on a swine shed.[76] Other work was more closely related to the building trades. He often put up scaffolding for masons to work from, and he did work on the lade and ark of a local water mill.[77]

As with many wrights of the day, we also see hints of undertaking, as when he made the 'dead cofean' for Janet Dawson.[78] As wrights built the coffins, many wrights also 'undertook' the care and burial of corpses.[79] At least one other burial was mentioned, though Dickson's role in this is not wholly clear.[80]

A perennial problem for Dickson was the sourcing of his raw materials, and many entries deal with obtaining timber. Three types of timber are visible: recycled, imported and locally

---

[74] DSL/DOST: 'Reb, *n.*', 2.a. In November 1736 he repaired ribs (B2, f11v), and then again in September 1737 (B2, f12r), possibly indicating the annual need for repairs of kiln ribs. As they were wooden parts in a stone structure which was regularly heated and cooled, this would make sense.

[75] B2, f41r and B1, f14v, respectively. The stall and manger may have been in the stables still visible in the western wing of Cockenzie House.

[76] B1, f26r and f35r.

[77] E.g.: B2, f41r and B1, f14v, respectively.

[78] B2, f19r.

[79] For more on this, see E. C. Sanderson, *Women and Work in Eighteenth-Century Edinburgh* (London: Macmillan, 1996), 64-71, and A. Allen, *Building Early Modern Edinburgh: A Social History of Craftwork and Incorporation* (Edinburgh: Edinburgh University Press, 2018), 75, 174-5 and 196, note 179.

[80] B1, f44r.

sourced. Due to the scarcity of larger timber in Scotland, old wood would have been reused where possible. It is known that wooden railways in England made use of recycled timbers from shipwrecks, and Dickson cryptically mentions 'wrack' and 'deall' in one entry relating to timbers, though how much of his work was done with reclaimed timber is not clear.[81]

More certain are the entries for imported timber, which fits our understanding of Scotland's reliance on Norwegian and Baltic imports. Scotland had limited supplies of oak, let alone old-growth timber, meaning that most building timbers needed to be imported. Indeed, the timber trade with Denmark-Norway was so important in the early seventeenth century that Norwegian historians today refer to the period as the 'Scottish Period', and the actual timber trade as the *Skottehandelen*, or 'Scottish Trade'.[82] Even by the early eighteenth century we can see how important such imports were. Dickson makes several references to timber coming in on Danish ships. We see full trees and deals, or planks, showing both unprocessed and processed timber.[83]

---

[81] Richard Carlton and Alan Williams 'The Discovery and Excavation of the Willington Waggonway', in Dominique Bell (ed.), *Setting the Standard: Research Reports on the Willington Waggonway of 1785, the Earliest Standard Gauge Railway Yet Discovered* (Newcastle: Tyne & Weir Archives & Museums, 2018), 58-9; B1, f47r.

[82] K. Newland, 'The Acquisition and Use of Norwegian Timber in Seventeenth-Century Scotland', in *Vernacular Architecture*, 42 (2011), 72; M. Lorvik, 'Mutual Intelligibility of Timber Trade Terminology in the North Sea Countries During the Time of the 'Scottish Trade'', in *Nordic Journal of English Studies* 2:2 (2003), 225; A. Lillehammer, 'The Scottish-Norwegian Timber Trade in the Stavanger Area in the Sixteenth and Seventeenth Centuries', in T. C. Smout (ed.), *Scotland and Europe, 1200–1850* (Edinburgh: John Donald, 1986), 97; and A. Crone and C. M. Mills, 'Timber in Scottish Buildings, 1450-1800: A Dendrochronological Perspective', in *PSAS*, 142 (2012), 329-69.

[83] E.g.: B1, f17r and f29r.

Finally, we see Dickson cutting timber locally. While it is not always clear how he transported the timber, he clearly felled trees in the Lothians, and also sought timber in Fife. He tells us that he cut a 'plan trie' at Seton for waggon wheels, and ash trees at Newton Hall in Yester Parish.[84] Unfortunately, we do not learn if this was prearranged felling, or a response to trees downed in storms, but we can clearly see that some locally-cut timber was used by Dickson. It is known that the Winton estate had considerable 'ornamental' timber resources in the 1780s, including numerous ash, plane and elm, though whether these were utilised in Dickson's generation is not clear.[85]

Interestingly, we also find the full range of technologies being employed for processing the timber, including both riving and sawing. We see him 'cutting and cleaving' wood for use during Cockenzie's annual fair in late October or early November.[86] We see him 'breaken out the timer' and 'pearten the trieas that cam out of John Mathe shep'.[87] Such references to *riving*, or splitting wood apart with wedges before planing the pieces into boards, can be contrasted with the many instances of *sawing* timber, which often involved a two-man saw and a saw pit.[88] Indication is also given of the size of the trees being processed, as with the list of 'bignes' of the trees at the harbour, which ranged from 37

---

[84] B2, f25r and f27v respectively. Newton Hall is found on one of Adair's maps, south-west of Yester and Gifford. NLS, Adv.MS.70.2.11 (Adair 10), John Adair, 'East Lothian', 1682 (manuscript).
[85] Seton, *History of the Family of Seton*, 1014-15.
[86] B2, f13r. For more on the time of the fairs and the events, such as horse racing, see J. D. Marwick, *List of Markets and Fairs Now and Formerly Held in Scotland: With Notes as to the Charters, Acts of Parliament, and Other Documents by Which the Right to Hold Them has been Conferred* (Glasgow: Royal Commissioners on Market Rights and Tolls, 1890), 31, and Whatley, 'A Saltwork and the Community', 52-3.
[87] B1, f14v and f26r.
[88] E.g.: 'an day with Adam Buernet at Seaton sawen a pies of wood'. B1, f3r.

to 60 inches - presumably meaning diameter - and from 13.5 to 17 feet in length.[89]

In terms of the *places* where Dickson worked, he recorded a wide range of geographical locations, both around Cockenzie and Port Seton, and much further afield (see Figure 4). He occasionally travelled for work, with jobs in Fife, Midlothian and various places across East Lothian. We find him working on a pan at Pickletillum, near Kirkcaldy.[90] In February 1744 he noted down 'goien to Abedouer for wagen whell'. With a series of entries below reading '6 days' and 'ditto', it would appear that he was working on waggon wheels in Fife for over a month. Finally, on 2nd April he noted down, 'now returned from Fieff'.[91]

In the Lothians, Dickson had unspecified business at Dalkeith.[92] Occasionally he travelled for specialist metalwork, as with his trip to Edinburgh for copperwork.[93] Other destinations were in his home shire, Haddingtonshire (East Lothian). While much of the timber was imported via the harbour, he also travelled to obtain his raw materials, from places like the Heugh at Tranent, Clerkington, Humbie Wood, and Newton Hall, in Yester Parish.[94] Work on the Waggonway occasionally involved at least a forty-five minute walk, as when taking timber up the hill to Tranent, or working on the coal gin which lifted the coal out of the pit on Tranent Moor.[95] Wear and

---

[89] B2, Front Endpaper.
[90] B1, f16v.
[91] B2, f26r.
[92] B2, f2r. Whatley mentions that iron plates for repairing the salt pans were purchased from the iron mill at Dalkeith, though whether Dickson had anything to do with this is not clear. Whatley, 'A Saltwork and the Community', 48.
[93] B1, f36r.
[94] B1, f9r; B2, f3v, f4r, and f27v.
[95] B1, f3r, f47r; B2, f27r. M'Neill tells us that the last use of a gin to remove coal in the area was in 1844. *Tranent and its Surroundings*, 30.

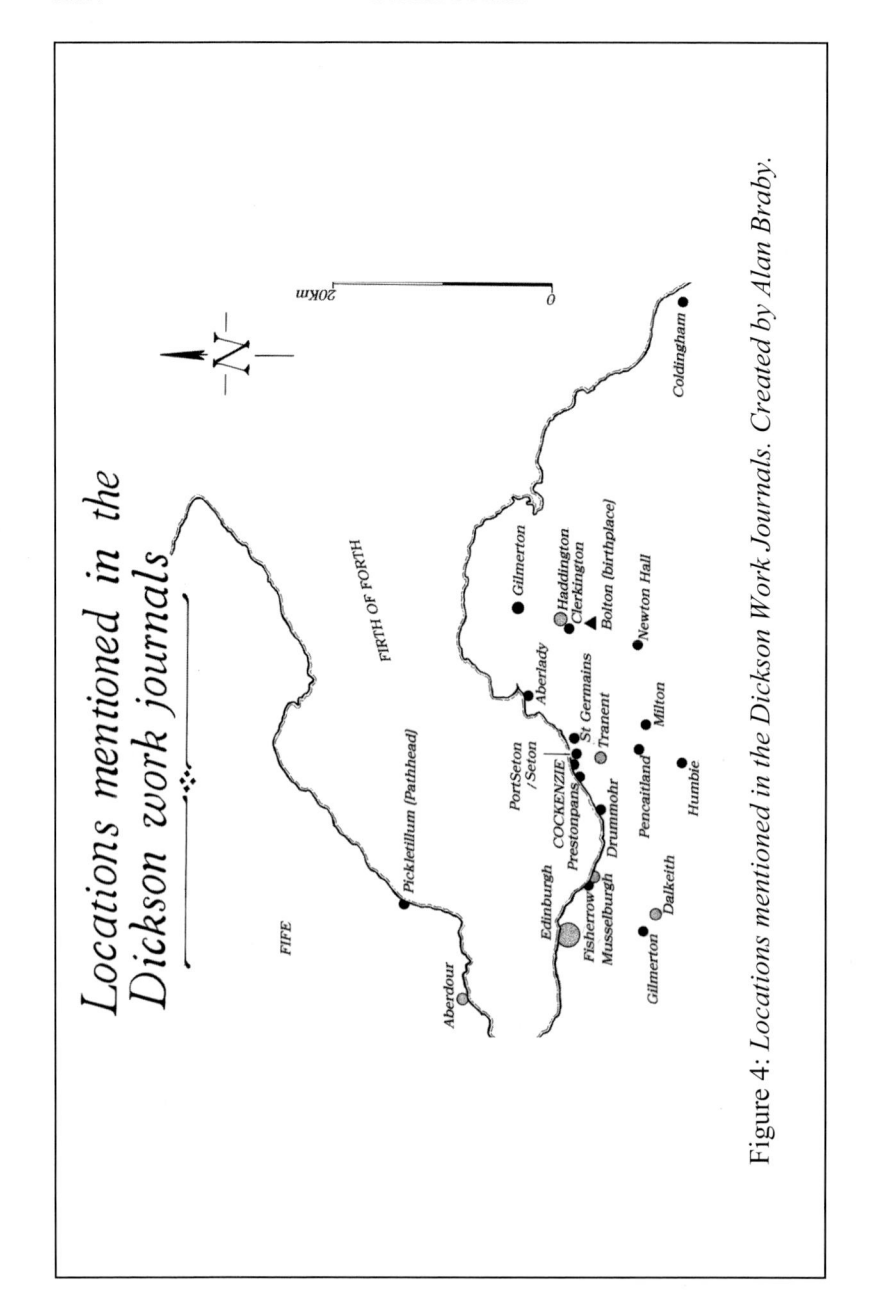

Figure 4: *Locations mentioned in the Dickson Work Journals. Created by Alan Braby.*

tear in the Waggonway system meant much work had to be done making new wheels, and he often travelled to places like Pencaitland, Milton and Clerkington for wheels, though it is unclear if this was outsourcing of labour or simply obtaining the materials and making them on the spot.[96] Other work was nearer the coast, as with the many jobs done at Musselburgh or Aberlady.[97] For some work, only a customer is mentioned rather than a place of work, as with the lath sawn for St Germains, or the deals sawn for Lord Drummore's house, which is likely to have been Drummohr House near Musselburgh.[98]

Most of Dickson's work took place in and around Cockenzie, and several place names are mentioned in the work journals. Much work was done in the settlement to the west, Prestonpans, including work for the local merchant family, the Mathies.[99] He occasionally worked at the neighbouring settlements of Seton and Port Seton, which like Cockenzie were associated with the Seton family before the forfeiture of the Earl of Winton's estates in the wake of the failed 1715 Jacobite uprising.[100] Several places relating to the estate are mentioned. When held by the Seton family, the seat was Seton Palace in Seton, but from the seventeenth century Cockenzie House had been the administrative hub of the Cockenzie elements of the Winton estate, and Dickson often worked at 'the House'. Details are given, including the Nursery, Kitchin, Green Room, and Garret

---

[96] B1, f15v, f51r; B2, f3v, and f4r.
[97] Musselburgh: B2, 22v and Aberlady: B2, f6r.
[98] B2, f5r and f32r respectively.
[99] For work in Prestonpans see: B1, f33v, f34v, f35r, f36r, f36v, f37r, f44r, f45r, f46r; B2, f7r, f10v, f13v, f14r, f23v, f33r, f42v. For more on the Mathie family, see the appendices.
[100] Seton: B1, f41v, B2, f25r; Port Seton: B2, f12r, and f19v; forfeiture: M'Neill, *Tranent and its Surroundings*, 197-8.

in the east end, not to mention the brewery and malt facilities.[101] Mention is also made in the journals of 'the wearhous', which may refer to the Hanseatic barn attached to Cockenzie House.[102] Naturally he worked on a 'salltgirenell', but does this also refer to the Hanseatic Barn?[103] Clearly more work is needed on the history of this early industrial complex, and Dickson's journals will prove useful in this endeavour.

Aside from the House, mention is made of other sites in Cockenzie. As the coal was mainly exported via the harbour facilities, the 'coal falde', or storage yard, was clearly an important depot.[104] Dickson gives important details of this facility, as with his references to working on the barn at the coal fald.[105] He also tells us he hung gates and worked on a dyke around the coal fald, giving the impression of a reasonably-secure yard for storing this important export.[106]

Other places were mentioned in Dickson's Cockenzie, including a smithy and a school.[107] While Dickson often worked away from home, he also did a great deal of work in properties associated with his own trade. Dickson mentions a 'wright workhouse'. He often refers to 'the close', which presumably

---

[101] For Dickson's work on 'the House', or Cockenzie House, see B1, f1r, f5r, f8v, f9v, f11r, f14r, f14v, f15r, f17r, f19r, f21r, f22v, f25r, f25v, f26r, f27v, f34r, f37r, f37r, f41r, f42v, f43v; B2, f12r, f12v, f14v, f23v-f24r, f24r, and f27r. See also appendices 2 and 4A.

[102] B1, f7v, f28v, etc. See the Canmore entry for the House and Barn (Canmore ID: 53644).

[103] B1, f17r. Note also John Greg's salt girnel in Prestonpans: B2, f7r.

[104] See for example, B1, f10r, etc. Even today, the 1722 Waggonway Heritage Group's Museum, to the south of Cockenzie Harbour on West Harbour Road, includes the place name 'Coalfauld' as part of the postal address.

[105] Barn: B1, f21v and f23r.

[106] Gates: B1, f10r, 30r and f44v; Dike: B1, f10v.

[107] B2, f9r.

was where he lived. Finally, he mentions a 'sawing shed'.[108] As such, we see a wright with a varied work pattern which encompassed several shires and spanned the Firth of Forth.

One of the most compelling elements of the work journals is what they tell us about the people of eighteenth-century Cockenzie; especially when set alongside other records. For example, much can be learned of Dickson himself, and of his family. William Dickson was baptised on 22nd December 1688 in Bolton, near Haddington, East Lothian.[109] His parents were Robert Dickson and Sibilla Henderson. This is possibly the Sibilla Henderson who was baptised on 20th October 1669 in Alyth, near Blairgowrie, who was the daughter of an Alexander Henderson.[110] No record could be found of Dickson's parents' marriage, nor of his own marriage to Bessie Watson, which is noted down in the work journals as having taken place on 18th June 1717.[111] However, he had three daughters baptised in Tranent Kirk: Elizabeth in October 1719; Jean in February 1722; and Cibilla, whose birth in 1726 he also recorded in his work journals, together with the death of his mother and the anniversary of his marriage.[112] These human touches give glimpses into the character of the man beyond his work.

Dickson was 32 when he started recording these work journals in 1720, a married man and father. For the first few

---

[108] B1, f22r; B1, f34r; and B2, f21r, respectively.

[109] 'December 22 [1688] Robert Dickson & Sibilla Henderson had a child baptised called William witnesses Robert Henderson Robert Proven'. NRS, Old Parish Registers, Births, 704/10, Bolton Parish, 15.

[110] NRS, Old Parish Registers, Births, 328/10, Alyth Parish, 181.

[111] B1, f51v. Dickson's wife, Bessie, is mentioned in the baptismal records for their children. E.g.: NRS, Old Parish Registers, Births, 722/30, Tranent Parish, 58, 11th October 1719.

[112] NRS, Old Parish Registers, Births, 722/30, Tranent Parish: 58, 11th October 1719 (Elizabeth Dickson); 92, 25th February 1722 (Jean Dickson); and 138, 11th September 1726 (Cibilla Dickson); and B1, f42r and f51v, respectively.

months he seems to have worked alone. From June 1723 he refers to an unnamed apprentice three times.[113] This may be John Bredwood who 'eantread hom to me' on 31st October 1722, which is recorded towards the back of his first journal.[114] On that same page he also refers to James Curreth. He then refers to his helper as a lad, but there is no way of knowing if he is referring to the same person. Later he refers frequently to 'myseallf and my man' suggesting some kind of business relationship, which may have been with casual day labourers, possibly assigned by the Winton estate to assist him. However, on 20th September 1726, he enters into an agreement when Gorg (George) Maknis 'eantered to work to me his agriment with me is 13 punde and a pear of shues'.[115]

It is usually clearer for whom Dickson worked. A major employer was John Mathie, merchant in Cockenzie who was involved in the shipping trade. Other shipmasters requiring the services of a wood wright such as William Dickson included Stephan Jolly, James Beal, Andrew Young, John Hutton, John May, Alexander Thomson, Stephen Sead and Messrs Cullen, Miller, Hunter, McDougall and White. He assisted Adam Burnet at the coal gin on Tranent Moor, John Barclay at Seaton, John Carens at Gilmerton and James Pillan in Pencaitland. He spent time working for local householders too, probably a lot more than is mentioned in his work journals. There are long periods when he does not note the work he is doing, possibly because it was for local householders who would pay in cash or kind at the time, and would not need to be reminded with a note in his work journals.[116]

---

[113] B1, f10r-f10v.
[114] B1, f48v.
[115] B1, f41v.
[116] It may also have been related to the various work stoppages observed in the salters of the community. Whatley, 'A Saltwork and the Community', 53-4.

Dickson worked in collaboration with many other tradesmen in the community. For example, he refers to working with '2 wrights that day and a carpenter' on John Mathie's ship in the harbour.[117] Sometimes they are unnamed, at other times we know both trade and name, as with James Paterson, the blacksmith, who ran the smiddy and made nails for Dickson. Dickson made a 'ruff' for the smiddy,[118] and sometimes they worked together on the ships in the harbour. There was still a Paterson at the Cockenzie smiddy in August 1762 when Scotland's first recorded railway death was noted down for eleven-year-old James Paterson, who was 'bruised by a wagon' on the Waggonway.[119]

A great deal of work was done at the twelve saltpans strung along the rocky coastline of Cockenzie. These were tended by salt making families who worked in the area for generations. Some of the salter surnames mentioned by Dickson, such as Donaldson, Fleuchar, Brown and Watson, also appear in the earlier Prestonpans Kirk Session records from the period 1674-7, when they were chastised for working their pans on a Sunday.[120] The same names appear in Edinburgh lawyer James Nicolson's account of the salters at Cockenzie dated 31st December 1695,[121] together with the maiden names of their wives, the names of their children, and the names of their servants, and their wives and children. Two Watson brothers married two Fleuchar sisters; James Watson's wife was a Fleuchar, and their son was Nicol Watson whose son died young

---

[117] B1, f49r.
[118] B2, f42v and f7r respectively. See also Whatley, 'A Saltwork and the Community', 49.
[119] Joy Dodd (ed.), *Tranent Mortality Book, 1754-1781: East Lothian* (Edinburgh: Scottish Genealogy Society, 2015), 79.
[120] NRS, CH2/307/6, Prestonpans Kirk Session, Accounts (1671-7) and Certificates (1699-1716), 47-8.
[121] Quoted in full in M'Neill, *Tranent and its Surroundings*, 208-11.

and was noted in Dickson's journals.[122] Indeed, many of the salters mentioned in Whatley's socio-economic study of the salter community around Cockenzie are also mentioned in Dickson's work journals.[123]

For example, Christopher Fleuchar is scored out in Dickson's work journal, perhaps because he had paid for the deals needed for his panhouse. This Fleuchar's mother was Barbara Nimmo, who in 1715 was paid £1, 'for teaching two poor scholars a quarter' according to the Tranent Parish Kirk Session Accounts.[124] It is heartening that education was considered important in the community, despite the time commitment that education brought, which was often in competition with the work needs of the family. Many of these families are still found in the area today, as are other salter families mentioned by Dickson, such as Mathieson, Balvaird and Greig.[125]

In conclusion, there is much to be learned from Dickson's work journals. They offer a crucial window into the early industrial history of Scotland, bringing technical detail on the coal and salt industries on the eve of the Industrial Revolution. They show more traditional craft practices related to pre-modern woodworking, not in the corporate context of a burgh, but instead in a more rural, coastal settlement, offering insights and comparative material to set alongside the well-documented wright craft within the towns. They give glimpses of early-eighteenth-century social life, adding detail to Whatley's

---

[122] B1, f44r.
[123] Whatley, 'A Saltwork and the Community', 47-54, including: Christopher Fleuchar (47), John Donaldson (47-8), Robert Donaldson (53-4), John Greig and Widow Greig (47, 51 and 54), Alexander Mathieson (49), and Nicol Watson (49 and 54).
[124] NRS, CH2/357/9, Tranent Kirk Session Accounts (1711-1734), 52, 6th November 1715.
[125] For more on the salters and their community, see Whatley, 'A Saltwork and the Community', 45-59.

previous work on the salter community, or Turnbull's work on the glassmakers. Importantly, they have been crucial in the interpretation of the archaeology of Scotland's first railway, bringing clarity and confidence to the interpretation of multiple phases of wooden waggonway found during recent excavations. As such, it is fitting that in this 300th anniversary year of the building of the first Waggonway that Dickson's work journals should be published by the SRS, affording greater opportunities for historians to make use of these rich resources.

Conventions

Dickson's spelling was usually phonetic, and he often mixed up the order of letters. For example, in B1, f5v, the word 'which' is rendered 'wchich'. Similarly, the word 'two' was rendered as 'tow' with transposed letters. Such idiosyncratic spelling was faithfully reproduced, with the exception of certain standard conventions for the sake of clarity and consistency with current practice. While Dickson mainly used 'th-', a few letter thorns were present, and these were changed to 'th-'. Likewise, at least one example of a letter yogh was changed to 'y', though it appears that the original spelling of 'Cockenȝie' (Cockenny) was already being written with 'z' by the early eighteenth century, so we went with the modern spelling of 'Cockenzie'.[126]

Interchangeable letters, such as u/w/v have been modernised for the sake of clarity, unless they were clearly Dickson's idiosyncratic spelling. If a 'u' made no more sense than a 'w', then the 'w' was left alone. For example, for the word 'floor', Dickson gave 'fllwer', and 'flluer' is not much closer to 'floor' than Dickson's spelling, so the original spelling was left alone.

---

[126] Compare Dickson's use of 'Cokkini' on B1, f41v, and 'Cokkensie' on B2, f23v, with 'Cockenzie' as clearly rendered in the *Caledonian Mercury* (see Appendix 2).

Similarly, capitalisation was added for proper nouns, such as people or place names. While some were clear, as with Prestonpans, others were more ambiguous. Did 'the pans' refer to Prestonpans, as is still the colloquial usage today?[127] Or did Dickson mean to informally reference a group of salt pans? As it is not always clear, 'the pans' has been rendered exactly as Dickson wrote it, and readers may make their own interpretations.

With numerals, where Dickson wrote 'i' we have modernised it into Arabic numerals as '1', as all other numbers were already in Arabic. Hence, the entry for 'Ocktober 2i' has been rendered as 'Ocktober 21' to avoid confusion, while the 'ii day' on f3r has been rendered as '11 day'. The former is obviously 21, whilst the latter is precisely seven days after the 4th and seven days before the 18th.[128] The use of 'i' for '1' is also a well-known practice in early modern Scotland.

For dates, while Scotland did not formally change to the Gregorian calendar until 1752, James VI did change the date of the *start* of the new year from 25th March to 1st January from the year 1600. So, although Dickson's dates are all on the older Julian calendar, the start of each new year is still 1st January. Most dates were given in Arabic numerals, though in Appendix 5, in the testament of John Mathie, we find the older, Roman numeral 'Jaj' dates being used.[129]

---

[127] It certainly did in the case of Mr Buell. Compare B2, f23v, where Dickson mentions 'worken about Mr Bwell house in Prestonpans', with the very next side of the page (f24r), where he writes 'Bwells hous in the pans'.
[128] B1, f31r and f3r, respectively.
[129] In Appendix 5 only, the manuscript dates were given as 'Jaj' dates, as, for example, with 1711: 'Jaj vij c& and Eleven years', meaning one thousand seven hundred and eleven, or 1711. In this older form, which uses Roman numerals, the 'j', is 'I', or 'one'; the 'aj', is an established corruption of 'm', for 'thousand'; and the 'c&' is a contracted form of *centus*, or hundred. While the 'jaj' part of the date is a well-known

Aside from these conventions discussed above, our rule of thumb was to reproduce the text as faithfully as possible. Line breaks have been kept, except where Dickson attempted to cram extra text in. For example, where Dickson got too close to the gutter, he often wrote the last word or last letters either above line or below line. As we did not have the same problem of thin pages, we simply carried on as if the text was on the same line for the sake of clarity. This will be seen where one line in the transcription seems longer than the others. Wherever clarity was lacking, we have added a footnote explaining our approach.

---

convention, the 'c&' is less obvious, so we have rendered them all as a superscript 'c' for *centus*.

BIBLIOGRAPHY

Manuscript
British Library (BL)
Caledonian Mercury
Roy Military Survey of Scotland, 1747-55
Cockenzie House and Gardens
Photograph of Sir Robert Cadell, 1854
University of Edinburgh Library, Special Collections
C18:14/1, J. Adair, c.1686 'A mapp of the parioch of Tranent with the port of Seaton belonging to the Right Honorable the Earl of Wintoun'
National Library of Scotland (NLS), Map Library:
Adv.MS.70.2.10 (Gordon 47)
Adv.MS.70.2.11 (Adair 10)
EMS.s.737 (15), John Adair (c.1650-1722), *A Map of East Lothian Survey'd by J. Adair* (Edinburgh: Cooper, c.1736)
'Fish Auction', Cockenzie, photograph, late 19th century, Mackinnon Collection
Forrest, William, Map of Haddingtonshire, 1802 (surveyed 1799). See https://maps.nls.uk/index.html
OS, 25 Inch, Haddingtonshire IX.1, 1892 (1894)
OS, 25 Inch, Haddingtonshire IX.2, 1892 (1894)
National Records of Scotland (NRS)
CC8/8/95, Edinburgh Commissary Court, 1733 Testament of John Mathie
CH2/307/6, Prestonpans Kirk Session, Accounts (1671-1677) and Certificates (1699-1716)
CH2/357/9, Tranent Kirk Session Accounts (1711-1734)
CS133/421, 'Representation for the York Building Company Annuitants, 1736'
Old Parish Registers, Births
RH9/1/212, 'Journals (2) of William Dickson, [wright in Cockenzie,] giving an account of work done and time taken. He appears to have worked in Midlothian and East Lothian, and there

are extensive references to the Tranent-Cockenzie wagonway, salt and coal workings and the harbour, 1720-1745'

RHP29/1, 'Plan of the runrig lands of Tranent, relative to the accomplished scheme of division, East Lothian', 26th July 1776.

Published

Adamson, Donald, 'A Coal Mine in the Sea: Culross and the Moat Pit', in *Scottish Archaeological Journal*, 30:1–2 (2008)

Allen, A., *Building Early Modern Edinburgh: A Social History of Craftwork and Incorporation* (Edinburgh: Edinburgh University Press, 2018)

Bell, Dominique (ed.), *Setting the Standard: Research Reports on the Willington Waggonway of 1785, the Earliest Standard Gauge Railway Yet Discovered* (Newcastle: Tyne & Weir Archives & Museums, 2018)

Bethune, Ed, Donaldson, Gary, and Braby, Alan, *The Quietus Account of Tranent Parish: Strange Tales of Old East Lothian* (Cockenzie: 1722 Waggonway Press, [2020])

Crone, Anne, and Mills, Coralie M., 'Timber in Scottish Buildings, 1450-1800: A Dendrochronological Perspective', in *Proceedings of the Society of Antiquaries of Scotland*, 142 (2012)

Cummings, A. J. G. and Devine, T. M. (eds), *Industry, Business and Society in Scotland Since 1700: Essays Presented to Professor John Butt* (Edinburgh: John Donald Publishers Ltd, 1994)

Dear, I. C. B., and Kemp, P. (eds), *The Oxford Companion to Ships and the Sea*, (Oxford: Oxford University Press, 2005)

Dodd, Joy (ed.), *Tranent Mortality Book, 1754-1781: East Lothian* (Edinburgh: Scottish Genealogy Society, 2015)

Dodd, Joy (ed.), *Bolton, East Lothian Burial and Mortcloth Records* (Edinburgh: Scottish Genealogy Soctiety, 2018)

Duckham, Baron F., *A History of the Scottish Coal Industry, Vol. I 1700-1815: A Social and Industrial History* (Newton Abbot: David & Charles, 1970)

Gentleman's Magazine: or, Monthly Intelligencer. For the Year 1731, Vol. I (London: F. Jefferies, 1731)

Gifford, John, *William Adam 1689-1748: A Life and Times of Scotland's Universal Architect* (Edinburgh: Mainstream Publishing Company, 1989)

Hustwick, Ian, *The George of Port Seton* (Caithness: Whittles, 2000)

Kjærheim, Steinar, 'Norwegian Timber Exports in the 18th Century: A Comparison of Port Books and Private Accounts', in *Scandinavian Economic History Review*, 5:2 (1957)

Lewis, M. J. T., *Early Wooden Railways* (London: Routledge & Kegan Paul, 1974)

Lillehammer, A., 'The Scottish-Norwegian Timber Trade in the Stavanger Area in the Sixteenth and Seventeenth Centuries', in Smout, T. C. (ed.), *Scotland and Europe, 1200–1850* (Edinburgh: John Donald, 1986)

Lodge, R. Anthony, 'Kellie Lodging, 23 High Street, Pittenweem, Fife: A Reappraisal of its Origins and History', in *Proceedings of the Society of Antiquaries of Scotland*, 150 (2021)

Lorvik, M., 'Mutual Intelligibility of Timber Trade Terminology in the North Sea Countries During the Time of the "Scottish Trade"', in *Nordic Journal of English Studies* 2:2 (2003)

Louw, H., and Crayford, R., 'A Constructional History of the Sash-Window, c.1670-c.1725 (Part 2)', in *Architectural History*, 42 (1999)

M'Neill, Peter, *Tranent and its Surroundings: Historical, Ecclesiastical, & Traditional* (Edinburgh: John Menzies & Co., 1884)

M'Neill, Peter, *Prestonpans and Vicinity: Historical, Ecclesiastical, and Traditional* (Tranent: P. M'Neill, 1902)

Maitland of Lethington, Sir Richard, *The History of the House of Seytoun to the Year M.D.LIX* (Glasgow: Maitland Club, 1829)

Marwick, J. D., *List of Markets and Fairs Now and Formerly Held in Scotland: With Notes as to the Charters, Acts of Parliament, and Other Documents by Which the Right to Hold Them has been Conferred* (Glasgow: Royal Commissioners on Market Rights and Tolls, 1890)

Murray, David, *The York Buildings Company, A Chapter in Scotch History Read Before the Institutes of Bankers and Chartered Accountants, Glasgow 19th February 1883* (Glasgow: James Maclehose & Sons, 1883)

National Coal Board, Scottish Division, *A Short History of the Scottish Coal-Mining Industry* (Edinburgh: National Coal Board, Scottish Division, 1958)

Newland, K., 'The Acquisition and Use of Norwegian Timber in Seventeenth-Century Scotland', in *Vernacular Architecture*, 42 (2011)

Peachey, S., *Food and Cookery in Elizabethan and Early Stuart England, Volume 18: Brewing and Malting Equipment and Ingredients* (Bristol: Stuart Press, 2019)

Pride, Glen L., *Dictionary of Scottish Building* (Edinburgh: Rutland Press, 1996)

Rowand, David (ed.), *The Jobbing Book of Mr Waterston, A Paisley Glazier 1736-1744* (Gourock: Renfrewshire Family History Society, 2016)

(*RPC*) Burton, J. H., *et al.* (eds), *The Register of the Privy Council of Scotland* (Edinburgh: H. M. General Register House, 1877-2009)

Sanderson, E. C., *Women and Work in Eighteenth-Century Edinburgh* (London: Macmillan, 1996)

Seton, George, *A History of the Family of Seton During Eight Centuries*, 2 vols. (Edinburgh: T. & A. Constable, 1896)

Smout, T. C. (ed.), 'Journal of Henry Kalmeter's Travels in Scotland, 1719-1720', in *Scottish Industrial History: A Miscellany* (Edinburgh: Scottish History Society, 1978)

Steffy, J. R., 'Illustrated Glossary of Ship and Boat Terms', in Ford, B., Hamilton, D. L., and Catsambis, A. (eds), *The Oxford Handbook of Maritime Archaeology* (Oxford: Oxford University Press, 2013)

Turnbull, Jill, *The Scottish Glass Industry, 1610-1750: 'To Serve the Whole Nation with Glass'* (Edinburgh: Society of Antiquaries of Scotland, 2001)

Turnbull, Jill, 'Venetian Glassmakers in the Prestonpans Area in the Seventeenth Century', in *Scottish Archives*, 23 (2017), 103-13

Whatley, C. A., 'A Saltwork and the Community: The Case of Winton, 1716-1719', in *Transactions of the East Lothian Antiquarian and Field Naturalists' Society*, 18 (1984), 45-59

Whatley, C. A., *The Scottish Salt Industry: An Economic and Social History 1570-1850* (Aberdeen: Aberdeen University Press, 1988)

Worling, M. J., *Early Railways of the Lothians* (Dalkeith: Midlothian District Libraries, 1991)

Zickermann, K., 'Scottish Merchant Families in the Early Modern Period', in *Northern Studies*, 45 (2013)

Unpublished

Cummings, A. J. G., 'The York Buildings Company: A Case Study in Eighteenth Century Corporation Mismanagement', 2 vols (unpublished PhD Thesis, University of Strathclyde, 1980)

Murdoch, Alexander, 'Andrew Fletcher, Scotland, and London in the Eighteenth Century' (University of Edinburgh Working Paper: School of History, Classics and Archaeology Website, 2013

BOOK ONE
1717–1732

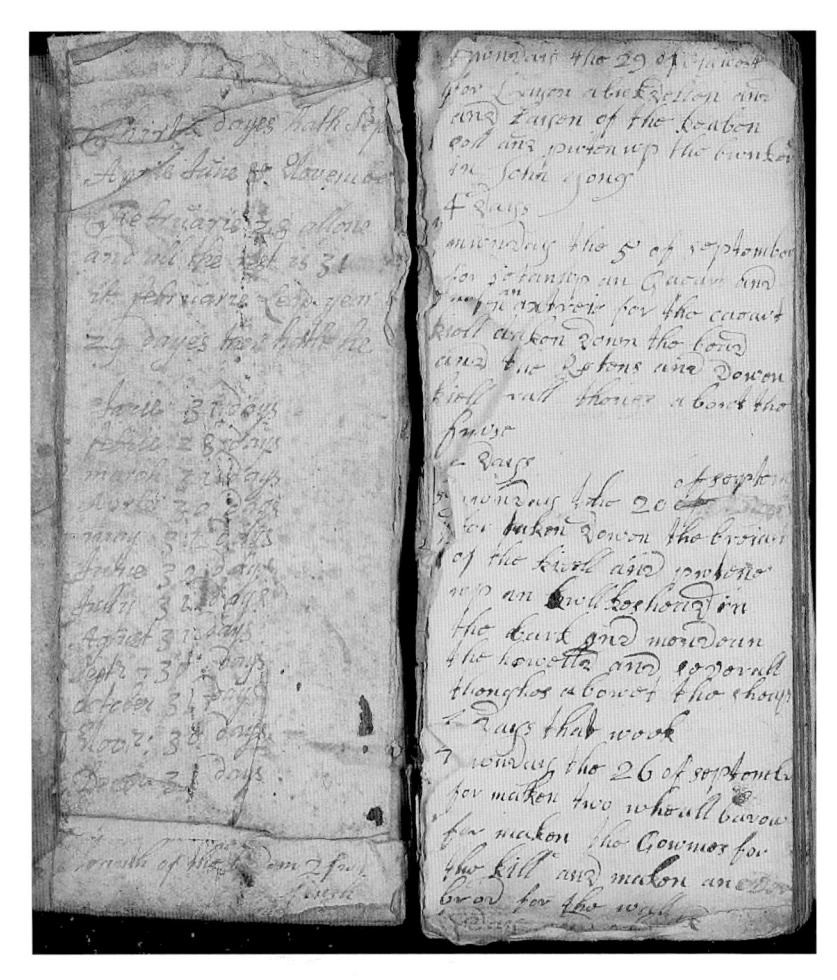

B1, Front Endpaper/Pastedown, f1r

[B1, Front Endpaper/Pastedown]

Thirty dayes hath September
Aprile June & November
Februarie 28 allone
and all the rest is 31
if Februarie Leap year
29 dayes then hath he

Januarie 31 days
Februarie 28 days
March 31 days
Aprile 30 days
May 31 days
June 30 days
Jully 31 days
Agust 31 days
September 30 days
October 31 days
November 30 days
December 31 days

leanth of the bodem 2 fut
   4 ensh

[B1, f1r]

Munday the 29 of Aguest
for Layen a buk dellen[1] and
and layen of the keaben
soll[2] and puten up the bunkers

---

[1] See DSL/DOST: 'Buk-denning' – A plank-lining in the hold of a vessel.
[2] See DSL/DOST: 'Sole, *n.¹*' – 4. a. The foundation or part of the foundation of a structure; the beam or joist (of wood or stone) forming the main member or one of the main members of such a foundation.

in John Yong
4 days
Munday the 5 of September
for setan up an Caeart and
[k]en[3] an axtreie for the caeart
[ta]ken[4] down the bead[5]
[t]he[6] Retens and dowen
[seve]rall[7] thengs about the
[ho]use[8]
[2][9] days
Munday the 20 of September
for taken dowen the breiast
of the kieell and putene
up an bullkeshead in
the bark and mendean
the howelld and severall
thenghes abouet the sheap
3 days that week
Munday the 26 of September
for maken two wheall barow
for maken the Cowmes for
the kill and maken another
brod for the wall
4 days and a [   ][10]

---

[3] Page torn – likely to be 'maken'.
[4] Page torn.
[5] See DSL/DOST: 'Bed, Bede' – 1. A bed.
[6] Page torn.
[7] Page torn.
[8] Page torn – likely to be 'house'.
[9] Page torn – tail of '2' visible.
[10] Last line partially missing.

[f1v]

June 25 for 1827 Gorum(?)
2 days that week
monday the 24
4 that week at sorton
Simon follor 2 mell
December the 2 days

thursday the 4 day
5 days at rowsaven
onder barn windows a[nd]
and mend the boll of[...]
and puton to the wall plo[...]

and puton up the mensen
cases

monday the 12 day
for maken at the brew for
windows and maken 3 trevs
for the gades windows
6 days that week
monday the 20
4 that week at kingson the
brods

[f2r]

3 days the 10 of forwary
1 day faren afrot at the
kenstor to the barke
monday the 23 day
2 days transport for the
shop for in the bates in the
roll and the chores and
and the boss for the
kill

thursday the 26
2 days bosson the hearth
stones and puton about
the bondron

north boxons on wasora(?)
bosoon to the bark for
taken down the thongs after
and boron for the carpinter
4 days that week
mousing for boron and
monday the 6 day
boren that week and
puton up of a burell beer(?)
6 days that week

B1, f1v, f2r

[B1, f1v]
Friday the 18 of November
2 days that week
Munday the 21
4 that week at sorten
Stephan Jollee[11] dealls
Desamber the 2 day

Munday the 4 da[y   ][12]
5 days at reaparen [   ][13]
onder baren windows a[   ][14]
and mend the kell [   ][15]
and puten to the wallple[it][16]

and puten up the measen
caflod[17]
Munday the 12 day
for maken at the brods for
windows and maken 3 brods
for the garets windows
6 days that week
Munday the 19
4 that week at hingen the
brods

---

[11] 'Stean' is expanded throughout to Stephan. This is most likely the Prestonpans skipper Stephen Jolly who sailed to Scandinavia and the Baltic, and died on a voyage to Norway in 1728. K. Zickermann, 'Scottish Merchant Families in the Early Modern Period', in *Northern Studies*, 45 (2013), 102 and 106-7.
[12] Page torn.
[13] Page torn.
[14] Page torn.
[15] Page torn.
[16] Page torn.
[17] scaffold.

[B1, f2r]

    1721
Tisday the 10 of Jenwarie
1 day sawen a trei at the
hearber to the barke
Munday the 23 day
1 day 4 hanspeak for the
shep for puten in the bates in the
kiell and the cheans and
and the bead for the
kiell
Furrsday the 26
2 days boksen the hearth
stones and puten abut
[t]he[18] bordren
[M]arth[19] begens on Wadsnday
begean to the bark for
talken down the sheap quarter
and boren for the carpinter
4 days that week
~~Munday for borean and~~
Munday the 6 day
borean that week and
puten up of a buellkhad
6 days that week

---

[18] Page torn.
[19] Page torn.

monday the 13 day
puton wp an bull shour in
John Mather shoup
puton wp an bull behaind
Johan Goallor
and puton an seamoure
in the koull and makon
new niches fe the kieull
5 days that work
puton that clondon on thi
bak of the harp and makon
the boxe for harp
4 days that work
monthe the 30 day
for makon an fram for
the harpe and makon a
axtrio for the hornes an
rails on the trios from
an day
wadsday the 5 of Aprealle
for reparon the Lofts for
the moullo
half a day
Apprealle the 24
for rason alwbeaten in
mathow whouth thoup
4 a day and a half

6 [[illegible]] of my days
fram brunet at the ghous
munday the 15 day of Noveamb
5 days that work
monday 18 day
5 days that work two days at
swaton and on at the ghous
on day with Adam Brernet
at swaton sawon a pies of wood
munday the 19 day
4 days that work
monday 28
4 days that work   1720
monday the 4 of Jeenuari
5 days that work and a hallf
monday the 11 day
4 days that work
monday the 18 days
5 days that work and a hullf
munday 25 day
5 days that work [[illegible]]
monday the first of Febr
5 days that work

[B1, f2v]

Munday the 13 day
puten up an bullkshead in
John Mathe sheap
puten up an bullkshad in
Stephan Geallee
and puten an seamear
in the keall and maken
newe riebas to the kieall
~~days that week~~
puten the clleaden on the
bak of the harp and maken
the boxe for harp
4 days that week
Marthe[20] the 30 day
for maken an fram for
the harpe and maken [ ][21]
axtrie for the keart an[d][22]
ranieon the tries from fallean
an day
Wadsnday the 5 of Aprealle
for repearen the Loftt for
the mealle
haf a day
Aprealle the 24
for Layen a bukdeallan in
mastear Whieitt sheap
2 a day and a hafe[23]

---

[20] March.
[21] Page torn – 'an'.
[22] Page torn.
[23] Half.

[B1, f3r]

    Meamerandom of my days
to Adam Burnet at the ghene
Munday the 7 day of Deseamber
5 days that week
Munday 14 day
3 days that week two days at
Seaton and on at the ghean in the muor[24]
an day with Adam Buernet
at Seaton sawen a pies of wood
Munday the 19 day
4 days that week
Munday 28
4 days that week
Munday the 4 of Jwenwari 1720
~~Munday the 11 day~~
[ ][25] days that week and a hallf
Munday the 11 day
[ ][26] days that week
Munday the 18 day
5 days that week and a hallf
Munday 25 day
5 days that week and a hallf
Munday the fuerst of Feubruary
5 days that week

---

[24] Tranent Moor.
[25] Page torn.
[26] Page torn.

B1, f3v, f4r

[B1, f3v]

    Maye fuerst
for puten up an buelkshead
and steallen in James Bealles
and maken an wheall for the
geakes an day and an haf
Juen be geans on Furesday
maken an Bockes for the
geak and begening to the
callendear
4 days that week
Munday the 4 day
worken at the callender and
puten up two bullksheades
in ~~Alleax~~ Androw Yong she[ ][27]
and maken two dubeall br[od][28]
for great back
6 that week   W W [D][29]
    Wia Jun 4 1720 W D
Munday 4 day   W D
for taken down the pump
wall and puten up a gean
and puten up an bunkear
and seaverel others
theangas in the ceaben
2 days Aandrow Yonge
    the eand of my year a
    a cowent
        W
W Wallam Dickson

---

[27] Page torn.
[28] Page torn, but loop of 'd' visible.
[29] Page torn.

[B1, f4r] [Page torn]

[   ]
[   ]
[   ]
[   ]
[   ]
[   ]
[   ]
[   ]
[   ]
[   ]
[   ]
[   ]
[   ]
[   ]
[   ]
[   ]
in [   ]
4 day[s   ]
the [   ]
being eand[   ]
WWiallim Dickson
   W Wiallim
        Dickson
W William Dickson
    W   W
William Dickson
 Wiallim Dickson D D
   Wiallim Dickson D D
Wiallim Dickson   D
WWiallim Dickson D D

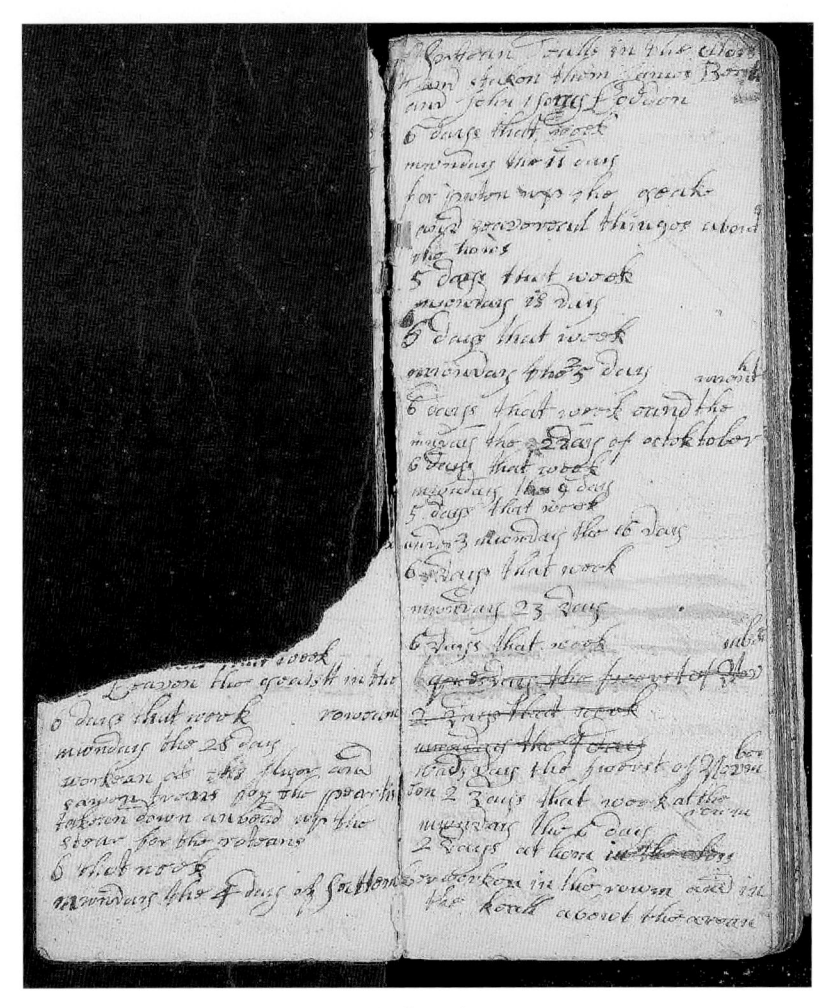

B1, f4v, f5r

[B1, f4v] [Page torn]

[   ]
[   ]
[   ]

[   ]
[   ]
[   ]
[   ]
[   ]
[   ]
[   ]
[   ]
[   ]
[   ]
[   ]
[   ]
[   ]
[   ]
[   ]x[30]
[   ]
[   ]
[that] week
[Leayen] the geaistt in the roweam
6 days that week
Munday the 28 day
workean at the flwor and
sawen treais for the peartision
takean down an bead up the
stear for the roteans
6 that week
Munday the 4 day of Secttember[31]

[B1, f5r]

Sortean dealls in the cllois

---

[30] On the next folio are the letters '-ander' divided from the other text by a '}'. Perhaps it is the name 'Alexander' written across the gutter onto the next folio.

[31] September.

~~st~~ and staken them James Beal
and John Yong Lodden
6 days that week
Munday the 11 day
for puten up the geake
and seavereall thinges about
the hous
5 days that week
Munday 18 day
6 days that week
Munday the 25 day
6 days that week eand the munth
Munday the 2 day of Octoktober
6 days that week
Munday the 9 day
5 days that week
ander}[32] Munday the 16 day
6 days that week
Munday 23 day
6 days that week
~~Qensday the fuerst of November~~
~~2 days that week~~
~~Munday the 7 day~~
Wadsday the fuerst of November
   2 days that week at the rown
Munday the 6 day
2 days at hom ~~in the closs~~
   worken in the rowm and in
   the keall about the arean

---

[32] Across the gutter on f4v is a letter 'x', but the rest of the word is lost to the torn page. Dickson often wrote across the gutter. Was this the name 'Alexander' written across both folios? Note the bracket Dickson used to separate the text.

work and 4 days in the [hoar?]
in ameroow young sheap
6 days that week
monday the 15 day
3 days in Andrew Jones
sheep workeing in the [barn?]
and 3 days in [stoun folls?]
sheep which is all [in heall?]
6 days that work

monday the 20 day
on day in [stoun folls?]
at the [wastker?] work
and one day [?] to the [wright?]
sawen in the [?] which is
on heall
3 days that work

[crossed out lines]

monday 2 days
2 meten sawen on day
[?] for the [?] and
maken the [?] for the
[?]
2 days that week

monday the 4 day of
Desember
for dighton the [?] for
[?] and [?] thomen
5 days that work

monday 11 days
for [?] the [?]
and taken a way the
waphents and [?] them
togeven and [?] them
[?] the Coftos and
maken [?] [?] and makes
[?] for the brewhous
6 days that work

Jenerari 1 o 22 22 day
for [?] [?] in the ellow
be longen to the [Schonettelt?]
[?] the caben of the and
master Coalton
on day that work

J[?]n [?]

[B1, f5v]

work and 4 days in the hearbre
in Androw Yong sheap
6 days that week
Munday the 13 day
3 days in Andraw Yonge
sheap workean in the keaben
and 3 days in Stephan Jolley
sheap which is all in heall
6 days that week
Munday the 20 day
an day in Stephan Jolley
at the buellkeshead
and an day to two wright
sawen in the cleas wchich is
an heall
3 days that week
~~Munday 27 daye~~
~~2 mean sawen treis for~~
~~the keall and worken at~~
~~the fream of the keall~~
Munday 27 day
2 mean sawen on day
treis for the kell and
maken the fream for the
keall
7 days that week

[B1, f6r]

Munday the 4 day of
Desember
for dighten the rebs for
kell and leayen them on
5 days that week
Munday 11 day
for finisen the keell
and taken a wae[33] the
waplleats and puten them
to agean and pllaster them
wadgen the Loftes and
maken an Leather and maken
an terles for the breweshous
6 days that week
Janeuar 1722 22 day
sortene dealls in the cllose
be Longen to the Johen Mah
and the caben Mathe and
master Ceallen
an day that week
    Wiallam Dickson

---

[33] away.

Jinowaris the 27 day 1722
an easin sorton woulls in the
clos to Longne John Mathr
James Mathr and Mr
febrovars the 26 day
makon an gantros botomn 3
chears shuton an bron graff
2 days that work

the Last of febrovars
puton up two biell thorn in
James Boal sheap and an
Stoulton
2 days that work

monday the 12 of March
for yukon two standors
makon an axtr and puton
to an Loumor to an uets
puton up 4 bolstons in
Stoun fotts shorp and
Sason a pllott foron
and makon clos with matt
5 days that work

monday the 26 day martho
makon two mustrothers and
mondon the fram for the bell
and makon of an wouget loab
5 days that work and a half
monday the 2 of March
workon at the toable and sorton
the woulls that cam out of the
yoans shorp
5 days that work

monday the 9 day
sorton out the woulls and
finowon out the toable
4 days that work

monday the 23 day
workon at the toabroon
5 days that work

monday the 30 day
workon at the yoan work
and sortoan woulls that
cam out of Moustov
Moulloar shorp
6 days that work

[B1, f6v]

Janeuare the 22 day 1722
an day sorten dealls in the
cllos be Longen John Mathe[34]
James Mathe and Mr Cellen
Febreware the 26 day
maken an gantres bedeinn 3
chears maken an bwn Leaff
2 days that week
the Last of Febreware
puten up two bullkhead in
James Beall sheap and an
steallen
2 days that week
Munday the 12 of Marth
for maken two standerts
maken an axtrie and puten
to an Leamer to an carte
puten up 4 bulkshead in
Stephan Sead sheap and
Layen a plleat forem
and maken clos with mats
5 days that week

---

[34] Probably the Prestonpans merchant and shipowner. Ian Hustwick, *The George of Port Seton* (Caithness: Whittles Publishing, 2000), 93, 95-6. See also his 1733 testament in Appendix 5.

[B1, f7r]

Munday the 26 day Marthe
maken two masstrothers and
menden the fram for the kell
and maken at an weanget teabell
3 days that week and a haf
Munday the 2 of Aprealle
worken at the teablls and sorten
the dealls that cam out of the
Deans[35] sheap
5 days that week
Munday the 9 day
sorten out the dealls and
fineasen out the teabells
4 days that week
Munday the 23 day
workean at the Leatrean
5 days that weak
Munday the 30 day
workean at the seam work
and sortean dealls that
cam out of Measter
Meallear sheap
6 days that week

---

[35] Danish.

munday the 7 day of May
I mason the Cauldron and
maken at the wall
4 and a half days
munday the 14 day maken
at the same walle
5 days that week and a half

munday the 21
waken at the cleaning of
the rooms
6 days that week

munday the 29
worken at the cleaning and
conten James Bealls loosing
conten 4 days wicks is in all
6 days that week

munday the 4 day of June
worken at the cleaning
and Cayson and pthat
haven in the warehouse and
putten up an Ould Shead
6 days that week

munday 11 day
maken the Linen renewes
and locken down the Linen
of the rooms

Cockson prece in the isher
room hieth
5 days that week

munday the 18 days
locken up the newe Linen
and repecaon the olde
Linen about the closet
5 days that week

munday the 25
6 days that week

munday the 2 days of July
6 days that week

munday the 9 days
forwarn Bealls that came
out of James Boall
6 days

Cayson about Cotton to
Joan Godfrey in days

Cayson about Cotton to
Joan Jouse in days
Agreest $9/22$

[B1, f7v]

Munday the 7 day of May
fineasen the Leatren and
maken at the reall[36]
4 and a heaf day
Munday the 14 day maken
at the same realle
5 days that week and a haf
Munday the 21
workean at the Lieanin of
the roowm
6 days that week
Munday the 29
worken at the Lieanin and
sorten James Bealle Loding
sorten 4 days wiche is in all
6 days that week
Munday the 4 day of Juen
workean at the Lieanin
and Layen an plleat
forem in the wearhous and
puten up an bulkshead
6 days that week
Munday 11 day
maken the Linen readay
and taken down the Linen
of the roowm
~~4 days that week~~

---

[36] This is the first instance of Dickson working on the 'rails' for the Waggonway.

[B1, f8r]

~~Munday 18 day~~
bockesen a preas in the ister[37]
rowm high
5 days that week
Munday the 18 day
seaten up the newe Linen
and repearen the olde
lienen about the closet
5 days that week
Munday the 25
6 days that week
Munday the 2 day of Jully
6 days that week
Munday the 9 day
sortean dealls that cam
out of James Beall
3 days
Layen a bukdellen to
Stephan Golley an day
Layen a bukdellen to
Stephan Siead an day
Aguest 1722

---

[37] Eastern.

September 14 for makein
down the bark at the hourbr
6 days short woke

November 13
two mon sawin deall for the
the dinet rowm bragh and new
them and zaagin the floor
preton on two locks
4 ½ days

mekon an toubl head and
makon an sevorell a boweth
the loft and severll things
about the hows makon 4
4 days 3 spoarton locks

december 1722
countod and cleard
with John gowan
of all moedons

Januar 1723
spoarton an stack in Sams
Boull ellos of doalls and an
stack of doalls in the oldyird
S mather S ovrie
an day and an haff days

monday 15
makon a chiest of draworos
for the libott ellout makon
an fuller bronn for the fett
and makon an torm for the
chimli howr
6 days

monday 4 day febroro
for makon up an bronlow in
the yaird for a camimork
south going to fornant with
the court for two courts
full of azis that cem out
of the hoough sorton doalls
at the henrbor and at hom
and mowon the close corrit
of that work
moalton at the panwrofs and
mekon four treaws for the
mesons
6 days

[B1, f8v]

Seaptember 17 for takean
down the bark at the hearber
6 days that week
   November 13
two men sawen dealls for the
the eiast rowm heagh and worken
them and deagin the fllowr
puten on tow Locks
4 days
maken an teabl head and
maken an sowdell aboveth
the kell and severll things
about the hous maken 4
~~4 days~~ } speaten bockes

Desember 1722
counted and cleard
with John Gowen
of all precidens

[B1, f9r]

Januar 1723
pearten an stack in James
Beall cllos of dealls and an
stack of dealls in the olld yeard
T Mathe T Curie
an day and an haff day
Munday 15
maken a chiest of drawers
for the Litell clloset maken
an falles bodem for the fatt
and maken an Lowm for the
chimlihead
6 days
Munday 4 day Febreware
for maken up an bunkear in
the yeard for a camimeill
seatt going to Terneant with
the ceartt for two ceartt
full of aeis that cam out
of the heough sorten dealls
at the hearber ~~and at hom~~
and mendean the close ceartt
4 that week
neallean at the panrowefs and
maken four treases for the
measens
6 days

monday 11 day
forgerton are the walls
3 days and worken at the
parrowes and repearen
the spowles to Robet watson
6 to my sealfe and my man
monday 18 dayes
for worken about the young
mason an hewores for the
climate here and mason
fowr roasmonth for wast
souther from the beares
of the other woreks and puttn
them on the roow and seavn
things about the hous
6 days that wor 6
monday 25 dayes
worken about the pans and
begoning to the new pan ron
6 days
Month monday 4 Day
wralten con worken at the rouff
and panthered
4 days and this
monday 11 days
15 days that work
monday 25
same ahalf that work

monday the fewrst oppers
worken at the panstones
and ronf
6 days that work
monday 8 day
worken at the seam work
6 days that work

friday the 14 Day of Juon
an way to mey fouthr of pearton
the walls that com olet of
John Yong

20 Day meruven the
brolbeevers cavens
monday 21
1 day at the brenkastle
coltalve mey sealf and
preantis
monday the fwerst of feurlty
worken at the brenke in
the coltalve and wroken at
the young hous in the pouls
in the sile
6 days that work to my seavlf
and my preantis
3 of the days at the pan
rose cupoles

B1, f9v, f10r

[B1, f9v]

Munday 11 day
for sorten out the dealls
3 days and worken at the
panrowefs and repearen
the spoutes to Nekel Watson
6 to my seallf and my man
Munday 18 daye
for worken about the pans
maken an hwerds for the
chimle head and maken
four keasments for wast
seallear altrean the bandse
of the other windowes[38] and puten
them on the wendowes and seavrelle
things about the hous
6 days that week
Munday 25 daye
worken about the pans and
begening to the now[39] pan rouf
6 days
Marth Munday 4 day
meallen and worken at the roufs
and panstands
4 days and a haf
Munday 11 day
5 days that week
Munday 25
6 and a haff that week

---

[38] The manuscript reads 'wndes'.
[39] new.

[B1, f10r]

Munday the fowrst Apreal
worken at the panstands
and rouf
6 days that week
Munday 8 day
worken at the sam work
<u>6 days that week</u>
Friday the 14 day of Juen
an day to my seallv of pearten
the dealls that cam out of
John Yong

20 day meanden the
hwrelbarows ~~haf~~ a day
Munday 24
1 day at the trunk at the
coll falde my seavelf and
preantic
Munday the fuerst of Juelly
workean at the trunke in
the coll falde and maken at
the panruf hingein the geats
in the fald
6 days that week to myseavlf
and my preants[40]
3 of the days at the pan
rufe cupels

---

[40] apprentice.

monday the 8 day
worken at the penn-rig and
s[...]off thingr abowt the
penn
5 dayr to my scolly and
prentes

munday 15 day J I W
that work workin at the
collhall puten up thes
gemoun on the collsoll the
[...] my scolls and mean
6 dayr that work

munday 22 day
[...]n the oggalla work
and monden the wagon and
[...]n tho wor [...] ceven
at the worboxy and wagon
6 dayr that work was
to my scoly and mean

munday the 29
mounen on the wagon was
5 dayr that work to my
scolls and man

Agrees the 1 day
maken at the goods for
the horsgh and maken at the
broods for the scolly winro
5 dayr that work

munday the 5 day
maken out the broods and
maken the shots hall in the
and puts on the even work
and puten on the bowing
and sawon latho for the
bowen
6 dayr that work to my
self scall and 2 dayr to my
munday the 19
sawon scally for the wagon
sawon deals for the wenr
and maken dowls tasl for
John govens habren and
sarveal thingr abowt
[...]

[B1, f10v]

Munday the 8 day
worken at the panruf and
seavrell things about the
pane
5 days to my seallf and
preantes

Munday 15 day   W W[41]
that week worken at the
collfald puten up that
framenen on the collfallde
diek my seallef and man
6 days that week
Munday 22 day
finesin the collfalld dieke
and menden the wagenway
menden the hwerll barows
at the herbour and wagenway
6 days that week
to my seallf and man
Munday the 29
meanden the wagen way
3 days that week to my
seallf and man

---

[41] Here he is practising his 'W's using the same colour ink as used on the opposite folio (f11r).

[B1, fl 1r]

~~Aguest begens on Tusday~~
~~maken at the[ ] yeats [   ]~~[42]
Aguest the 1 day
maken at the yeats for
the howgh and maken at the
broods for the sealler windows
3 days that week
Munday the 5 day
maken out the brods and
maken the shots holl in them
and pute on the aren worke
and puten on the bands
and sawen Lathe for the
baren
6 days that week to my
~~my~~ seallf and 2 days to my Lad
Munday the 19
sawen dealls for the wagens
sawen dealls for the windows
and maken dukit holls for
John Gowns Leatren and
savreall thinges about
hous

---

[42] Text obliterated and now unclear.

the yeare rowld things to
the meadors
6 dayes to my sealf and my
heat *Sepemb.*
monday 26 sawon dealls for
worken at the windows my the windows
sealf and my sead
6 dayes that work
Sepetembear begans on
sabath
monday the 2 day
worken at the windows
my sealf and the sead
6 dayes that work
monday the 9 day
6 dayes that work to my
sealf and my sead that
week worken at the
enon of the rowm
monday the 16 day
worken at the same of
the work of rowm

6 days that work to my
sealf and my sead
monday the 23
worken at the rowm my
sealf and my sead
6 days that work
monday the 30
toosday the furst of ocktobr
6 days that work to my sealf
and my men worken at
at the rowm
monday the 7 day
worken at the rowm and
makn the brethrin
6 days to my sealf and my
men
monday 14 day
makn the doe holls and casin
ge on the beem and fixen the
brethrin and worken about
the rowm
4 days and a half days to my
sealf and my men

[B1, f11v]

and seavreall things to
the measons
6 days to my seallf and my Lad
that week
~~Aguest 16~~
Munday 26 sawen dealls for
        the windows
worken at the windows my
sealf and my Lad
6 days that week
Seaptembear begeans on
Sabath
Munday the 2 day
maken at the windows
my sealf and the Lad
6 days that week
Munday the 9 day
6 days that week to my
seallf and my Lad that
week worken at the
Linen of the rowme
Munday the 16 day
worken at the same ~~of~~
~~the~~ work of roowm

[B1, f12r]

6 days that week to my
seallf and my Lad

Munday the 23
worken at the rowm my
seallef and my Lade
6 days that week
Munday the 30
Tuesday the furst of Ocktober
6 days that week to mysealf
   and my man worken at
   at the rowm
Munday the 7 day
worken at the rowm and
maken the Leatrean
6 days to my sealf and my
man
Munday 14 day
maken the dou holls and sayin-
ge[43] on the bands and fixen the
Leatren and worken about
the rowm
4 days and a haf day to my
seallf and my man

---

[43] Assaying, or 'trying'.

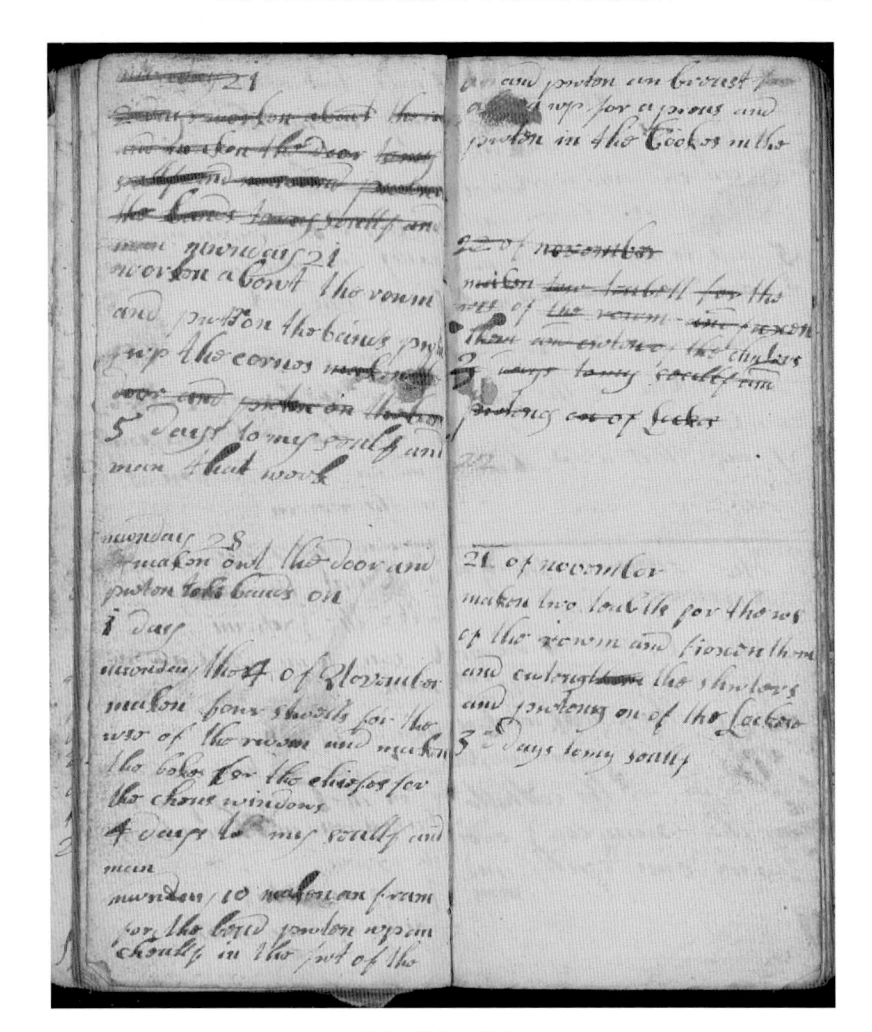

~~...workon about the~~
~~...workon the door~~
~~...~~
~~the dore...~~
men niuoweis 21
worken about the room
and pwtton the beams py...
up the corners ...
... on the ...
5 daest to my selfe and
men that work

munday 28
maken out the door and
putton the beams on
1 day

tuisuday the 27 of November
maken four sheuils for the
use of the room and meakin
the boks for the cluisfos for
the chore windous
4 days to my selfe and
men

munday 10 ... fram
for the lord powton upoun
chonly in the pwt of the

... and pwton on ...
... ... up for e[y]nous and
pwton in the Cook[e]s milke

22 of november
maken ... toubell for the
...st of the room ...
than ... the elinbers
3 days to my selfe
pwtong on of ... Leker

21 of november
maken two ladell for the use
of the rowm and fionen them
and enlargeth the shulvers
and pontong on of the Leckor
3 days to my selfe

[B1, f12v]

~~Munday 21~~
~~2 days worken about therin~~
~~and maken the door to my~~
~~sealf and man and puten~~
~~the bands to my seallf and~~
~~man~~ Munday 21
worken about the rowm
and putten on the bands puten
up the cornes ~~maken the~~
~~door and puten on the bars~~
5 days to mysealf and
man that week

Munday 28
maken out the door and
puten [   ][44] bands on
1 day
Munday the 4 of November
maken four shoells for the
use of the rwem and maken
the bokes for the chiefes for
the cheas windows
4 days to my seallf and
man
Munday 10 maken an fram
for the bead puten up an
cheallf in the fut of the

---

[44] It appears that Dickson mistakenly wrote 'tow' for two, and then changed it to 'the'. As the exact word is unclear, we have left it blank.

[B1, f13r]

and puten an breast ~~for~~
~~a~~-[   ]⁴⁵ up for a preas and
puten in the bookes in the⁴⁶

~~22 of November~~
~~maken tow teabell for the~~
~~wss of the rowm and fioxen~~
~~them and cuten of the chuters~~
~~3 days to my seallf and~~
~~puteng on of Lockes~~

21 of November
maken two teabells for the us
of the rowm and fioxen them
and cuteng ~~them~~ the shuters
and puteng on of the Lockese
3 days to my seallf

---

⁴⁵ Several words have been erased or smudged out here.
⁴⁶ Line incomplete.

monday 25 of November
worken at the bruck in
the cellpolls and worken at
the stone and sawen boath
5 days to my soulf
6 days to my man that week

monday the 2 days desember
Dito worken at this same
worke
4 days that week to my
soulf and man

the seven of the 10th
a account

Sauvew Corpus on monday
1721 ?
fridey the 5 days worken
at the salth power maken
an iren for the cellhills
for the penwoed poder
2 days to my soulf and
man

monday the 6
dito worken at the salt
panes my soulf andman
4 days that week
an day sawen abuk dotton
in the hourbor my soulf
and man all within that
week

monday the 13
dito worken at the salt
panes my soulf and man
5 days that week

monday the 13
puten in four casment
in the garret windowes
and dreven the benes of the
oll and puten them on the
neew and sowrrout thing
about tirhows
an day to my soulf

[B1, f13v]

    Munday 25 of November
worken at the trunk in
the collfolld and worken at
the shead and sawen dealls
5 days to my seallf
6 days to my man that week

Munday the 2 day Decamber
dito worken at the same
worke
4 days that week to my
seallf and man

---

    the eand of the year
    accountt
Januar begens on Wadensday
        1724
Frideye the 3 day worken
at the salltt panse maken
a fram for the coll hille
for the panwood Lodes
2 days to my seallf and man

[B1, f14r]

    Munday the 6
ditto worken at the salt
panes my seallf and man
4 days that week
an day Layen an bukdellen
in the hearbur mysealf
and man all within that week

Munday the 13
ditto worken at the sallt
panes my seallf and man
3 days that week
Munday the 13
puten in four casment
in the garrat windowes
and altren the banes of the
olld and puten them on the
neow and seavreall things
about the hous
an day to my sealf

munday the 20 day
pwton wp of the youn
stands mr. scally an ma
6 days hint work

munday 24
half aday to mr. scall[...]
at delor

the [...]ast of the month[...]
an day to mr. scalf att[...]
the [...]icad of the mill ark
and dorcen sceuroll thing[...]
about the hous

febuarie the 5 day
sorten the death that cam
out of John asons
an day to mr. scallf an[...]
and anaf me staken th[...]
munday 10 day
straken the cart
axtrie pwton wp the
horshe triosth and manger
and yowen scevrouh thin[...]
about the hous and breaken
out the timer for the
mason lafth
2 days to mr. scalf and man

frdeay 17 day
worken in the brewhous
2 days that week to mr.
scalf

munday 19
worken at the bad
and maken the trouble
for the cappour
6 days to mr. scalf an
[...]

munday 24
maken the the sige
beam for the sad
an[...] gaorden the fe[...]
and serven sourvoll
things about the hous
4 days to mr. scalf
and man

munday 28 hoerbow
menden the the collbak
and collmeath and pwton
on the new[...] tandes
and otherdin the gree[...]ge
all day to mr. scal[...]
and man at the
hoerbow

[B1, f14v]

    Munday the 20 day
puten up of the pan
stands my seallf and ma[n]
6 days that week
Munday 29
hallf a day to my sealf and man
at ditoe
the Last of the munthe
an day to my sealf alltren
the Liead of the mill arke
and dowen seavrell things
about the hous
Febrewarie the 5 day
sorten the dealls that cam
out of John Yong
an day to my seallf and man
and a haf and stakin theam
Munday 10 day
    streaken the cart
axtrie puten up the
horshe triefish and manger
and dowen seavreall things
about the hous and breaken
out the timer for the
masken fatt
2 days to my sealf and man

[B1, f15r]

Frideay 14 day
worken in the browhous
2 days that week to my
sealf
Munday 17
worken at the faat
and maken the creabe
for the cappear
6 days to my seallf and man
Munday 24
maken the the fase
bodam[47] for the faat
and gearden[48] the fat
and dowen searvell
thinges about the hous
4 days to my seallf and man
Munday 28 hearbour
menden the the collbakets
and collmeats and puten
on the newk bandes
and clleadin the gange
an day to my seallf
and man at the hearbour

---

[47] false bottom.
[48] girding.

March begins on
Saboth
Laiken & we & Collen in
Strain Gothy shop and
proton wp two brollkstons
3 days to my soulf and
col half day takon denn
the brollkshoud an proton
a goau to my soulf the man
~~the day of the ~~
Friday the 13 day
Cancon at the wagon
wholls at millton
2 days to my soulf
mondayß 16
Sawen waigon wheulls
at millton my soulf
4 days S Wallaue Dickson
mundayß 20
proton wp the cassell ho
about the capor and the
foot
an day to my soulf an
man

mondays 23
mowen the wholl bow'd
and makon fower coll bake
at the howsebrie my
soulf one man
i day that week
wwwwww
the cause of that account
given in this
222222
the [r]est of apriuoll
makon an long cart an
mowen the saltcart
wholl
an day and an hulp to
my soulf

May the 11 day
makon the wasolls for
the meadow at the dam
an day to my soulf

[B1, f15v]

    Marth begins on Sabeth
Layen a buckdellen in
Stephan Golly sheap and
puten up two bullkshead
3 days to my seallf and man
an haf day taken down
the bulkshead and puten up
agean to my sealf and man
~~an day in the b[ ]s puten up~~
~~the caffolden about the caper~~
Friday the 13 day
sawen at the wagen
whells at Millton[49]
2 days to my seallf
Munday 16
sawen wagen whealls
at Millton my seallf
4 days Willam Dickson
Munday 20
puten up the caffellton
about the caper and the
fatt
an day to my seallf and man

---

[49] Near present-day West Saltoun, East Lothian. Milton is shown on the c.1736 edition of Adair's map of East Lothian: NLS, EMS.s.737 (15), John Adair (c.1650-1722), *A Map of East Lothian Survey'd by J. Adair* (Edinburgh: Cooper, c.1736).

[B1, f16r]

Munday 23
menden the whellborows
and maken four collbackets
at the hearbrie my
seallf and man
1 day that week

the eand of that account
given in this year

the Last of Aprieall
maken an Long cartt and
menden the sallt cart
whelle
an day and an haf to
my seallf
Maye the 11 day
maken the scafellts for
the measens at the chimleheads
an day to my seallf

Mars the 18
makon the spouts &
putou up the stoun and
down sindery things
a bout work a pick
pickol tellon pane
6 days to my soullf and
man.

Monday 2 5 day 2
mendon the whellborows
on monday Duckon
grain flour
on day and on half day
to my soullf and man

Agust the 6 day
sorton the doulls that cam on
of stoan gelly shup my soulf
and man   man
3 days to my soulf and

Agust 19 day
gawen two doulls and makon
the dow hell in his clost and
doing other things about
the hows
3 days to my soulf and man

monday the 24 day
sorton the bergs that cam out
of the down sherys of the
harbowr my soulf and man
all day my man
all day with John frito

Septomber 23
sorton the doulls that cam
out of John muther ship
my soulf and man
on day

Thursday 2 5 day
takon down the salt givon
on of and makon the chapells
and souskut it a gorn one
gawen trio for takes for the
old cupoll
4 days to my soulf and man

[B1, f16v]

    May the 18
maken the spouts and
puten up the stand and
dowen sevreal things
about the work at Pick[50]
Pickelltillem pane[51]
6 days to my seallf and
    man
Munday 25 day
menden the whellborows
and menden Dunken
Gream fllwer
an day and an haf day
to my seallf and man
Agust the 6 day
sorten the dealls that cam out
of Stephan Golly sheap my sealf
and man
4 days to my seallf and man

---

[50] This appears to be an abortive attempt at 'Pickelltillem'. See next line.
[51] This is likely to be a salt pan associated with Pickeltillim near Kirckaldy. See NLS, Adv.MS.70.2.10 (Gordon 47): Robert Gordon (1580-1661), 'An outline map of the Tay estuary round Fife Ness and on to Kirkcaldy'. It is also shown on Blaeu, but not on Roy.

[B1, fl7r]

Aguest 17 day
sawen two dealls and maken
the dow holl in his closet and
dowing other things about
the hous
3 days to my seallf and man
Munday the 24 day
sorten the treys that cam out
of the Dean[52] sheap at the
hearbour my seallf and man
an day my man ~~half an day~~
an day with Johen Tintoo
Seaptember 23
sorten the dealls that cam
out of John Mathe ship
my sealf and man
an day
Fursday 25 day
taken down the salltgirenell
ruf and maken the cupells
and searknet it agean and
sawen tries for bakes for the
olde cupells
4 days to my seallf and man

---

[52] Danish.

the 24 ocktober
highton Robert Donollson
spowts and mekon a noow
spowts mekon a noow stoow
to his cow
my soulf and jorns jonson
an day to his Colho

the 2 days of November
altoren tho stadoll
2 days my soulf and ma[n]

24 day mowin the tow
lofts in the waist sood
of the clos
2 days to my soulf and lad
and on half day to my soulf
and lad

November the 24
proton up an timboar hows
in the clos my soulf and lad
3 days that wook
29 days my soulf and lad
2 days that wook
the end of this year
work being the year 1724

Janovari 1725
mekon an covon chiost
monday 18 my soulf and lad
3 days that wook

2 day mekon at the satt
my soulf and lad
1st day

monday 25
mekon at the satt
my soulf and lad
5 days

martts 19 day
for laying a buck salmin
got stons 3 hors cars prdon
up two coll hoads
my soulf and lad

2 days to my soulf and
man

Martts 24 mekon 6 collbr
bays a day my soulf and man
half a day at maetsom pan
spowts and
my soulf and man

[B1, f17v]

the 24 Ocktober
highten Robert Donellson
spouts and maken a neow
spouts maken a neow stanerrt
to his cowp
my sealf and James Jonson
an day to his bothe
the 2 day of November
alltren the stabell
2 days my seallf and man
24 days mendin the two
   Lofts in the wast siead
   of the cllos
2 days to my seallf and laed
and an haf day to my sealf
and laed
~~an day and af a haf~~
Deasamber the 24
puten up an timbear hous
in the clos my sealf and laed
3 days that week
29 day my sealf and laed
2 days that week
   the eand of that year
   work being the year 1724

[B1, f18r]

    Januari 1725
maken an coren chiest
Munday 18 my seallf and lad
    3 days that week
22 d~~ay worken at the sallt~~
    ~~pans my seallf and lad~~
    ~~an day~~
Munday 25
    ~~worken about the sallt~~
    ~~pans my sealf and lad~~
5 days
Marthe 19 day
for Layen a buckdeilin in
John Yong shiep and puten
up two bullkheads
my seallf[53] and Lad
2 days to my seallf and man
Marth 26 maken 6 collbakets
haf a day my sealf and man
haf a day at Mathisin pan
spouts and ruf
my seallf and man

---

[53] Note that 'my seallf' was also written on the line above, but was erased.

Apreall the fayrst day
picton wp John gray his
poeuerne and seruts sepurall
at day long day day at the joinry
to my soull and man
and laying an brickelon in
the stoowp celoac the beats
and half a day at the shewp
my soull and man

Apreall the 15 day
maken six collackets for
the wherbove half a day to
my soull and man

The first of may
geven the deall for the
portion in the wright loft
for gallow room and fencld
oft one bed, and taken down
an bow in the woorsted
my soul and man and doing
sepurall things
6 days to my soull and man

May the 15 day
wollen below borwoen
pan ... and jowing
sepurall things aboout the still

half a day to my soull and
man
tasede the fuort of Jowen
to Jowton wp the norgreo
bow and taken of the bands
and poston them on a gown
and doing sepurall things
about the hows my soull
and man on day

Jully 13 for poston the
coulls that came owt of the
downshewp and the trees
at the heartsow my
soull and man
2 days   Jully 21 mondonthe
an haf beglivo elescoets my soull
and man
Jully 22 for doparon
the wheull carros in the
clowweor hons my soull
and man
2 days
24 day calon liros of the
for the ios of the wagons
an day my soull and
man
works

[B1, f18v]

Apreaill the furst day
puten up John Greag his
panruf and duing seavreall
an day and a haf day at the panruf
to my sealf and man
and laying an bukdllen in
the sleoup calead the Beatte
and haf a day at the sheap
my sealf and man
Apreaill the 15 day
    maken six collbakets for
    the hearbour haf a day to
    my seallf and man

the furst of May
sawn the dealls for the ~~pea~~
pearticen in the wright Lofte
for gallow rowm and puten
up ane bead and taken down
an bead in the nursrie
my seaf and man and duing
    sevreall things
6 days to my sealf and man

~~May the The 15~~
    ~~neallen Petr Beveard panruf~~
May the 15 day
    neallen Pitear Beveard
    panruf and and duing
    sevreall things about the salltworks

[B1, f19r]

haf a day to my sealf and man
Tusday the furst of Juen
~~Tus~~ puten up the nursree
bead and taken of the bands
and puten them on agean
and duing sevreall things
aboout the hous my seallf
and man an day
Jully 13 for sorten the
   dealls that cam out of the
   Dean[54] shieap and the tries
   at the hearbeare my
   seallf and man
2 days
an haf day
[Jully 21 mendn the
two clos carts my seallf
and man][55]
Jully 22 for reparen
the wheallbarows in the
cllose warkhous my seallf
and man
2 days
24 day cuten tries at the
for the us of the wagens
an day my seallf and
man

---

[54] Danish.
[55] Note that the entry 'Jully 21...and man' was added afterwards, so he inserted it where he had blank paper. As the order is confusing, we have rendered it in date order.

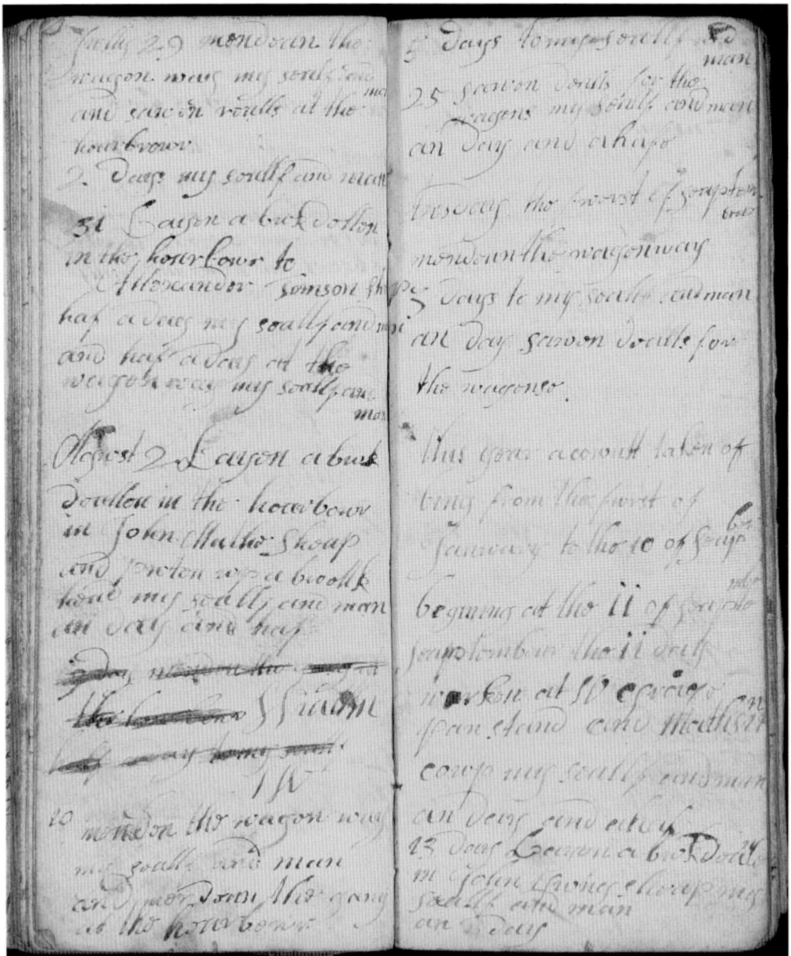
Jouly 29 mondoun the
wagon way my soull and ma
an seaven roulls at the
houerbour
2. days my soull and man
31 Laijen a beck dotton
in the houerbour to
Alexander Simson sho[p]
hof a days my soull and man
and hoef a days at the
wagon way my soull and
man
Agust 2 Laijen a buck
dowllon in the houerbour
in John Mathe Shoup
and foreton was a bootk
hand my soull and man
an day and hoef
[illegible]
Swam
half way home
10 mondon the wagon way
my soull and man
and mor John [illegible] gang
at the houerbour
5 days to my soull and man
25 seaven roulls for the
wagons my soull and man
an day and a haf
tosday the furst of Seaptember
mondon the wagon way
5 days to my soull and man
an day seaven roulls for
the wagons.
this is a account taken of
tims from the furst of
Janury to the 10 of Seap[tember]
begining at the 11 of Seaptember
seaptomber the 11 day
workon at [illegible]
[illegible] stand and [illegible]
corps my soull and man
an days and a haf
12 days Laijen a beck dotton
in John [illegible] shoup my
soull and man
an day

B1, f19v, f20r

[B1, f19v]

Jully 29 mendean the
wagen way my sealf and man
and sawen realls at the
hearbrour
2 days my seallf and man
31 Layen a bukdellen
in the hearbour to
      Allexander Tomson sheep
haf a day my seallf and man
and haf a day at the
wagen way my seallf and man
Agust 2 Layen a buk
deallen in the hearbour
in John Mathe sheap
and puten up a buellk
head my seallf and man
an day and haf
~~19 day menden the gang at~~
  ~~the hearbour~~ Wiallm
~~haf a day to my seallf~~
               W[56]
10 menden the wagen way
  my seallf and man
  and mendean the gang
  at the hearbour

---

[56] Note what appears to be a false start to another 'W' just before this W.

[B1, f20r]

5 days to my seallf and man
25 sawen dealls for the
   wagens my seallf and man
an day and a hafe
Tusday the fuerst of Seaptembear
mendean the wagenway
3 days to my seallf and man
   an day sawen dealls for
   the wagense

   this year acountt taken of
   being from the furst of
   January to the 10 of Seaptember
   begining at the 11 of Seaptember
Seaptembear the 11 day
   worken at W Grage[57]
   pan stand and Mathsin
   cowp my seallf and man
   an day and a haf
13 day Layen a bukdealen
   in John Yung sheap my
   seallf and man
   an day

---

[57] Widow Greig? See C. A. Whatley, 'A Saltwork and the Community: The Case of Winton, 1716-1719', in *Transactions of the East Lothian Antiquarian and Field Naturalists' Society*, Vol. 18 (1984), 51.

19 day worken at the
waggonway my soull
and man
5 days

20 days woken at the
waggonway my soull
and man
5 Days that week

25 sorten the coalls
that cam out of Steam
Johns sheap and maken
a goutter to felon i sen
sheep
on day to my south coal
pitt
27 day worken at the
waggonway my soull and
man
4 days that week

friday the first of october
souten coalls for the crast
rem hord and worken at
stone my soull and man
2 days that work

5 days worken at the
waggonway my soull
and man
5 days that work

11 day worken at the
waggonway my soull and
5 days that week   man
12 days worken about the
hous my soull and man
1 day that week
tuinsday the 18 day
worken about the hous my
soull and man
5 days that week
20 day worken at the
waggonway and souten
my soalt and man double
5 days that week
monday 26 woiken at the
waggonway my soul and
all days that work man
25 worken about hous my
soulf and man
2 day that work

[B1, f20v]

17 day worken at the
wagenway my sealf
and man
5 days
20 day worken at the
    wagenway my seallf
    and man
5 days that week
25 sorten the dealls
that cam out of Stephan
Jolye shieap and maken
a Leather to John Yong
sheap
an day to my seallf and
man
27 day worken at the
    wagenway my seallf and man
4 days that week

Frideay the furst of Ocktober
sawen dealls for the eiast
rowm hight and worken at
theme my seallf and man
2 days that week

[B1, f21r]

5 day worken at the
   wagenway my seallf
   and man
   5 days that week
11 day worken at the
   wagenway my seallf and man
5 days[58] that week
12 day worken about the
   hous my seallf and man
1 day[59] that week
Munday the 18 day
worken about the hous my
seallf and man
5 days that week
20 day worken at the
   wagenway and sawen dealls
   my sealf and man
5 days that week
Munday 26 worken at the
wagenway my sealf and man
an day that week
25 worken about hous my
sealf and man
2 day that week

---

[58] Note that he started with 'an day', changed it to '4 days' and then finally to '5 days'.
[59] Note '5 days' was changed to '1 day'.

2 November 9 day
sewen douls for thens
of the waegens
an days mays salt wa-
10 days maken wyden good
in the morein
an day to my soulf
and man ~~in the waegon at the~~
~~the waegon way my~~
~~soulf and man~~
~~3 days that week~~

12 day maken at the cryp
for the beam at the
colsate
7 days to my soulf and
that week
15 sewen at the feitha
sewen douls for me at
the waegon
2 days at the feitha
an day at the sewen at
doull my soulf and man
3 days at the waegon
my soulf and man
22 days worken at
the waegon way

6 days that week to my
soulf and man
29 worken at the waegon way
man
and sewen doull for wag-
ens and piston and an
stewen wedew in the
wreight werk hous
4 days at the waegon way
2 days at the doull
sewen and stewen wedew
my soulf and man that week

~~nesember the first of~~
~~man on the 5 day of november the~~
~~December worken at the~~
~~the waegon way my~~
~~5 days that week~~

December the 6 day
worken at the waegon way
my soulf and man
6 days that week

munday the 13 day
worken at the waegon way
my soulf and man
6 days that week

[B1, f21v]

    November 9 day
sawen dealls for the us
of the wagens ~~my sealf~~
~~and man~~
an day m~~y~~y salf and man
10 day maken up an preas
    in the nursre
an day to my seallf
and man
~~11 day worken at the~~
    ~~the wagenway my~~
    ~~sealf and man~~
~~3 days that week~~
12 day maken at the cupels
    for the baren at the
    colfald
    2 days to my sealf and man
    that week
15 sawen at the Lathe
sawen dealls for us of
the wagens
2 days at the Lathe
an day at the sawen of
dealls my seallf and man
3 days at the wagenway
    my sealf and man
22 day worken at
    the wagenway

[B1, f22r]

6 days that week to my
   sealf and man
29 worken at the wagenway
   and sawen deall for wagens and puten out an
   storem window in the
   wright workhous
4 days at the wagenway
2 days at the dealls
   sawen and storem wondow
   my seallf and man that week

~~Wadenesday the fuerst of~~
   ~~Munday the~~ 6 day of thes munthe
~~Deseambear worken at the~~
   ~~the wagenway my seallf and man~~
~~5 days that week~~
Desambear the 6 day
   workean at the wagenway
   my seallf and man
6 days that week
   Munday the 13 day
   worken at the wagenway
   my sealf and man
6 days that week

13 day altroan the
window brickwork in the
fresh drawingroom of the
Lymeno my selfe and man
all day
5 days at the waggonway coalls
muneday the 20

boujon a bro Rosten at the
hour tower in the stoops
my selfe and man
buy a days

22 days makon a drawen
for drayers the pieces in batten
and doreon goeined thinges
about the hows my selfe and
man all day
29 gaven coulls for the m's
of the wagons
all day

the record of the last year
before the year 1725
[crossed out]
gaun 45 statens

1x26 founeed the 13 day
repearen the saltworks my
selfe and man
3x days that week
muneday the 19
workon about the salt
works my selfe and man
6x days that week
muneday the 24 day
6x days at the saltworks my
selfe and man
tusday the 25 day
makon at the colleorpes my
selfe
4 days that week

tusday the 25 day my man
workon at the waggonway
with cleam grund
4 days that week

[crossed out]
bosday the frost of foubruwar
altroan the poorticon in the
barum at the coll feld and
workon at the saltwork my
selfe
3 days to my selfe

[B1, f22v]

    13 day alltrean the
    window briests in the
    high dinin rowm of the
    Linene my seallf and man
an day
5 days at the wagenway sealf man
    Munday the 20
    Layen a bukdellen at the
    hearbour in the slloup
    my seallf and man
haf a day
22 day maken a draneer
    for drayen the pweri in kitsin
    and dowen seavrel things
    about the hous my sealf and man
an day
29 sawen dealls for the us
    of the wagens
an day __ __ __ __ __
    the eand of the Last year
    bigen[60] the year 1725
    ~~Januar 22 Recved from~~
    ~~John Gown 15 shilens~~

---

[60] Bygone – see DSL/DOST: 'Bygane', with the spelling variant 'bygene'.

[B1, f23r]

~~1~~1726 Januar the 13 day
   reparen the saltworks my
   seallf and man
3 x days that week
   Munday the 17
   worken about the sallt
   works my seallf and man
6 x days that week
   Munday the 24 day
2 x days[61] at the salltworks my
   seallf and man
   Tusday the 25 day
   maken at the collcorfes my
   seallf
4 days that week
   Tusday the 25 day my man
   worken at the wagenway
   with Adam Grant
4 days that week
~~Tusday the furss day~~
Tusday the furst of Feaberuari
alltrean the pearticen in the
barean at the collfalld and
worken at the salltworks my
seallf
3 days to my seallf

---

[61] Note that the '2 x' was written over 'an' as a correction from one day to two.

tuseday the fyrs of febuary
my men worken at the
waigonway
5 days that work
tysday the 3
proton on the waenworke
on the course and proton the
aeon work the waigon doors
2 days that work my soull
satterday the fifte day
X worken the grieat for the
colhill my soull and men
on day
monday the fryday
+ worken at the poont my souly
and men
6 days that work
newsday the 19 day
X worken at the grieat my
soull and men
2 days of that work
wadensday 16 day
worken at the saltworks
my soull and men
4 days that work
monday the 21
maken still waves for the
saltworks
2 days that work to my
soull and man

wedensday the 25 day
maken an othere vilod
cort for the colhill
2 days that work to my
soull and man
friday the 25
[struck through]

friday the 25 proton up
the maison of my ons
maken ther trosses and
maken there sewolls and
evrey fearwell things about
the works my soull and man
2 days

[B1, f23v]

Tusday the furs of Febrewari
   my man worken at the
   wagenway
5 days that week ~~day that week~~
   Fursday the 3
   puten on the arenworke
   on the corefs and puten the
   aren work on the wagon doors
2 days that week my seallf
   Seaterrday the fifte day
X worken at the great for the
   collhill my seallf and man
an day
   Munday the 7: day:
X worken at the great my sealf
   and man
6 days that week:
   Munday the 14 day
X worken at the great my
   seallf and man
2 day of that week
   Wadensday 16 day
   worken at the salltworks
   my sealf and man
4 days that week
   Munday the 21
   maken whillbarows for the
   salltworks

2 days that week to my sea[62]
  seallf and man

[B1, f24r]

  Wadensday the 23 day
  maken an othear ribed
  corf for the collhill
2 days that week to my
  seallf and man
  ~~Friday the 25~~
  ~~Layen a buckdellen in the~~
  ~~hearbour to Mastear: Mack-~~
  ~~duekell my seallf and man~~
~~2 days to that~~
  ~~Friday the 25~~
  ~~worken about the salltwork~~
  ~~my seallf and man~~
~~2 days that week~~
  ~~Munday the last of~~
  ~~Febrewarie worken at Donellson~~
  ~~panruf my seallf and man~~
  ~~and puten the measen gang~~
  ~~puten in new gistes in his hous~~
  ~~and~~
  Friday the 25 puten up
  the measen gang and
  maken thear treasses and
  maken thear scafellt and
  duing seavrell things about
  the works my seallf and man
2 days

---

[62] Note this is an abandoned attempt at 'seallf', which he wrote on the next line.

tuesday the first of
ffebrewary
taken down the olde roof
of denellson pour and mekon
the new cupolle and worken
about the beam and purloin
[struck] girts in the barnhous
and [thuroen] the [fellor] my
soull and man
6 days that work
wensday the 9 day
worken at the [work] the new
barnrof and other things
about the poor houses
4 days that work at the [fatty]
friday the 11 [works]
taken [corp] the [crook] to
the Coll hill my soull and man
on day and chap that week
munday the 14
worken at the [quee] at the coll hill
at the [putin] together
my soull and man
2 days that work

Month 25
Bloken out the tombou
for the corp my soull and
man
2 days that work

munday 18
worken at the Corp my
soull and man
6 days that work

ffebruary the 1 day bious
munday
worken at the Cors
my soull and man
3 days that work

munday 11 day
worken at corps my soully
and man
6 days that work
munday the 18
worken at the corps my soull
and man
6 that week
the here worke

munday 25 of ffebruary
worken about the hogs and
porken the depths that Common
of John [Maker] and
[Elion] [folly] [hoops] my soull
and man
6 days that week

[B1, f24v]

    Tusday the furst of
    Marthe
    taken down the olld rufe
    of Donellson pan and maken
    the new cupells and worken
    about the seam and puten in
    new[63] gists in the panhous
    and menden the fllwr[64] my
    seallf and man
6 days that week
    Munday the 7 day
    worken at the at the new
    panruf and other things
    about the pan houses L[   ][65]
4 days that week at the salltworks[66]
an haf day[67]
    Frideye the 11 day
    taken up the great to
X the Collhill my seallf and man
an day and a haf that week
    Munday the 14
X worken at the great at the collhill
    at the putin up ther
    my seallf and man
2 days that week

---

[63] Note that 'new' is written over another word beginning with 'd'.
[64] Floor.
[65] He appears to have made a mistake as he then smudged out the word beginning with 'L'.
[66] The 'works' in 'salltworks' was written belowline.
[67] Note: 'an haf day' is written perpendicular to '4' and is clearly an afterthought addition.

[B1, f25r]

Marth 25
    Blloken out the tembear
    for the corf my seallf and
    man
2 days that week
    Munday 28
    worken at the Corfs my
    seall and man
6 days that week
    Apriell the 4 day biene
    Munday
    worken at the Corfs
    my seallf and man
3 days that week
    Munday 11 day
    worken at corfs my seallf
    and man
6 days that week
    Munday the 18
    worken at the corfs mysealf
    and man
6 that week
      the hous worke
    Munday 25 of Apreall
    worken about the hous and
    sorten the dealls that cam out
    of John Mathe and
    Stien[68] Jolley sheap my sealf
    and man
6 days that week

---

[68] Normally we have expanded 'Stean' to 'Stephan', but here, as he has spelled it differently, we have left it.

6 May Goeing on Sabath
monday the 2 day
worken about the hous
Staken doull in the cley
and goeto up the gabants
6 days that work

May 11
worken at the sall
worke my selfe and man
3 days that work
worken at Jones Brown
rom
2½ day worken about
the hous my selfe and man
yeild out the gabants
in the ottings and maken
bords for the rome Simi[lar]
2 days that work

gun the 11 day
maken bords to the chimtes
my selfe and man
on a thard day
[crossed out] XX
[crossed out]
the [crossed out] the [crossed out]
the grand of this account
a bup viton tacked of to
be comeing upon the how
account

monday 23 July of July
worken about the hous
my selfe
half [crossed out] a day for[...]
worken about the hous
my selfe and man
5 days this week
half a day to my selfe in
the sam week
monday the first of
August worken about the
the hous and pontes the
bras that cam out of
Solon Mothe hous and
forton the cords
6 days to my selfe and
man
monday the 15 day
upon toup this garillon in
sexton work about hous
Steck my selfe
on day on other
the [crossed out]
the [crossed out] hous [crossed out]
the 24 day taken down
the Larn in the upper rom
on day to my selfe

[B1, f25v]

    May begens on Sabethe
    Munday the 2 day
    worken about the hous
    staken dealls in the cllos
    and pute up the gabealls
6 days that week
    May 11
    worken at the sallt
    works my seallf and man
3 days that week
    worken at James Brown
    pan
    24 day worken about
    the hous my seallf and man
    rightean the gabearts
    in the olleard[69] and maken
    brods for the rume chimlle
3 day that week
    ~~Jun the~~ 11 day
    ~~maken brodes to the chimllis~~
    ~~my sealf and man~~
~~on half day~~ X X
    ~~the end of the taken~~

the eand of this acount
abuf writen takeat of be-
gening upon anothear
acount

---

[69] Did he mean 'oll[d y]eard'? See f9r where he states: 'in the olld yeard'.

[B1, f26r]

Munday 25 day of Jully
~~worken about the hous~~
~~my seallf~~
~~haf a day to my seallf~~
   worken about the hous
   my seallf and man
5 days of that week
haf a day to my sealf in
   the sam wek
   Munday the furst of
   Agust worken about the
   the hous and pearten the
   trieas that cam out of
   John Mathe shep and
   sorten the dealls
6 days to my seallf and man
   Munday the 15 day
   puten up the peallen in
   Seaton park about heay
   stak my seallf
on day and a haf
   ~~the 24 takn down the~~
   ~~in the Neursrie~~
~~on day to my seallf~~
   the 24 day taken down
   the Linin in the Nursrie
on day to my seallf

B1, f26v, f27r

[B1, f26v]

  Seaptembear the 20 day
 sorten the dealls that cam
 out of Stephan Jolly shalp
 my seallf and man
3 days that week
 26 day sortean dealls my
 seallf and man
2 days to my sealf and man[70]
 Ocktobear the furst
 maken the new Linine
 and beads stides in the
 Nursrie
6 days that week my sealf
 and man
 dito worken at dito
4 day that week my sealf
 and man
 Munday the 17
 maken at the windows
 to Dunken Grame
 hous
6 days to my seallf and man
 Munday 24
 worken at ditto that week
2 days
 Novembear the furst
 worken at ditto my seallf and man
6 days that week

---

[70] Note: this text was written over 'on and a haf day'.

[B1, f27r]

    Januar 1727
    worken at the salltworks
    and the pertisen for the
    grien Rowm[71] worken by
    Johen Jamson ordears
    bien the 23 of Januari
6 days to my sealf and man
    Munday the 30 day
    worken at ditto my seallf
6 days that wiek
    my man worken at ditto
4 days and a haf day
    an day and haf day to
    Isbeal Brown hous
    Munday the 6 of Febrewari
    worken at ditto maken the
    cleater cafelld[72] and polls
    and nealen the brwesruef[73]
2 days to my seallf and man
    at that work
10 day worken at James Watson
    panruf with James
    Johnston and sawen Lath
    myseallf and man
2 days at that work

---

[71] At Cockenzie House there is a room which is still called the 'Green Room' today, though it is unclear if it is the same room. It is painted green, and is on the first floor to the right of the stairs when looking from the front yard. We're grateful to Mr Gordon Neil, the current joiner for Cockenzie House, for providing this information.
[72] cleated scaffold.
[73] brewhouse roof.

monday the 20 day
worken at the greene roum
worken up the portheon
1 days to my soelf and
mein that week

24 day althon the
the portlicoin in the
kittein cut down
sawarwoll thing abort the
hows
on day to my soelf and mein

tuesday the 28 day
taken the Lenn in the gre-
roum agoun, sown
and althon the two windeys
ond sawen them about and
up on cwthe of the windos
on day one half to my soelf
on thes day an greett monday
maken spout to johns
and righted us stons

Mearth the 3 day maken
on speus to the poorbour
maken a spout for wrundo
the coils chito thir shew
on day to my soelf

Mearth the 2 day
maken 6 collbockots to harold
on day and haf day to my soelf
29 day
taken down ptons Broun
ries maken som erypoulk and
worken about the callwork
on day to my soelf and mein
accoumt
the erane of that yeare

foouweane 1728

rose at thee luxcep the
3 day of that month
the 2 day of Jonneare
worken at the house for
the callwoull
2 days one half over
five days the 15 worken
at the collthworks
2 that week

munday the 22
pactoin up the provisn
1 days that work

[B1, f27v]

Munday the 20 day
    worken at the grean roum
    puten up the perttisen
4 days to my seallf and
    man that week
    24 day alltren
    the pearttisean in the
        kittsin and down
    seavrell things about the
    hous
on day to my seallf and man
    Tusday the 28 day
    taken the Linen in the grin
    rowm window down ~~puten~~
    and altren the two windows
    and Linen them about puten
    up an cullie of the window
on day and haf to my sealf
on hay day an geatt menden
    maken spout to John P
    and rightn his stand
    Marth the 27 day maken
    an gang to the hearbour
    maken a spout for runin the
    the colls in to the ships
on day to my seallf

[B1, f28r]

    Marthe the 27 day
    maken 6 collbakets to hearbeour
on day and haf day to my sealf
      29 day
    taken down Pitear Beveard
    ruf maken som cupealls and
    workean about the salltworks
on day to my seallf and man
    the eand of that year acount
    Januarie 1728
~~worken at the harp the~~
~~2 day of that munth~~
    the 2 day of Januarie
    worken at the heape for
    the collheall
2 days and haff day
    Fuersday the 17 worken
    at the salltworks
2 that week
    Munday the 22
    puten up the panstands
6 days that week

munday the 29
werken et the granstean
3 days that work

fursdewerie the 13
werken at the sall work
and maken wheelbarrow
3 days that work

tnorsday 23 day 1725
Lousen a bie delton in
Storm Jollis sheep
and porten 10 p 3 bieth sheep
5 day

Weather the fuirst day
an day in the we ewr howr gowin
up on brott head for woull

wensday the ii
worken at John Penes son
4 days and a haf day

munday the 25
worken at Sanders medtson
penrws and stean
on day

fursday the 28
maken the penweinds
and dowing severall things
about the works
3 days

Aprell the 8
maken an pump and
taptew le Robert donelse
bucket pitt
an haf day

May the 10 day
sorten the deells that cam
oot of the denns sheep
3 days that work

May the 21
maken 6 lockers for porken
gellons at port seaton and put
on up a boord for the gillen
eye flowr
an day

wedensday the 3 day of Jueni 1725
enterwes to work at porteerdo
to the roof with John Jamson
2 days that work and
2 haf days that work

[B1, f28v]

    Munday the 29
    worken at the panstands
3 days that week
    Fuebuarie the 13
    worken at the salltwork
    and makn whillbarows
3 days that week

```
                  ┌─────────────────────────────────────┐
       Jolly sheap│ Fuersday 23 day 1728                │
                  │ Layen a bukdellen in                │
                  │ Stephan Jolly sheap                 │
                  │ and puten up 3 bullkshead           │
                  │ 5   day                             │
                  └─────────────────────────────────────┘
```

    Marthe the furst day
~~an in the~~
an day in the wear hous puten
    up an bullkhead for meall
    Munday the 11
    worken at John Donellson
    panruf
4 days and a haf day
    Munday the 25
    worken at Sanders Mathson
    panruf and stand
on day

[B1, f29r]

    Fursday the 28
    maken the panwands
    and dowing seavrell things
    about the works
3 days
    Apriell the 8
    maken an pump and
    tap trie to Robeart Donelson
    bucket patt
an haf day
    May the 10 day
    sorten the dealls that cam
    out of the Deans sheap
3 days theat week
    May the 21
    maken 6 bockess for paken
    glleas at Port Seaton and put-
    en up a boord for the gllea-
    eris thear
on day
    Wadensday the 3 day of Juene 1728
    entareen to work at Port Seaton
    to the ruef with Johen Jameson
2 days that week and
2 haf days that week

	mundays the 15 day
	werken at ditto
6	days that week
	munday the 19
	werken at ditto
6	days that week
	munday the 22 of...
	worken at portiton at the
	gests
5	days and half day
	munday the 29 day
	worken at portiton pr...
	to the gests to the cupo...
	and deacon on the right
	and sown severall things
	abouet the house
	days that week
	munday the 5 day of
	Ogueset worken at ...
	and makon treves for the
	masons and sown se...
	things ther
4	days that week
2	days at the call work
	Mecone or Mathson
	munday the 12 day
	makon newenes gests and
	braces and cowms and
	sown severall things

6	days that work
	munday 19 makon ...
	for the masons and sown
	severall things ther
4	days that work
	friday the 23
	hewen gerds at the coll
	sald and hangen the
	gerds and pinten to cut
	beads and taken pilens
	Bavour pan ruf down
	days
	munday the 26 Ogueset
	makon at the gerds at
	portgarden
	days that work
	thursday 29 day
	worken at pitour Bowan
	severuf
	days that work
	munday the 2 day of
	Souptembour
	worken at the pan ruf
	and sown severall about
	the workes
	days at ditto

[B1, f29v]

    Munday the ten day
  worken at ditto
6 days that week
    Munday the 17
  worken at ditto
6 days that week
    Munday the 22 of Jully
  worken at Port Siton at the
  geats
5 days and haf day
    Munday the 29 day
  woorken at Port Siton puten
  to the geasts to the cupells
  and drawen on the rufe
  and duen seaverall thengs
  abeout the heous
5 days that week
    Munday the 5 day of
  Aguest worken at deato
  and maken treases for the
  masens and dowen seavrel
  thengs thear
4 days that week
2 days at the salltworks
    Allexander Mathson
    Munday the 12 day
  maken measensis gangs and
  treaseas and cowms and
  dowen seavreall things

[B1, f30r]

6 days that week

    Munday 19 maken cowms
    for the measens and dowen
    seavreall things ther

4 days that week
    Fridey the 23
    Altren geats at the coll
    falld and hingen the
    geats and puten to cat
    bands and teaken Pitear
    Beveard pan ruf down

[Margin: 'salltwork']

2 days
    Munday the 26 Aguest
    maken at the geats at
    Port Seaton

3 days that week
    Fursday 29 day
    worken at Pitear Beveard
    panruf

3 days that week
    Munday the 2 day of
    Seapteambear
    workean at the panruf
    and dowen seavreall about
    the workss

[Margin: 'salltwork']

2 days at ditto

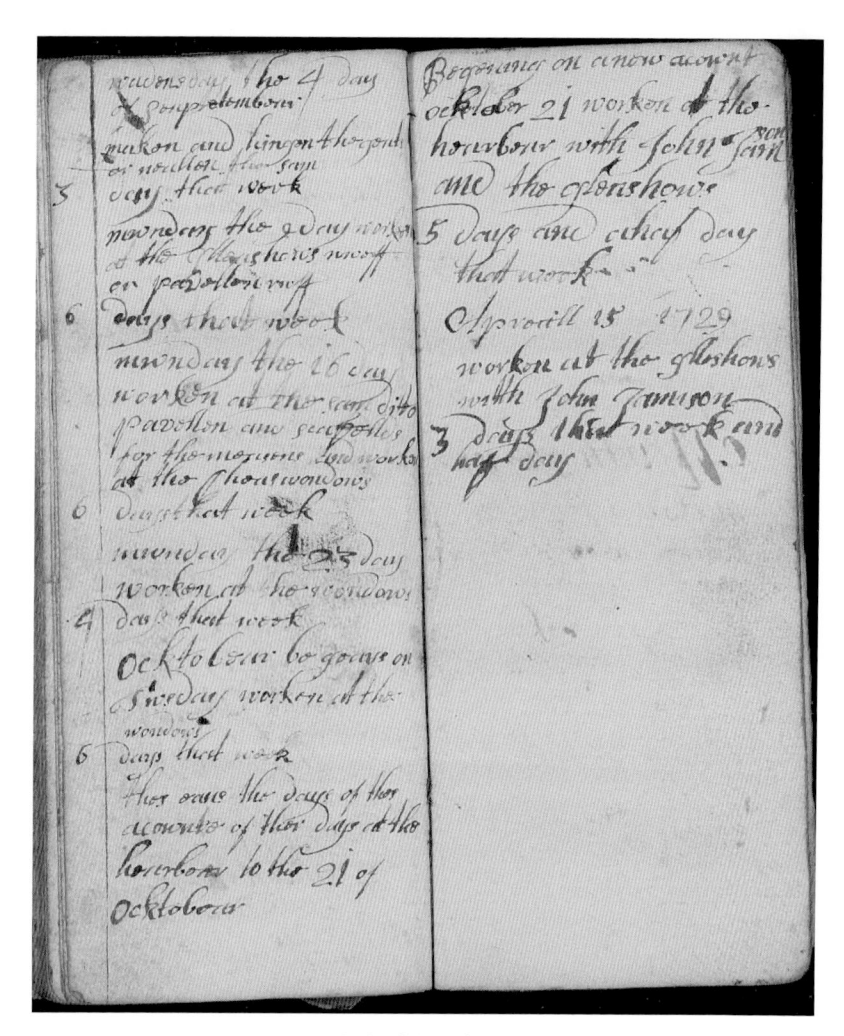

wedensday the 4 day
of September
makon and lieing on the yeards
or nowlles the sam
3 | day thet work

mondday the 9 day worken
at the ploughowrs rowoff
on padellon row
6 | days thet work

mondday the 16 day
worken at the sam dito
pavellon and seecpottes
for the mesume and works
at the hous wondows
6 | days thet work

mondday the 23 day
worken at the wondows
4 | days thet work

Oktober bogons on
fixeday worken at the
wondows
6 | days thet work

thes eads the days of thes
acounts of thes days at the
hoverbour to the 21 of
Oktober

Begenans on a now acount
oktober 21 worken at the
hoverbour with John son Jean
and the plowshowr
5 | days and othes day
thet work

Aprooill 15 1729
worken at the ploshows
with John Jamison
3 | days thet work and
half day

[B1, f30v]

    Wadensday the 4 day
    of Seaptetembear
    maken and hingen the geats
    or neallen the sam
3 day that week
    Munday the 9 day worken
    at the Glleashous rueff
    or Pavellen ruff
6 days that week
    Munday the 16 day
    worken at the sam ditto
    Pavellen and scafellds
    for the measens and worken
    at the Cheaswondows
6 days that week
    Munday the 23 day
    worken at the wondows
4 days that week
    Ocktobear begeans on
    Tusday worken at the
    wondows
6 days that week
    thes eans the days of thes
    acounte of ther days at the
    hearbear to the 21 of
    Ocktobear

[B1, f31r]

Begening on a new acount
Ocktober 21 worken at the
hearbear with John Jameson
and the gleashous
5 days and a haf day
   that week
   Apreaill 15 1729
   worken at the glleshous
   witth John Jamison
3 days that week and
   haf day

[B1, f31v]

   Feabwarie the 20 day
   1729
   sorten dealls in the
   cllos
3 days that week

   Munday the 24 day
   sorten dealls in the cllos
5 days that week
   Munday the 3 day
   sorten dealls
on day that week
   Marth the 17
   maken a preas for
   hingen clos in to standin
   garet
5 days that week

febrearie the 20 day
1629
sorton dealls in the
Clos
3 days that week

munday the 24 day
sorton dealls in the clos
5 days that week

monday the 3 day
sorton dealls
on deep that week

March the 17
makon a prees for
hanson clos in to standin
garet
5 days that week

Juen the 15 day
sorton the ousle that cam
out of John Mathe shoep
5 days that week

August the 12 day
sorton the dealls that cam
out of John Mathe sheep
7 days

octtobar the 11 day makon
the modell for the toun
2 days that week

November the 1 day
makon a pregn about todd
noall the cornner Godon
and workon about the
meall bouris and douen
seaurall thyngs
5 days and half

desambar the 8 day
workon about the meall bon us
haf day

[B1, f32r]

Juen the 18 day
sortten the dealls that cam
out of John Mathe sheap
5 days that week

Aguestt the 18 day
sortten the dealls that cam
out of John Mathe shep
7 days
    Octtobear the 11 day maken
    the modeall for the tome
2 days that week

    Novembear the 17 day
    maken a fram to a bead and
    neall the canmes[74] bodem
    and worken about the
    mallt bowns and dowen
    seavreall thengs
5 days and haf
    Desambear the 8 day
    worken about the mallbowns
    haf day

---

[74] Possibly a scribal error for 'canwes' or canvas.

January the 19 1750
workon in the yeard at
the portton my sontt
and man
on day on haf and haf to man
tusday the 21 workon in
the yeard my wallf at the
portton and the kelhwole
2 days that work
febrewary the 6 day
Layon a brok dollan
Allexcevexr yong sheepe

All thes formour
acount bieh taken of and
drawon out from the yare
2429 bieinging upon
a now account

March the 3 day 1750
workon at a portton up for
the mult loft
4 days that work

tusday the 10 day
workon at the same
porthion wall
4 days that week

Aprall the 8 day
Layon a brok dollan in
top of our Chaplwan sheep
cow portton up on stordon
on day

April the 9 day
mendon the kelhwole
on day

Aprall the 11 day
mendon the kelhle and
the cuwall abuf the
kell
on day and haf

May the 26 days
workon a broad of the
sheep at the horerbour
down, ser we all thomeye
ther
4 days thoud

Iuly the furst
portton up and portton out
of our Echon mathor sheep
haf day

[B1, f32v]

    Januari the 19 1730
  worken in the yeard at
  the peallen my seallf
  and man
an day and haf and haf day to my
  man
  Tusday the 21 worken in
  the yeard my seallf at the
  peallen and the kiellriebs
2 days that week
~~on day Layen a bukdllen~~
  Fubrewarie the 6 day
  Layen a bukdellan
  Allexander Yonge sllupe

  All thes formear
acount bien taken of and
  drawen out biean the year
    1729 bieanging upon

  A new acountt
Marth the 3 day 1730
  worken at a pertisen wa[ll] for
  the mallt Loft
4 days that week

[B1, f33r]

    Tusday the 10 day
    worken at the same
    pearthsion wall
4 days that week
    Apreall the 8 day
    Layen a bukdeallen in
    Sepkaar Cheapllean sheap
    and puten up an steallen
on day
    Aprll the 9 day
    menden the kellrebs
on day
    Apreall the 11 day
    menden the kellrebs and
    the cudell abuf the
    kiell
on day and haf
    May the 26 day
    worken abword of the
    sleuop at the hearbour
    dowen seavreall thengs
    ther
4 days thear ~~Jully the~~
      Jully the furst
    puten up an brist for matllt[75]
    in Johen Mathe sheap
haf day

---

[75] Presumably 'malt'. See appendices for a note of John's son Thomas and his dealings in malt.

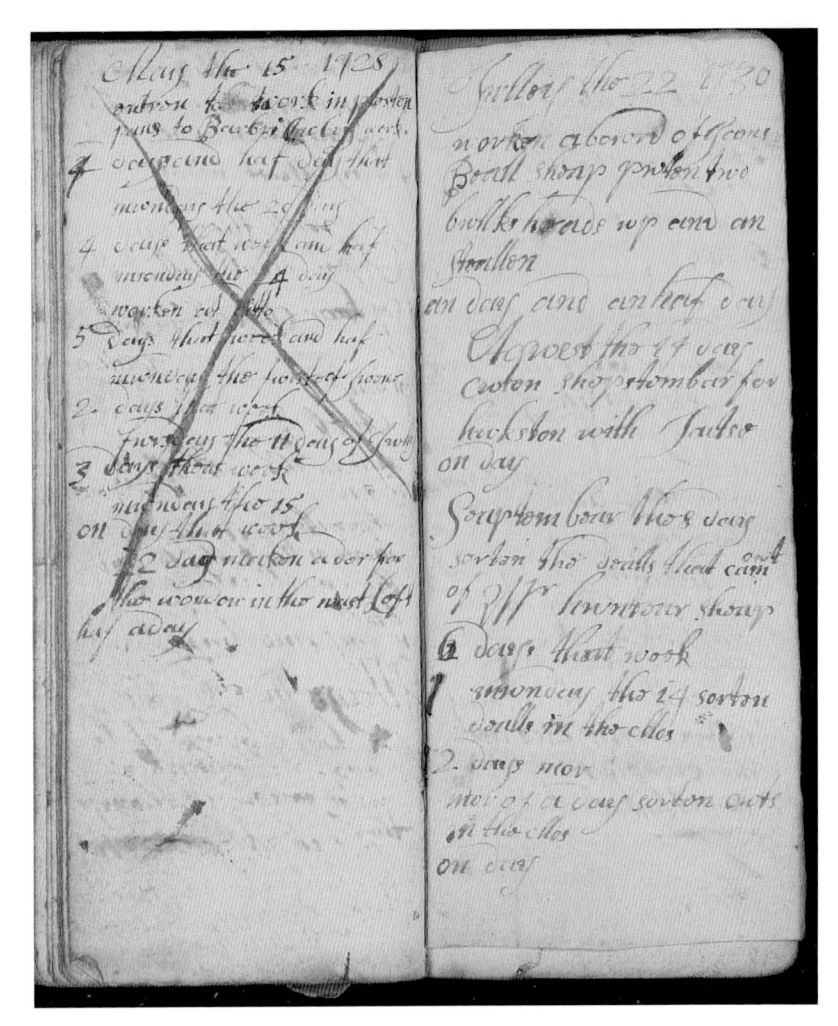

B1, f33v, f34r

f33v (crossed out)

Aug the 15 1728
entred to work in potten
puns to Bearbrithcter work
4 ocepeons half day that
mending the 20 ...
4 days that work one half
mending the 4 day
worken ed ...
5 days that work and half
mending the twist of ....
2 days ... work
tursdays the tt day of ...
3 days ... work
mending the 15
on day that work
2 day merken a der for
the woucow in the nust left
half day

f34r

Jully the 22 1730
worken aboword of scons
Boatt shoap porten two
bullks heads up eew an
Stoullon
on day and an half day
Agoust the 14 days
coton shoptember for
hackston with Sutso
on day
Soeptember two days
sorten the deals that cam
of R/R leumtover shoap
6 days that work
mendeay the 14 sorten
deals in the eller
2 days mor
mon of a day sorten outs
in the eller
on day

[B1, f33v]

~~May the 15 1728~~
~~entren to work in Presten-~~
~~pans to Barbri Cubey work~~
~~4 days and haf day that~~
~~Munday the 20 day~~
~~4 days that week and haf~~
~~Munday the 24 day~~
~~worken at ditto~~
~~5 days that week and haf~~
~~Munday the furste of Juene~~
~~2 days that week~~
~~Fursday the 11 day of Jully~~
~~3 days theat week~~
~~Munday the 15~~
~~on day that week~~
~~22 day maken a dor for~~
~~the wondow in the wast Loft~~
~~haf a day~~

[B1, f34r]

    Julley the 22 1730
    worken abowrd of James
    Beall sheap puten two
    bullksheads up and an
    steallen
an day and a haf day
    Aguest the 14 day
    cuten sheps tembar for
    Hukston with Jaitse
on day
    Seaptembear the 8 day
    sorten the dealls that cam out
    of Mr Huntear sheap
6 days that week
    Munday the 14 sorten
    dealls in the cllos
2 days mor
    mor of a day sorten cuts
    in the cllos
on day

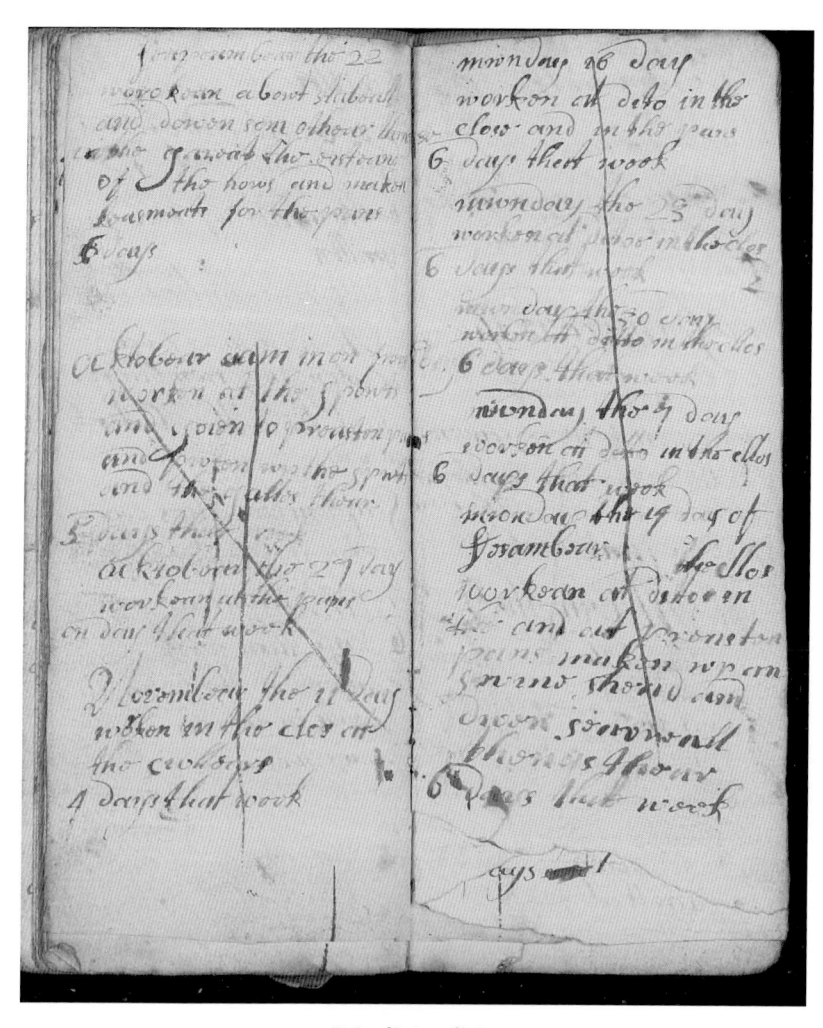

septembor the 22
worken about the boat
and down som other thing
in the ground the estovar
of the hows and makon
basmoth for the poor
6 days

octobor sixm in on
worken at the spout
and gown to prouston
and brogt home the spout
and the other ther
5 days ther

octobor the 27 day
worken at the
on day ther work

November the 11 days
worken in the cles on
the crocksot
4 days that work

monday 26 day
worken at deto in the
cles and in the pens
6 days ther work

monday the 28 day
worken at deto in the cles
6 days that work

monday the 30 day
worken at deto in the cles
6 days ther work

monday the 27 day
worken on deto in the cles
6 days that work

monday the 19 day of
November the cles
worken on deto en
the and out prouston
pens maken upon
swine shord and
oxen sorrow all
thongs ther
6 days ther work

days

[B1, f34v]

    Seapeambear the 22
  worokean about stabeall
  and dowen som othear thingse
in the gareat the eist eand
  of the hous and maken
  keasmeats for the pans
6 days

~~Ocktobear cam in on Fursday~~
   ~~worken at the spouts~~
   ~~and goien to Preastonpans~~
   ~~and puten up the spouts~~
   ~~and the gables thear~~
~~5 days that week~~
   ~~Ocktobear the 27 day~~
   ~~workean at the pans~~
~~on day that week~~

   ~~Novembear the 11 day~~
   ~~worken in the clos at~~
   ~~the cullears~~
~~4 days that week~~

[B1, f35r]

~~Munday 16 day~~
~~worken at dito in the~~
~~close and in the pans~~
~~6 days that week~~
~~Munday the 23 day~~
~~worken at ditoe in the clos~~
~~6 days that week~~
~~Munday the 30 day~~
~~worken at ditto in the cllos~~
~~6 days that week~~
~~Munday the 7 day~~
~~worken at ditto in the cllos~~
~~6 days that week~~
~~Munday the 14 day of~~
~~Desambear~~
~~workean at ditto in the cllos~~
~~and at Preasten-~~
~~pans maken up an~~
~~swine shead and~~
~~dowen seavreall~~
~~thengs thear~~
~~6 days that week~~

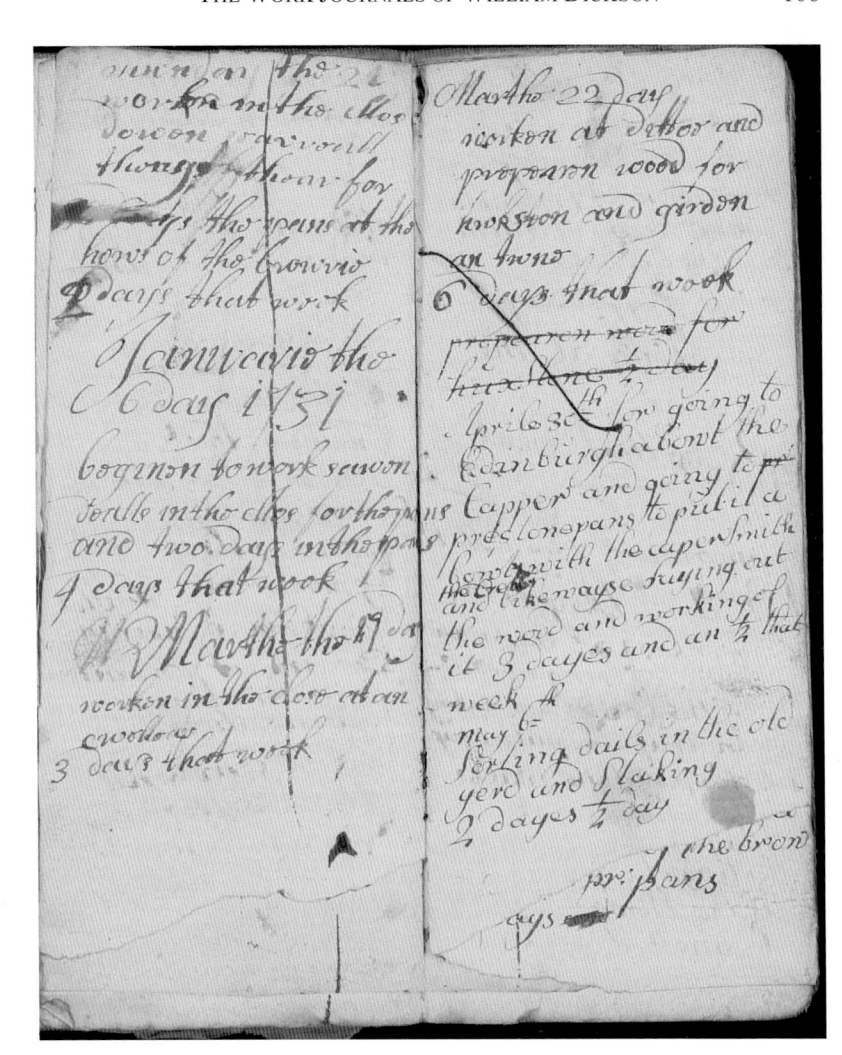

wrun on the 2[?]
workm in the clos
doroon [?] well
things [?] hour for
[?] the pans at the
hows of the browio
2 days that work

Janwarie the
6 day 1731
beginen to work sawon
[?] in the clos for the pans
and two days in the pans
4 days that work

Mawthe the 19 [?]
workon in the clos ab on
cwollores
3 days that work

Mawthe 22 day
workon at deker and
properann [?] for
workson and girdon
an iron
6 days that wook
[crossed out: properon new for]
[crossed out: [?]]
Aprile 30th for going to
Edanburgh about the
copper and going to pu[?]
preslonepans to pul it a
how with the copersmith
and likewayse buying out
the roed and working of
it 3 dayes and an ½ that
week

may 6 =
Perling dails in the ole
yerd and Plaking
2 dayes ½ day

[?] the brow
pr pans
[?]

[B1, f35v]

~~Munday the 21~~
~~worken in the cllos~~
~~dowen sevreall~~
~~thengs thear for~~
~~the pans at the~~
~~hous of the browrie~~
~~2 days that week~~
~~Januarie the~~
~~6 day 1731~~
~~beginen to work sawen~~
~~dealls in the cllos for the pans~~
~~and two days in the pans~~
~~4 days that week~~
~~Marthe the 17 day~~
~~worken in the close at an~~
~~cuellear~~
~~3 days that week~~

[B1, f36r]

Marthe 22 day
   worken at dittoe and
   prepearen wood for
   Hukston and girden
   an tune
6 days that week[76]
   ~~prepearen wood for~~
   ~~Huxstone 1/2 day~~
   Aprile 30th for going to
   Edinburgh about the
   Capper and going to ~~Pr~~
Prestonepans to put it a-
bout the Crebb with the capersmith
and likewayse laying out
the wood and working of
it 3 dayes and an 1/2 that
week
May 6th
sorting dails in the old
yerd and slaking
2 dayes 1/2 day

---

[76] Note the change in hand from this point forward. Someone else was writing in Dickson's work journals.

May the 12th day
working at the
browari in p:pans
making of Corppals
and fainy of faith
3 days) that weak
½

May 17th day
working at the
browari
4 days that week

May 22 day
mending the Mathifte
1 3 day

May 25 th
working at the browa=
=arie altring and seting
of the Coolers and making
an trap and piting up
1½ of a perlitione wall
day that week

worken at preston pans
preston wp an porellon
at prestonpans
from 1 day
day and half

worken at the harbowr
proten wp an Crollkhead
in john hirton shoop
and an stotton and nomwen
the skeapers head for Mr
Mathoins
dagg and half day
on 2

Sutter the 20
Seplm: 9th
for making a label
to betty Matthew
fixing of it and dong
some other things a=
bout the howse
2 day that week
Seplm: 13
for making a flote
for the use of the brow
=ari in mr pans
2½ days

[B1, f36v]

    May the 12th day
    working at the
    browari in Prestonpans
    making of coupals
    and laing of laith
3 1/2 days} that weak
    May 17th day
    working at the
    browari
4} days that week
       May 22^{d} day
    mending the Maltlofte
1} day
       May 25th
    working at the browa-
    arie altring and seling
    of the Collers and making
    an trap and puting up
    of a pertitone wall
1 1/2 day that week

[B1, f37r]

    worken at Prestonpans
    puten up an peallen
    at Prestonpans
    Juen 11 day
on day and haf
    worken at the hearbour
    puten up an bullkhead
    in John Huten sheap
    and an sttellen and menden
    the skeapers bead for Mr
    Mathe use
2 days and haf day
    Julley the 20
    September 8th
    for making a label
    to Betty Matthew &
    fixing of it and doing
    some other things a-
    bout the house
2 Day that week
    September 13th
    for making a flot to
    for the use of the brow-
    ari in Prestonpans
2 1/2 days ~~and~~

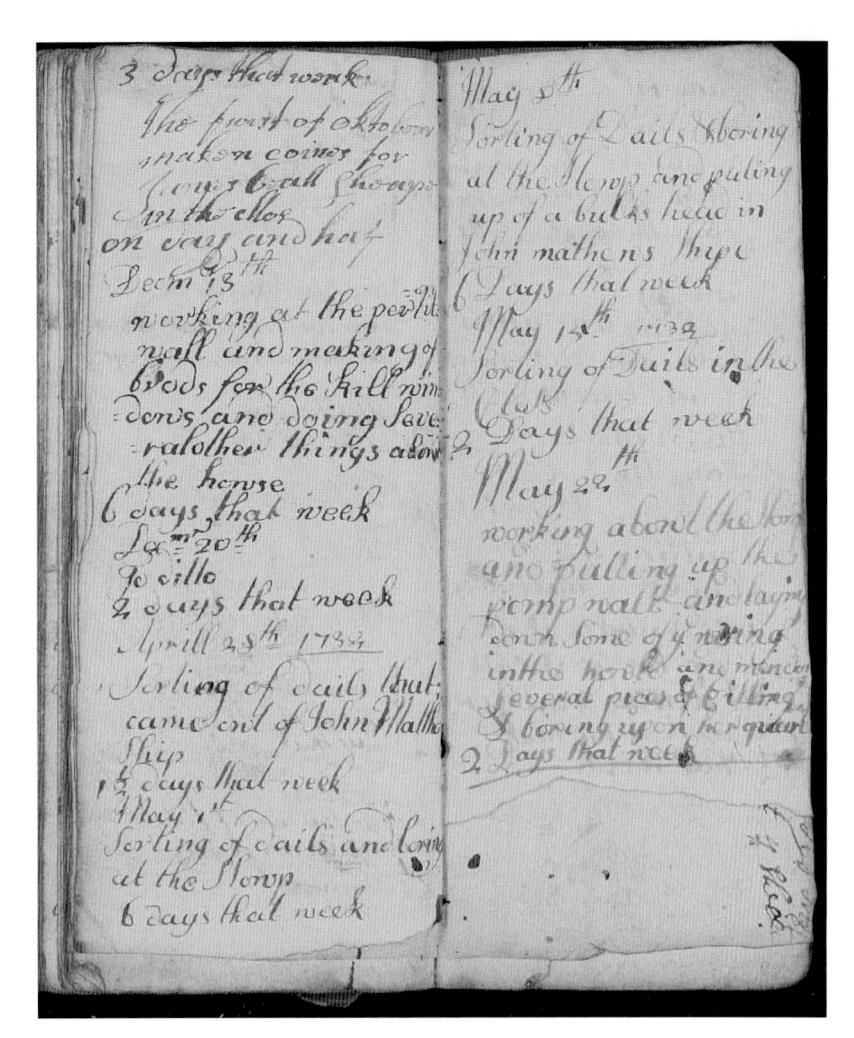

3 days that work
the frunt of oktober
maken corner for
[...] Coll [...]
in the clos
on day and ha[lf]
Decm 18th
working at the pertit[ion]
wall and making of
boeds for the hill win-
=dows and doing seve-
=ral other things about
the house
6 days that week
Jar 20th
To ditto
2 days that week
Aprill 28th 1733
Sorting of dails that
came out of John Mathe[ws]
ship
6 days that week
May 1st
Sorting of dails and bori[ng]
at the Sloop
6 days that week

May 8th
Sorting of Dails & boring
at the Sloop and puling
up of a bulks head in
John mathens Shipe
6 Days that week
May 15th 1733
Sorting of Dails in the
Clos
6 Days that week
May 22th
working about the Sloo[p]
and pulling up the
pomp nalls and laying
down some of y[e] nering
in the houks and mind[ing]
several pices of billing
& boring upon the quart[er]
2 Days that week

[B1, f37v]

3 days that weak
   the furst of Oktobear
   maken coines for
   James Beall sheape
   in the cllos
on day and haf
   December 13th
   working at the pertition
   wall and making of
   brods for the kill windows and doing seve-
   ral other things about
   the house
6 days that week
   December 20th
   To ditto
2 days that week
   Aprill 28th <u>1732</u>
   sorting of dails that
   came out of John Matthow
   ship
1 1/2 days that week
   May 1st
   sorting of dails and boring
   at the sloup
6 days that week

[B1, f38r]

May 8th
Sorting of Dails & boring
at the sloup and puting
up of a bulks head in
John Mathews shipe
6 Days that week
    May 15th <u>1732</u>
    Sorting of Dails in the
    Clos
2 Days that week
    May 22th
    working about the sloup
    and putting up the
    pomp wall and laying
    down some of the wiring
    in the hould and mending
    several pieces of cilling
    & boring upon her quarter
<u>2 Days that week</u>

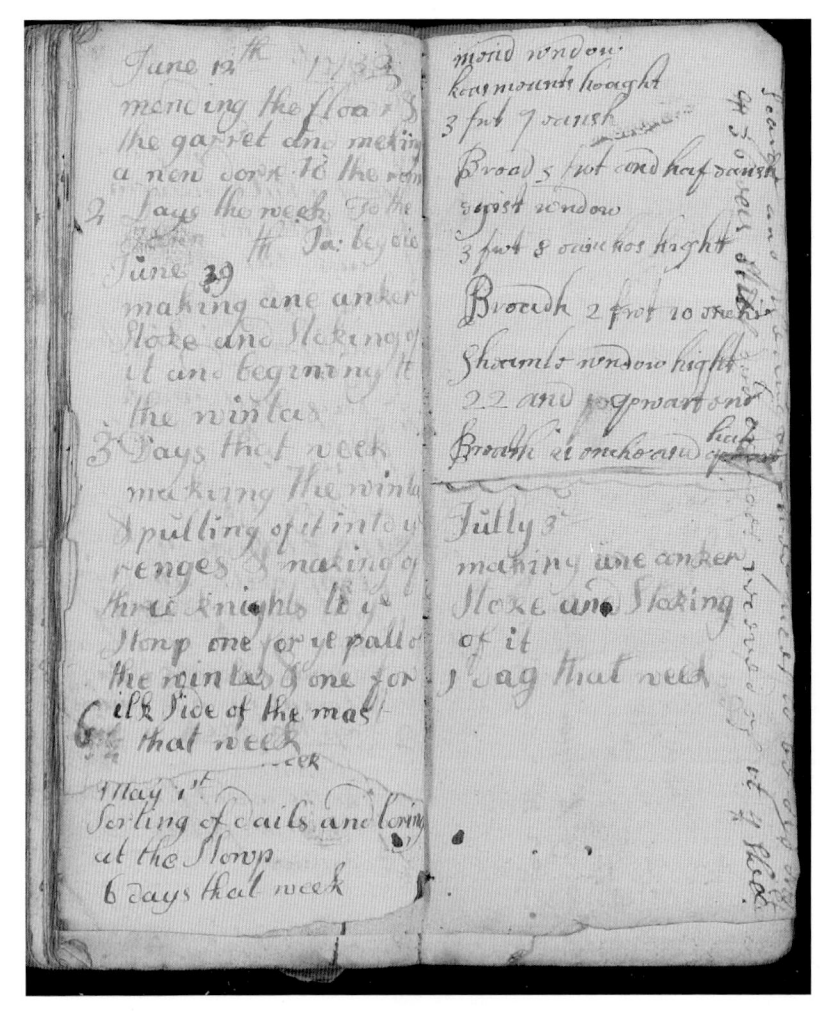

June 12th 17[..]
mencing the floar &
the garret and meking
a new door to the [..]
2 days the week. To the
[..] ffr Ja: be[..]
June 29
making ane anker
stoke and steking[..]
it and beginning [..]
the winter
3 Days that week
making the winter
& pulling of it into [..]
renges & making of
three knights [..]
stonp one for ye pall of
the winter & one for
ill side of the mas[t]
that week
[....]

May 1st
sorting of [..]ails and [..]
at the stonp
6 days that week

[..] window
[..] mounts hooght
3 foot 7 ranish
Broad 5 foot and haf ranish
[..] window
3 foot 8 ounches hight
Broadth 2 foot 10 on[..]
Sheamlo window hight
22 and [..]qwart on[..]
Broadth [..] onchorsw haf

fully 3
making ane anker
stoke and steking
of it
5 day that week

[B1, f38v]

 June 12th <u>1732</u>
 mending the floar &
 the garret and meking
 a new dorr to the rom
2 Days the week To the
   James Begbie
 June 29th
 making ane anker
 stoke and stoking of
 it and begining to
 the winlas
3 Days that week
 making the winlas
 & putting of it into the
 renges & making of
 three knights to the
 sloup one for the pall of
 the winlas & one for
 ilk side of the mast
6 that week

[B1, f39r]

mend window
keasmeants heaght
3 fut 7 eansh
Bread 3 fut and haf eansh
eaist window
3 fut 8 eanches hight
Breadh 2 fut 10 enchs
Sheamle window hight
22 and quarter
Breath 21 enche and ~~quarter~~ haf
Jully 3ᵈ
making ane anker
stoke and stoking
of it
1 day[77] that week

[Right margin:
    'searge and pleding on three peces to be dyd [ ][78]
       Item 36 ells stuf dyd oringes receved of it 4 shellens']

---

[77] The manuscript reads 'dag' by clear mistake, so we have corrected it here.
[78] Illegible – 'd[i]videt'?

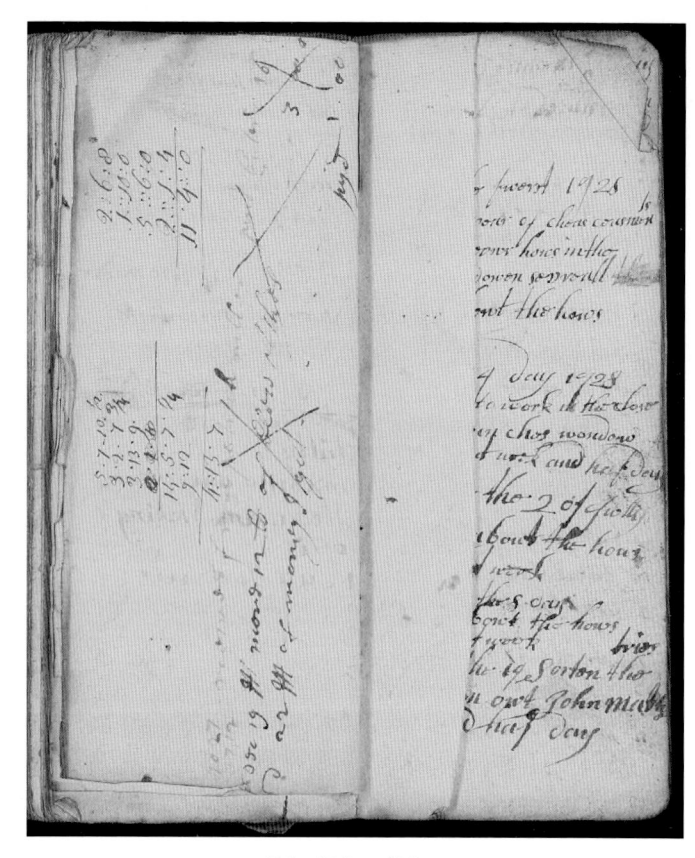

B1, f39v, f40r

[B1, f39v]

     5· 7·10 ½   2 : 6 :8
     3· 2· 7 ¾   ·1::10 :0
     3·13· 9·   5:: 6 :0
     ~~12· 1· 6~~   2:: 1 :4
     14· 5· 7 ¼   11· 4::0
     9: 12
     4: :13· 7

~~1027 received frae Patrick Miller 4 pund buter   0 16 0~~
~~1712~~
~~Dec 19 Item more 12 li of blew Ashes _____ 3 00 0~~
~~D 22 Item of money I get_____ 1 00 0~~
                                           pyd

[B1, f40r] [Third of a folio sewn into binding, blank]

[B1, f40v] [Third of a folio sewn into binding, blank]

[B1, f41r]

    Novembear 9
6 tweall fut dealls
8 cutes
Maye the fuerst 1728
   maken a pear of cheas ceasments
   for Seaameowr Hous in the
   pans and dowen sevreall
   things about the hous
3 days
   Jun 24 day 1728
   entren to work in the close
   maken an ches wondow
4 days that week and haf day
   Tusday the 2 of Jully
   worken about the hous
5 days that week
   Munday the 8 day
   worken about the hous
3 days thet week
   October the 14 sorten the tries
   that cam out John Mathe
a day and haf day

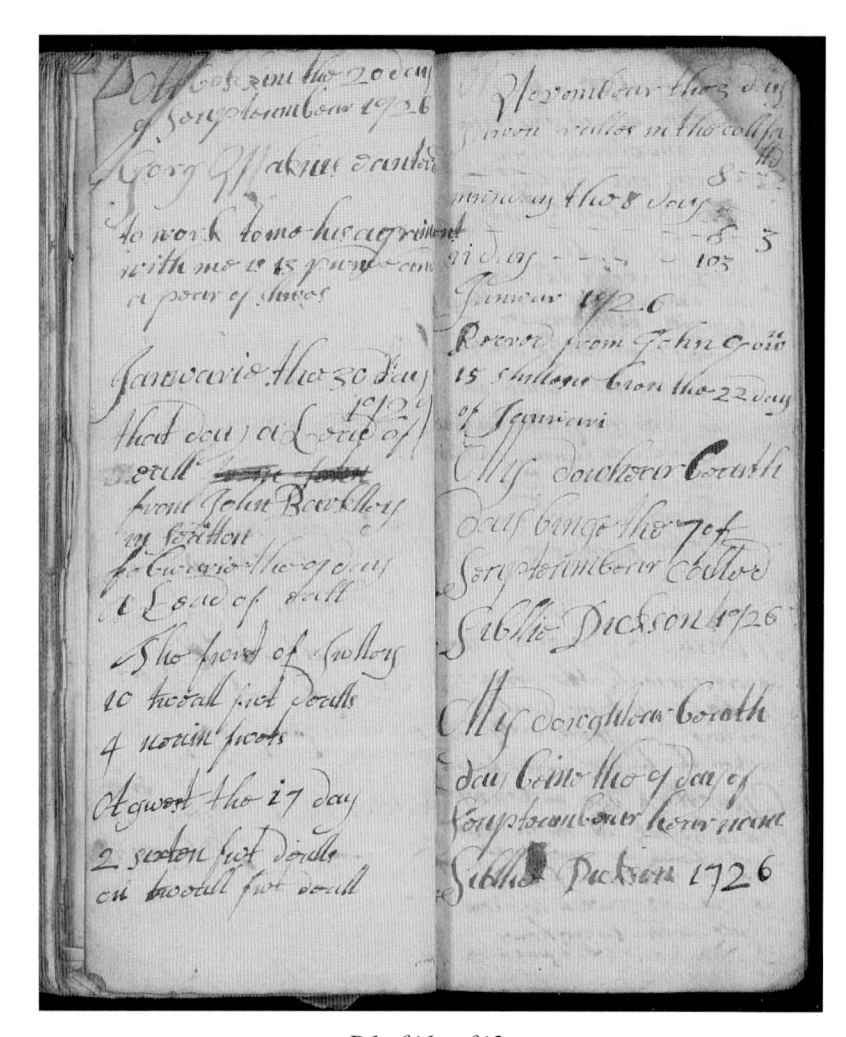

Oloboson tho 20 day
of Soxptombor 1926
Gorg Wakno sonted
to work tome his agriment
with me to is punne and
a pair of shoes

Janwarie tho 30 day
1725
that day a loup of
soul
from John Bowthors
in Sexton
foworie tho 9 day
a Load of soul

Tho prist of Nolors
10 twoall fut doulls
4 nouin fwots

Agwost tho 17 day
2 sexton fut doulls
a twoall fut soul

Desombor tho 8
noon roules in the colls
8
monday tho 8 day
8
21 day   103   3

Januar 1726
Resvd from John Croll
15 shilling tron the 22 day
of Jenuari

My dowhtor Grath
day bing the 7 of
Sorptombor boro
Sible Dickson 1726

My doughtar Grath
day bino tho 9 day of
Soxptombor horn noun
Sible Dickson 1726

[B1, f41v]

At Cokkini the 20 day
of Seapteambear 1726
Gorg Maknis eantered
to work to me his agriment
with me is 13 punde and
   a pear of shues

Januarie the 30 day 1727
that day a Lead of
   eall ~~from John~~
   from John Barklley
   in Seatton
Febrewarie the 7 day
a Lead of eall
   The furst of Julley
10 tweall fut dealls
4 neain fuets
Aguest the 17 day
2 sixten fut dealls
on tweall fut deal

[B1, f42r]

    Novembear the 3 day
sawen ralles in the collfalld
- - - - - - - - - - - - - - 8 - - 2
Munday the 8 day
- - - - - - - - - - - - - - 8 - - 3
11 day - - - - - - - - 103
Januar 1726
Recved from John Gown
15 shillens bien the 22 day
of Januari
My dowhear bearth
day binge the 7 of
Seapteambear called
Sibllie Dickson 1726

My dowghtear bearth
day beine the 7 day of
Seapteambear hear nam
Sibllie Dickson 1726

[November] 26
makon the cenves and soatin
floar and cladon therin
on day and on half day
to my soallf at Some Roberts

January the 18 day
worken about the galloy
and daying several thing
about it being rouseovr
2 days to my soallf and la[bour]
26 sawen the doalls for
the pertitions and putn
of up and [d]wing several
things about the hous
2 days and a half day to
my soallf and men

March 28 puton up the
mortessou soall titte firste d[ay]
X en half day to my soallf
X en half day to my soallf
makon the backe for the forur[nace]
May the 8 day makon up
one choss cart and morden[d]
cart wheels and stoores wh[en]
d oyr and throwhen the
axtres and puton up som
doalls in the brew hous
2 days to my soallf and men

May the 16 day
makon an great my soallf
and men
an day and an half
Spayeng makon at the doors
and window broad's for the
barren and puton up on
luthr and plustr well e[tc] the
shypston my soallf and men
6 days that work
September 8 day
worken at the steere that
gos up to the kill and maken
the Lytton doan m the flowr
and fittn in the broad's and
doors and hengin them
6 days that work
15 day worden the kilvil[log?]
my self half a day
puton on the ruf on the [wall?]
puton on two boad doors on an
End makon an plock great
an day to my soallf and men
October 22 culteren the gabes
of the wall makon an box to the
sponet makon an brey at the
kil brst an day to my soallf and [men]

[B1, f42v]

    November 26
maken the cowms and seatin
theam and claden theam
an day and an haf day
to my seallf at Thomas Robert
Januari the 11 day
    worken about the sealler
    and dowing seavreall things
    aboutitt bing neascear
2 days to my seallf and lad
26 sawen the dealls for
    the pearticone and puten
    of it up and dowing seavral
    things about the hous
    2 days and a haf day to
    my seallf and man

Marth 23 puten up the
    pertisen wall at the forsiede
x an haf day to my seallf
x an haf day to my seallf
    maken the bockce for the hearp
May the 8 day maken up
    an clloscart and menden the
    cart whealle and showen whell
    agean and streaken the
    axtrie and puten up som
    dealls in the brow hous
    2 days to my sealf and man

[B1, f43r]

May the 16 day

maken an geat my seallf
and man   q[79]
an day and an haf
Agwes[80] maken at the doors
and window broods for the
baren and puten up an
lathe and plaster wall at the
stipston my seallf and man
6 days that week
Seapteamber 8 day
    worken at the stare that
gos up to the kill and maken
the Liften doors in the flwer
and fittin in the broods and
doors and hingin them
6 days that week
15 day menden the kill ribes
my sallf haf a day
puten on the ruf on the sealler
puten on two bead door on an
bead maken an flleak geatt
an day to my sealf and man
Octobear 22 alltren the gattes
of the wall maken an box to the
spout maken an trap at the
kill brist an day to my sealf and man
    x

---

[79] Meaning unclear. Note that the ink is a slightly different colour and the font is larger.
[80] August.

worken at the peans
Tems Roberton worke
... wth my scadf...
and man the 15 day of
May 1727

an ...

Socuptember the 8
Jams Johnson and his man
1 day worken at the peans

~~the ~~

the 22 of october
mueken an ploak goat
maken an locks for the
port at the wall
and ... the gouller of
the wall mendon the ellow
and Dowing gearoll things
about the hows
an day to my scaff and
                    man
November 6 day
maken an noow sead an ... d...

Reve of monie ... 9 0/23
24 prins eets munie
goody the 10 days
Scuptember the 4 day
loan shillons 8 ... ton
November 23
munie shillons sharloxes at
that tiem
Tems Johnson and his man
worken at Tomer Roberttown
work at Prevstown peans
an day worken at the roof
hire soul and his man
an day puten on the roof
hime sadly and man
his man an day seaven latk
his man an other day seaven latk
him sadly half a day he ... en
the ... swipso that day ...kell
...sen ... was ...
an day proton on the swipers
and ... the stoe up ...
|||| ... ... hyme

[B1, f43v]

    worken at the panes
Thomas Robertsoun worke
sawen Lathe my sealfe
and man the 15 day of
May 1724
an day
Seaptember the 8
James Johnson and his man
1 day worken at the pans
~~the furst of Octtobear~~
the 22 of Octtobear
maken an flleak geat
maken an bocks for the
spout at the wall
and alltren the gealles of
the wall menden the sllead
and dowing seavrell things
about the hous
an day to my sealf and man
November 6 day
maken an neow slead an haf day

[B1, f44r]

Receved of munie thes year 1723
24 pund [S]cots munie
Jully the 10 day
Seaptember the 4 day
    tean shillens starlen
November 23
twentie shillens starlens at
that tiem
James Johnson and his man
worken at Tomei Roberttown
work at Preastownpans
an day worken at the rufe
him seallf and his man
an day puten on the ruf
him seallf and man
his man an day sawen Lathe
his man an other day sawen lathe
himseallf hallf a day heowen
the swipse that day Nikell
Wattson chielld was buried
an day puten on the swipes
and searken the sied of it
D ||||| _____ of tyme

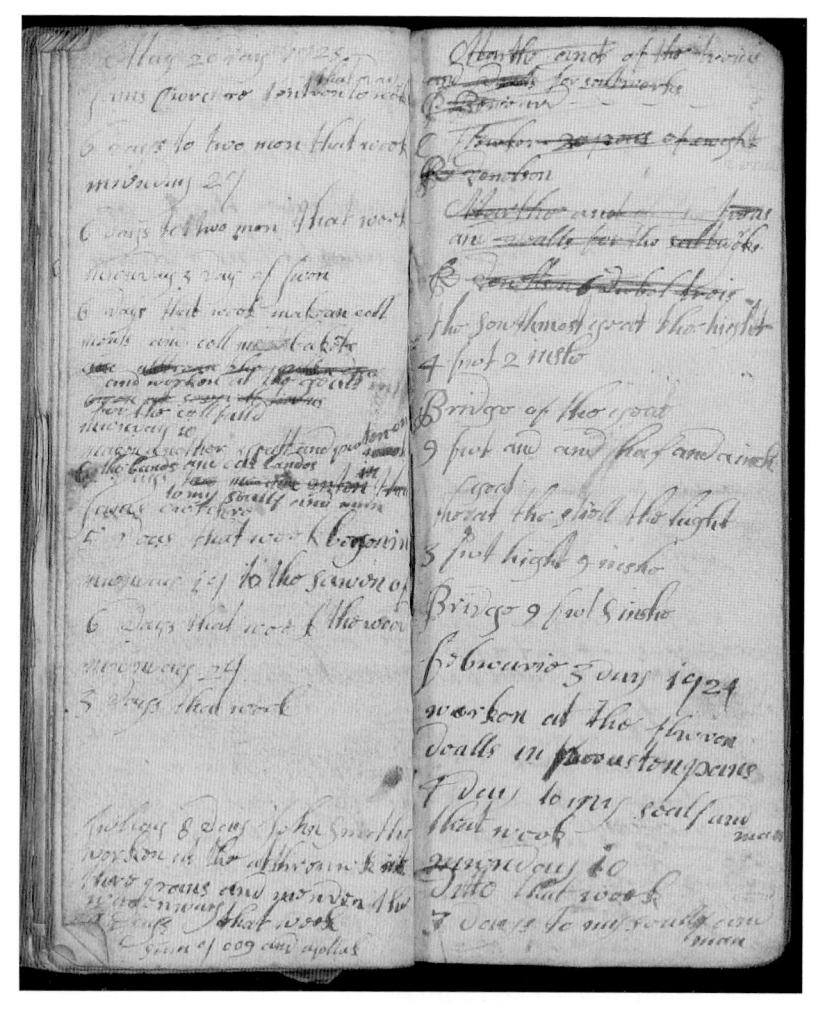

B1, f44v, f45r

[B1, f44v]

    May 20 day 1723

James Cwrchre entren that day to work

6 days to two men that week
Munday 27
6 days to two men that week
Munday 3 day of Juen
6 days that week makean coll
meats and coll bakets
~~and alltrean the pithied or~~
   and worken at the geats
~~digen at severell tiwms~~
   for the coll falld[81]
Munday 10
maken another yeatt and puten on
   the bands and cat bandes
6 days [ ][82] to my seallf and man
James Cwrchre
5 deas that week begenin
Munday 17 to the sawen of the wood
6 days that week
Munday 24
3 days that week

Jullay 8 day John Smethe
worken at the at thre nwk at[83]
thre pans and menden the
wagenway that week
4 days
      Sum of 0 0 9 and a pllak

---

[81] Note that this passage is a correction. Dickson crossed out the original two lines and added text above each line. His intended meaning is clearly: '6 days that week makean collmeats and coll bakets and worken at the geats for the coll falld'.

[82] Note Dickson crossed out some text here and replaced it with, 'to my seallf and man' below line.

[83] Meaning unclear.

[B1, f45r]

~~Marthe and of the treias~~
~~and dealls for saltworks~~
~~R Beweard - - - -~~
~~C Fleuker 20 peas of ewght~~ dealls
~~R Donelson~~
~~Marthe and of the treas~~
~~and dealls for the saltworks~~
~~R Donellson 6 dwbel treis~~
the southmost yeat the hight
4 fut 2 inshe
Bridge of the yeat
9 fut and and haf and a inch
   yeat
   the eat the stiell the hight
3 fut hight 9 inshe
Bridge 9 fut 8 inshe
Febrewarie 3 day 1724
worken at the sheven
dealls in Preastenpans
4 day to my sealf and man
that week
Munday 10
ditto that week
3 days to my seallf and man

March 23
my soulf and mean
2 days that wos
my mean
6 days that wrok
May the 16 day
makon an gord my
soulf and mean
on day and a haf
~~makon the flawer wols~~
~~my salf and mean~~
10 days
the lowst of augost
makon the dors and wind
ows brods and poten up
an lether and plaster hall
at the stipston
my soulf and mean
6 days that work
Souptomber the 8 day
~~fower wrights that day~~
~~workon at the stors~~
2 day my soulf and mean
lingen the dors ~~and~~ doning sontom
to my soulf 2 days monein
the kill riges and fenstones
the work makon the doors for

1704 my gebe at
aperstoun pane to Sons
Robroun
on haf day pon toning
the porteson at the pitor
stabes
on haf day makon the
botlos for the hous
to my son Mr
Sons Robroun
the 8 day of may
maken ~~our on other~~
~~the~~
monder co cont which
and shewn thow a horn
twee on the ox for
and puton up somoud
at the brew hous and
doweing soumoutt thing
not spokn of
and makon an bokes for the
houpo thow trons piten
the same which ie all intod
2 days to my soulf and my son
the stoars how up filled at the kill
crate

[B1, f45v]

    Marth 23
my seallf and man
6 day that wek

my man
6 day that hweek[84]

May the 16 day
maken an geat my
seallf and man
an day and a haf
~~Layen the flwren dealls~~
~~my sealf and man~~
10 days
the leastt of Aguest
maken the dores and wind-
ows broods and puten up
an lathe and plaster wall
at the stipston
my sealf and man
6 days that week
Seaptember the 8 day
four wrights that day
    worken at the stears
    2 days my sealf and man
hingin the dorrs and dowing seavrel things about the loaft
to mysealf 2 day mendin
the kill ribes and fineshing
the work maken the doors for the stear head in fllwer at the kill
buste

---

[84] Week.

[B1, f46r]

    1724 my Jobes at
Prestounpans to Thomas
Robr[t]own[85]
an haf day puten up
the pertisien at the faier
siead
an haf day maken the
bockes for the hearp
to my seallf

    Thomas Robrtown
the 8 day of May
maken up an clloscart
mendean the cart wheall
and shuen them aghean
streaken the axtrie
and puten up som deall
in the brow hous and
doweng seavreall things
not spokn of
and maken an bockse for the
hearpe ther 1 tiems fiten
the shead which is all in heal[86]
2 days to my sealf and man

---

[85] See seven lines below.
[86] in whole.

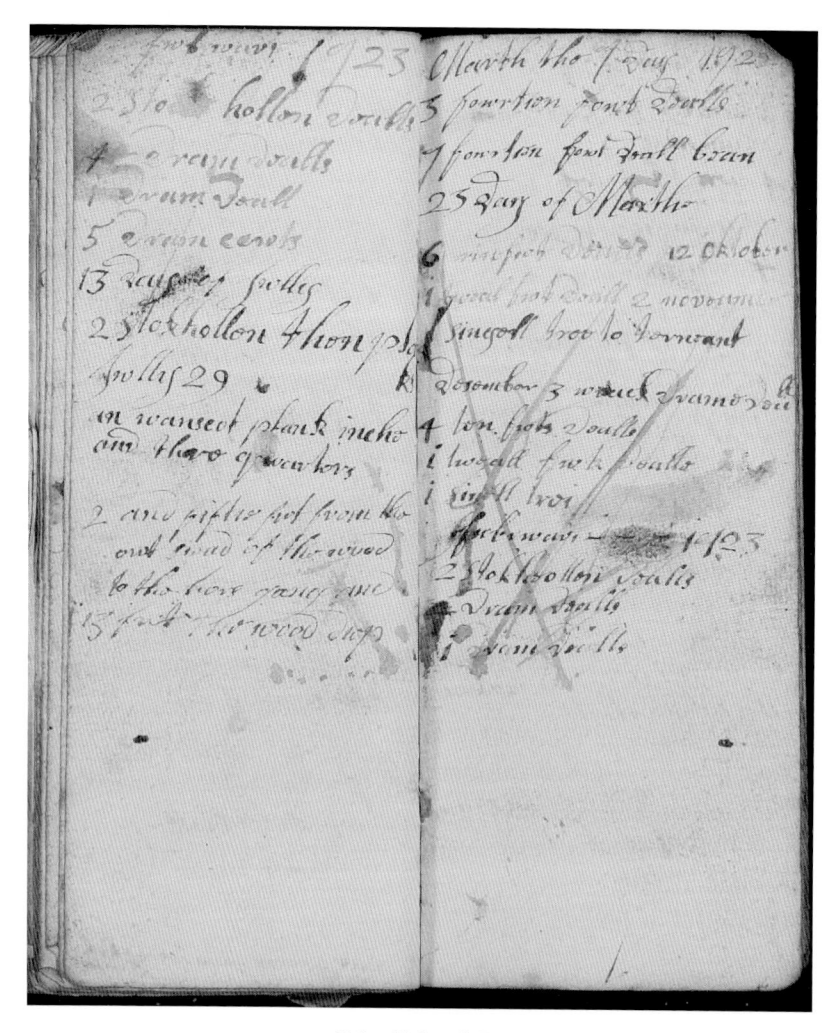

B1, f46v, f47r

[B1, f46v]

   Fubrewari 1723
2 stock hollen dealls
4 dram dealls

1 dram deall
5 dram cowts
13 day of Jully
2 stokhollen then planks
Jully 29
an wanscot plank inche
and thre quarters

2 and fiftie fut from the
   out siead of the wood
   to the hors gang and
13 fut the wood diep

[B1, f47r]

Marth the 7 day 1722
3 fourtien fout dealls
7 fourtien fout deall bean
23 day of Marthe
6 nin fut dealls 12 Oktober
1 tweal fut deall 2 Noveamber
   singell tree to Terneant
Desember 3 wrack drame deall
4 ten futs dealls
1 tweall fut dealle
1 singell trei
   Fubrewari ---- 1723
2 stokheollen dealls
4 dram dealls
1 dram deals

Gulvin to the Chapwork
Desember the 3 entrina
on munday
4 men that work 6
munday 10 days
4 men that work 6
munday 1st day   febr: 24
2 men that work 6
John Samson and his man
that work — 4 William
munday 24   leath 16
5 Days to my Cralfs

to my man gilon up the
mens bears and gulon in the
streets and brocken the woven
in the out sider and maxon
the cabon laboll
februari 25 1723
John Cruson and his man
4 days that work
munday monday 4 day
John Crosoto and his man at
the panwork
4 roils

Memorandom of my day
of the rem of them to Samsbord
pot roweare 5 day
munday 5 two men sawen som
boulls for the touben and
good for other things that
week
3 days that work
munday 15 day
an day to two mean
munday the 19
6 days to my Cralfs and
5 days to my Pigs
the last of march 1723
5 days that work
Appreall the firoret
6 Days that work
munday 18
3 days that work
to Gorey Brittherstons

[B1, 47v]

    Entrin to the shep work
Desember the 3 entrin
on Munday
4 men theat week 6
Munday 10 day
4 men that week 6
Munday 17 day Seatrday 17
2 men that week 6
John Jameson and his man
that week - - 4 wich is in heall 16
Munday 24
5 days to my sealf
4 to my man puten up the
mens beads and puten in the
sheafs and busken the window
on the out siead and maken
the caben tabell
Febrewari 25 1723
John Jameson and his man
4 days that week
Marth Munday 4 day
John Jameson and hes man at
the panwork
4 days

[B1, f48r]

    Meamarandom of my days
of the reas of them to James Beal
Febreware 5 day
Munday 5 two men sawen som
dealls for the keaben and
seaverll other thengs that
week
3 days that week
Munday 12 day
2
an day to two mean
Munday the 19
6 days to my seallf and
3 days to my Lade
the Last of Marth 1723
3 days that week
Apreall the furest
6 days that week
Wadsday 18
3 days that week
to Gorg Brotherstons

B1, f48v, f49r

[B1, f48v]

Janeuare the 22 day 1722
James Curreth eantrean to
worke
Munday the 22 daye
6 days
Munday 29
6 days
Munday 5 of Febrewari
4 days
Munday 12 day
6 days
           1722
Ocktobear 31 James Br-
edwod Eantread hom to me
~~the Last of Apreall~~
~~Gorge Brotherstons~~
~~6 days that week~~
on hunder small speaks out of
    the wast Loft
    and two hundear trinealls
    and four scor of biggspeak
    out of the eas lofte

[B1, f49r]

    Wadsday the 22 of Febrewari
Eantren to John Mathe
sheap
5 wrights that day
23 day 2 wright that day
and a carpnter
Wadsday the 24 of Maye

Gorge Menroe an day sawen
5 fourten fut dealls that day
an sawen chellef for a myseallf
    1722
John Jameson eanren
to work with me at
Cokkeani 18 of Juen
5 days that week
5 days to his man
Munday 25 day
5 days and haf day that
an day to his man

[B1, f49v]

Munday 17 of Agueste
worken at Terneant[87] to
Gorg Yung in Fisherae[88]
5 days that week

Seatrday the 12 of Marthe 1720
worken at John Mathe shepe
an day that week
Munday 21
4 days that week Layng the bukdlen on the Seatrday
Munday 28

---

[87] Tranent.
[88] Fisherrow, near Musselburgh.

munday 9 of agust
workon at fernouss to
Gorg yong in fishorow
5 days that work

satriday th 12 of Martch
workon at John Mathew sharp
an day that work
munday 21
4 days that work laying the
munday 26 C[...]ton on the [...]

W[...] of da[...]
John Cavens the 20 of Agust
workon at gotinorton
6 days that work

munday the last of Agust
6 days that work   10 29

satordays the 12 of Martch
workon at John Mathew shorp
an day that work
munday the [..] 2[..]
4 days that work
munday 28 Ben[jam]in [...]
an day that work two days
at the bickroton and took
that work puting up the sharon
housen and puton up the candel
and nonson the house   10
2 days that work and a half
munday the 4 of April
an half day 2 days to
at the bickroton who were out at
w[...]d

B1, f49v, f50r

[B1, f50r]

    Memarandom of days to
Johen Carens the 10 of August
worken at Gellmerten
6 days that week
Munday the Last of Aguest
6 days that week
Seaterday the 12 of Marth 1720
worken at John Mathe sheap
an day that week
Munday the 21
4 days that week
Munday 28 begenin to bukdlen on the Seatrday
an day that week two days
at the bukdellen and buelkhead
that week puting up the
steallen and puten up the cambows
and menden the howld
2 days that week and a haff[89]
Munday the 4 of Aprell
an haff day   days 10
        whearof two at
at the bukdlen and bulkhead

---

[89] The intended order of the words in this passage is not wholly clear.

december 29 day
rembrowne to work to wals Br-
shcap
2 Days that week
Janwari the 2 day
5 Days that week
monday the 8 day
6 days that week
monday the 15 day
5 days that week and a half
day
monday the 22 day
half day
tuesday an day
wensday an day
thursday half a day to his
friday an half to my brother
which is all in houell
4 days that week
monday 29 day
3 that work
[illegible]
monday the 16
[illegible] thad week of his sheap
[illegible] the 24 of febwari

[right page]
for days work at [illegible]
to saynphan the swarst
work
2 days and a half day
the cokonde work
2 days and a half day
the thorsday work
5 days that week
the fowrt week the prekt
wason work
2 days that week
monday 23 of Agwost
gorge Monro entered to
work with me
6 days that week
monday the 30
4 half week
all day aftour the far 1920
Agwost 3 day 17/21
gorge monro 28 days and
half day for sawen
days A
[illegible] 5 [illegible]
goads

[B1, f50v]

    Desember 29 day
eantrean to work to James Beal
sheap
2 days that week
Januari the 2 day
5 days that week
Munday the 8 day
6 days that week
Munday the 15 day
5 days that week and a haf
day
Munday the 22 day
haf a day
Tuesday an day
Wadsday an day
Fwersday haf a day to his
Friday an haf to my} bothe
which is all in heall } man[90]
4 days that week
Munday 29 day
3 that week

---

[90] As he says the list adds up to 4 days in total, the 'bothe man' probably corresponds to the Thursday, meaning two men had half days. This is, admittedly, an educated guess, and the passage has been reproduced exactly as it is given in the manuscript, including the brackets separating the text.

[B1, f51r]

for days worken at Pencatlen
to James Pllan the fuerst
week
2 days and a hallf day
the cekende week
2 days and a hallf day
the theread week
5 days that week
the fourt week the prokl-
measen week[91]
2 days that week
Munday 23 of Aguest
Gorge Menro entread to
work with me
6 days that week
Munday the 10
4 that week
an day aftear the far 1720
Agguest 3 day 1721
Gorge Menro 2 days and
haf day for sawen
May 24
an day sawen 5 sewrten deals

[B1, f51v]

    1717

Meamarandom of my mareth[92]
day 18 day of Jueni
Meamrandom of my maret
  day the 18 day of Juen

---

[91] The 'proclamation week'; meaning unclear.
[92] marriage.

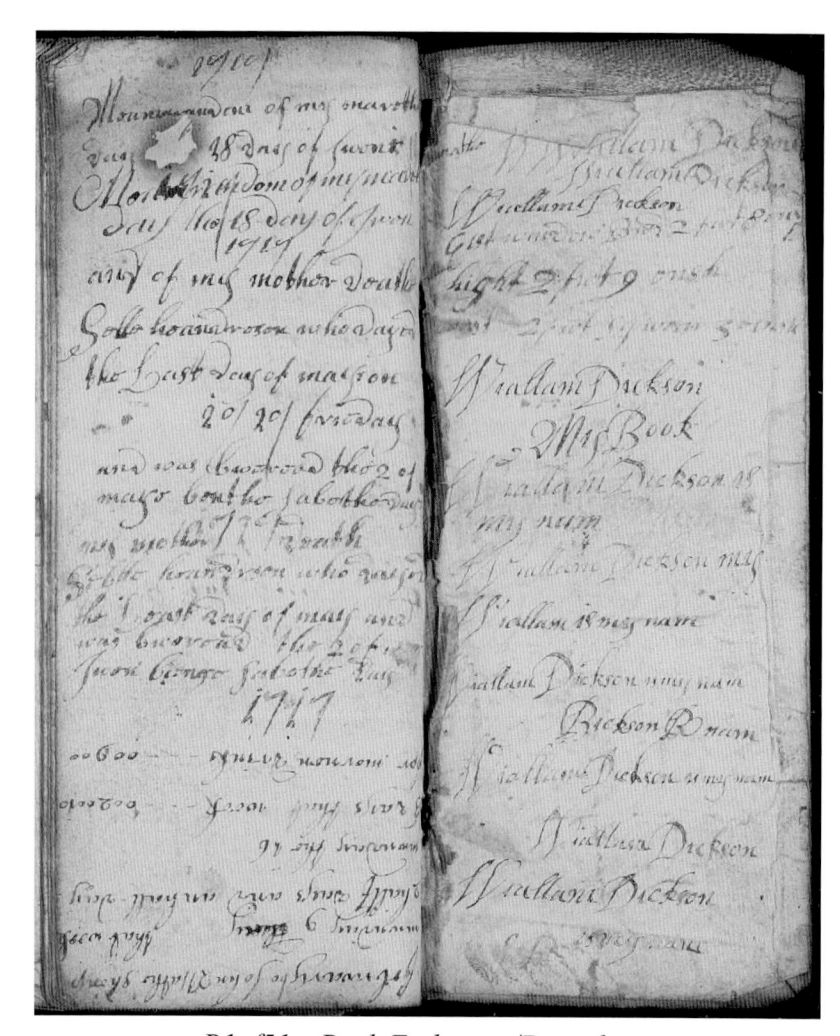

B1, f51v, Back Endpaper/Pastedown

    1717
and of my mother deathe
Seble Heandresen who dayed
the Last day of May on

　　　　1717 Frieday
　and was bueread the 2 of
　Maye ben the Sabethe day
　　　　1717
my mother death
Seblle Heandrsen who dayed
the Least day of May and
was bueread the 2 of
Juen bienge Sabethe day
　　　　1717

[B1, Back Endpaper/Pastedown]

^{Mathe} W Wiallam Dickson
　　　　Wiallam Dickson
Wiallam Dickson
Eist window Bred 2 fut 8 ensh
hight 2 fut 9 ensh
west 2 fut squear 3 einsh
Wiallam Dickson
　　My Book
Wiallam Dickson is
　my nam
Wiallam Dickson my
Willam is my nam

Wiallam Dickson is my nam
　　　Bickson R nam
Wiallam Dickson is my nam
　　Wiallam Dickson
Wiallam Dickson
　　　　is my nam

[The following B1 folios include the text which was upside down at the back of the volume. In this fairly-common practice, known as *tête-bêche*, the book was inverted to keep certain text, such as accounts, separate from the main text. The last folio effectively became a new first page, though Dickson only used a few folios in this manner. Some were paginated, from '2' to '7', with a few having no other (inverted) writing. It is reproduced below with corresponding foliation of f1r to f5v.]

B1, f1r (Inverted f51v)

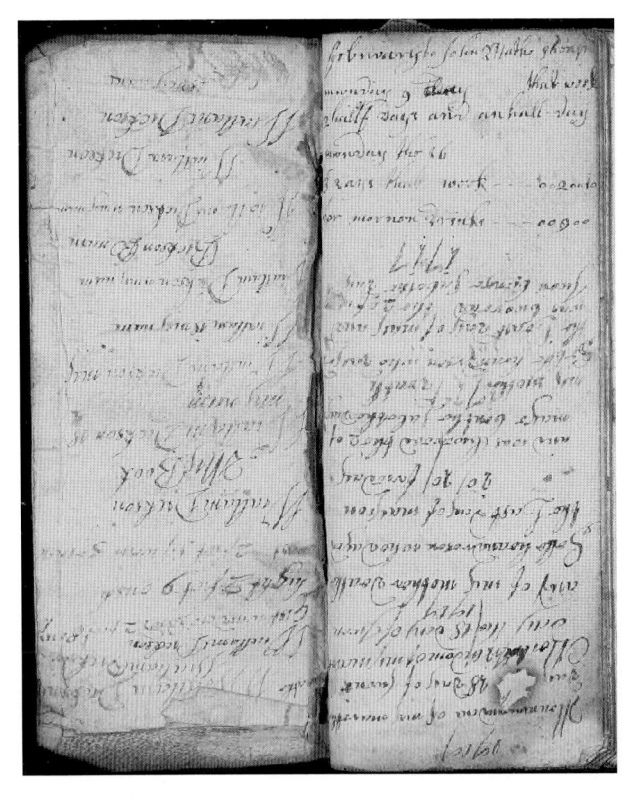

[B1, f1r (Inverted f51v)]

Febrewary to John Mathe sheap
Munday 9 day
2 hallf days and an hall day that week
Munday the 16
3 days that week - - - 0020010
for mornen drinks - - - 00900

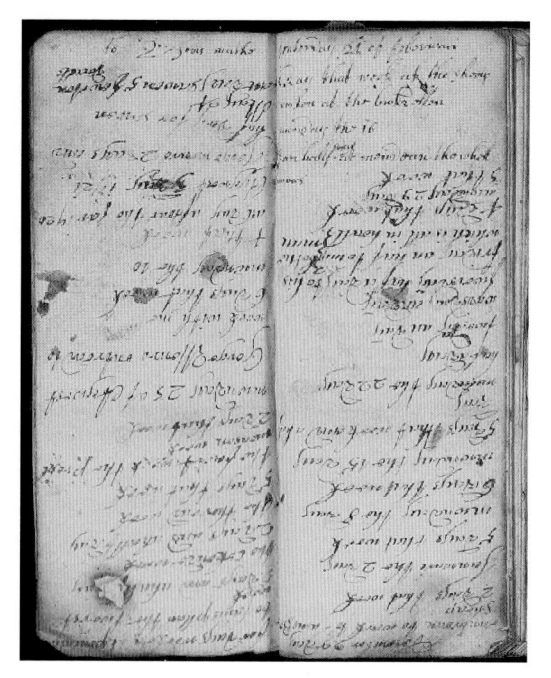

B1, f1v (Inverted f51r), B1, f2r (Inverted f50v)

[B1, f1v (Inverted f51r)]

    2
to Thomas Mathe[93]

[B1, f2r (Inverted f50v)]

Seaterday 21 of Feberwari
1 day that week at the sheap
worken at the bukdellen
Munday the 16

---

[93] Note that 'to' and 'Thomas Mathe' are on either side of the page number '2' as there was little space available at the bottom of f51r. Clearly this was a later addition.

3 an hallf day at mendean the whell
Barrows

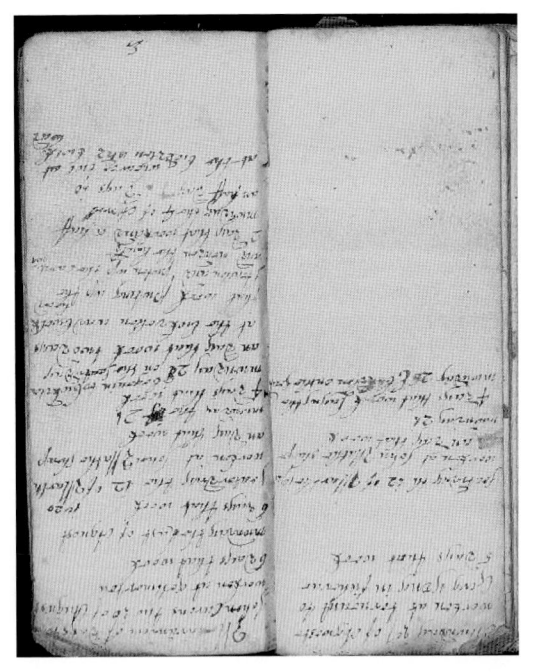

B1, f2v (Inverted f50r), B1, f3r (Inverted f49v)

[B1, f2v (Inverted f50r)]

    3

[B1, f3r (Inverted f49v)]

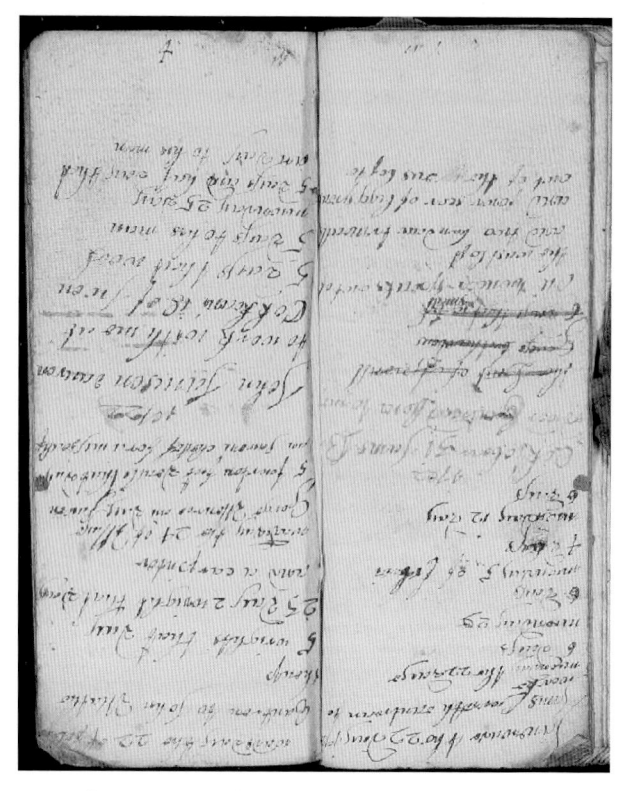

B1, f2v (Inverted f50r), B1, f4r (Inverted f48v)

[B1, f3v (Inverted f49r)]

    4

[B1, f4r (Inverted f48v)]

    w s

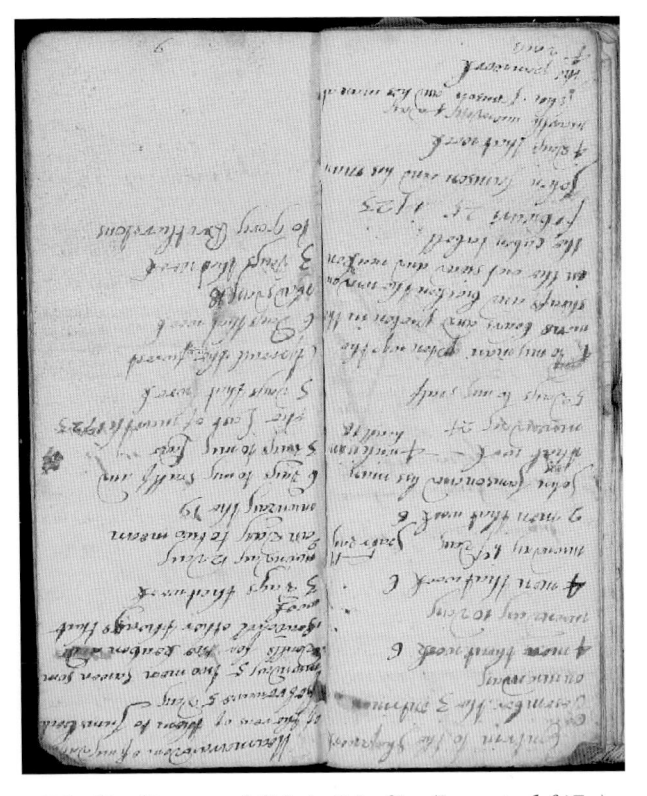

B1, f4v (Inverted f48r), B1, f5r (Inverted f47v)

[B1, f4v (Inverted f48r)]

6

[B1, f5r (Inverted f47v)]

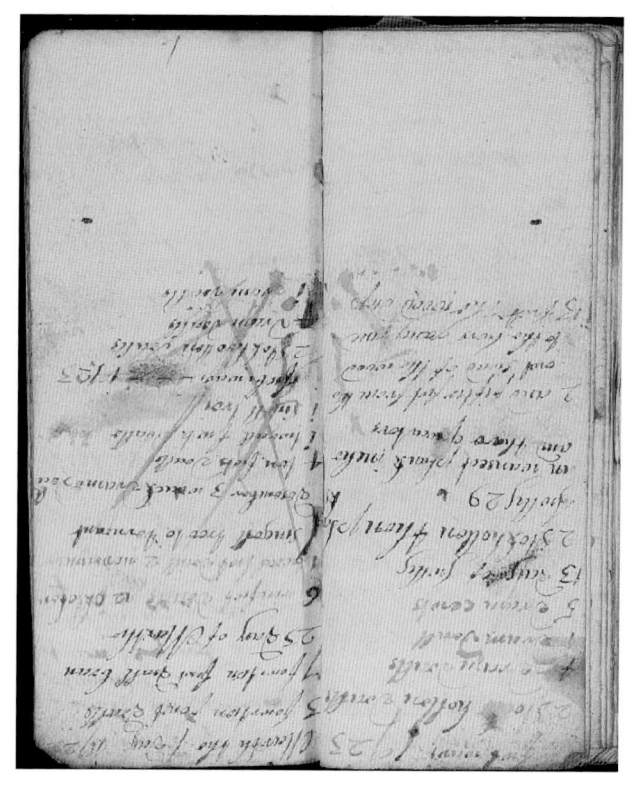

B1, f5v (Inverted f47r), B1, f6r (Inverted f46v)

[B1, f5v (Inverted f47r)]

7

[B1, f6r (Inverted f46v)]

BOOK TWO
1728–1745

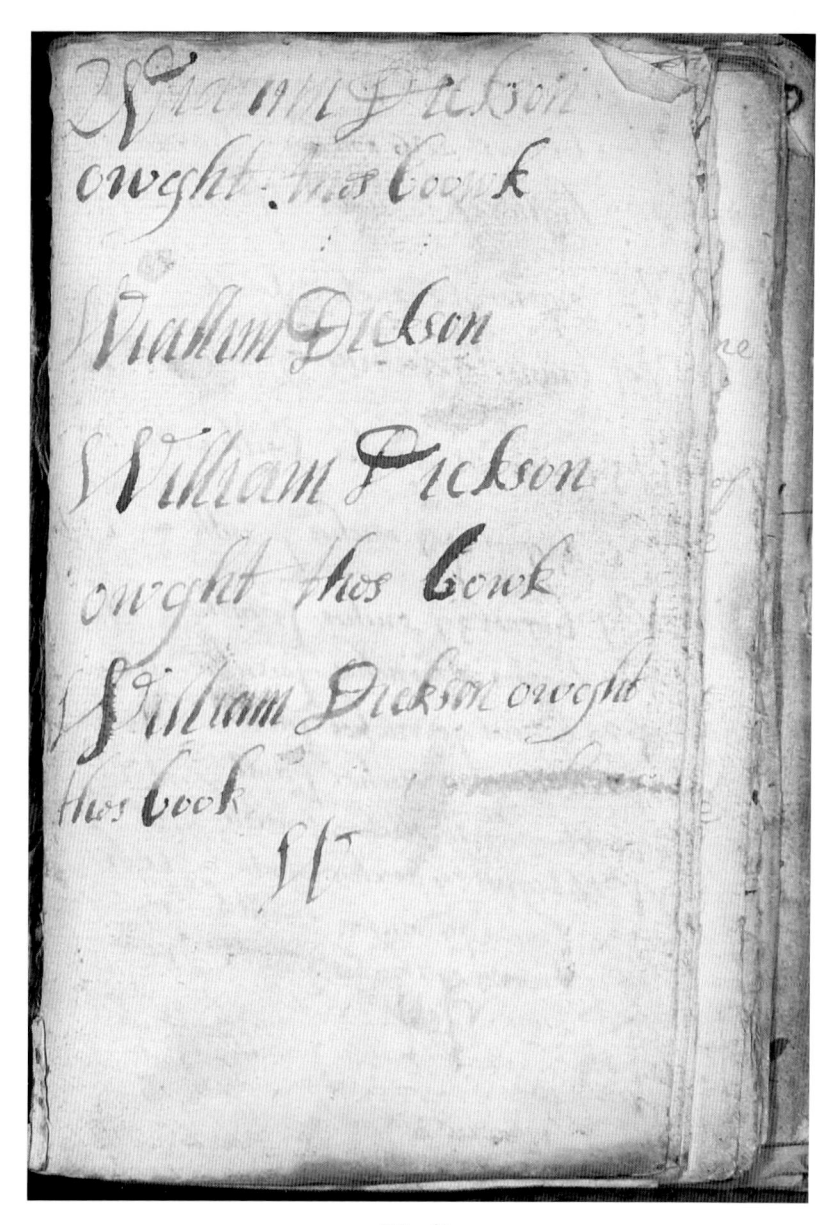

William Dickson
oweght thos Cook

William Dickson

William Dickson
owght thos Cook

William Dickson owght
thos Cook

[B2, Leather Endpaper/Pastedown]

[B2, f1r]

Wiallim Dickson
owght thes boowk

Wiallim Dickson

William Dickson
owght thes bowk
William Dickson owght
thes book
      W

B2, f1v, f2r

[B2, f1v]

    a not of the tris at the hearbour
N-1 bignes – 46 enches – Lenth – 16 fut
N2 bignes 42 – enches Lenth – 16
N3 – bignes 43 enches Lenth – 16
N4 bignes 44 enches Lenth – 16
N5 bignes 41 enches Lenth – 17
N6 bignes 49 enches Leanth – 14 haf
N7 bignes 37 enches Leanth 17
N8 bignes 37 enches Leanth 16
N9 bignes 48 enches Leanth 16 h
N10 bignes 38 enches Leanth 17
N11 bignes 45 enches Leanth 16
N12 bignes 37 enches Leanth 16 h
N13 bignes 49 enches Leanth 17
N14 bignes 47 enches Leanth 16
N15 bignes 39 enches Leanth 16 h
N16 bignes 57 enches Lennth 13 h
N17 bignes 55 enches Leanth 16 h
N18 bignes 60 inches Lenth 16 foot
N19 bignes 60 inches Lenh 16 a 2/1[94]

---

[94] It would appear that he meant 'and a ½', but put 'a 2/1'.

[B2, f2r]

    the begening of thes acountt
    from the 29 of Seaptembear
    1728
    Novembear the 4 day
    workean at the salltworks
    workean at the Wide[95] Huntear
    pan ruf and maken 4 wheall
    barows and dowinge seavreall
    others things about the
    workes
6 days that week
    Munday the 10 day
    worken at ditto
3 days that week about the
    salltworks

    Munday the 18 day goinge to
    Dullkith and cuten the treis
    and cuten at Cokkni
6 that week

---

[95] Widow.

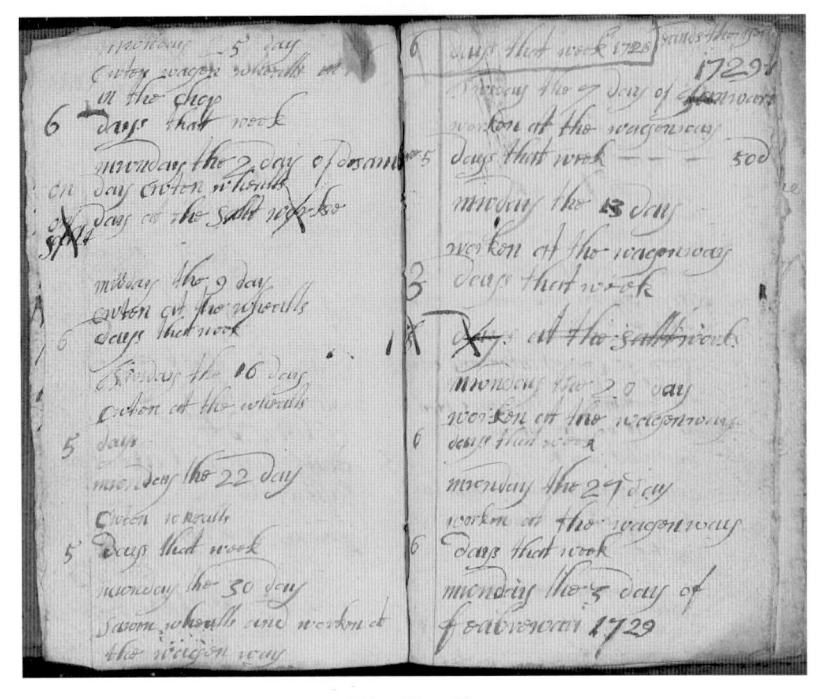

B2, f2v, f3r

[B2, f2v]

    Munday 25 day
    cuten wagen whealls
    in the chop
6 days that week
    Munday the 2 day of Desambere
on day cuten whealls
~~on day at the salltworkse~~
~~salt~~
    Munday the 9 day
    cuten at the whealls
6 days that week

    Tusday the 16 day
    cuten at the whealls
5 days
    Munday the 22 day
    cuten whealls
5 days that week
    Munday the 30 day
    sawen whealls and worken at
    the wagen way

[B2, f3r]

<u>6 days that week 1728</u> [96] eands the year
                                1729
    Tusday the 7 day of Januari
    worken at the wagenway
5 days that week - - - 50^d
    Munday the 13 day
    worken at the wagenway
3 days that week
~~3 days at the salltworks~~
    Munday the 20 day
    worken at the wagenway
6 days that week
    Munday the 27 day
    worken at the wagenway
6 days that week
    Munday the 3 day of
    Feabrewari 1729

---

[96] This line was carried over from the previous folio, and was delineated with a box of two lines.

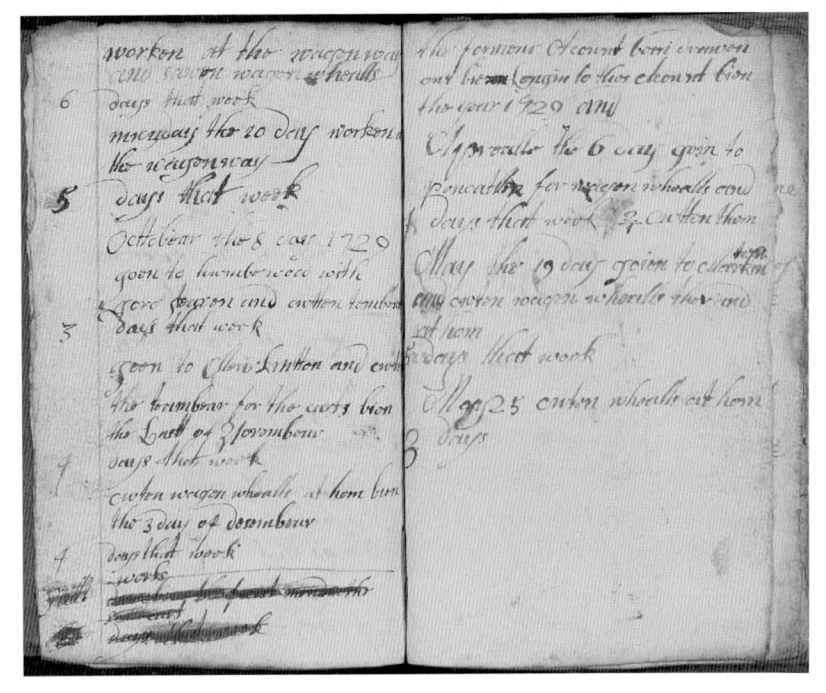

B2, f3v, f4r

[B2, f3v]

    worken at the wagenway
    and sawen wagen whealls
6 days that week
    Munday the 10 day worken at
    the wagenway
5 days that week
    Octtobear the 8 day 1729
    goen to Humbe Wood[97] with
    Gorg Steaven and cutten tembear

---

[97] Near Humbie, East Lothian. This place name is given by Adair on his 1682 map of East Lothian: NLS, Adv.MS.70.2.11 (Adair 10).

3 days that week
 goen to Cllearkintten[98] and cuten
 the teambear for the carts bien
 the Last of Novembear
4 days that week
 cuten wagen whealls at hom bien
 the 3 day of Desembear
4 days that week
~~sallt works~~
 ~~Desembear the furst menden the~~
 ~~sallt cart~~
~~2 days that week~~

[B2, f4r]

the formear Acount bein drawen
out bie Longin[99] to thes Acount bien
the year 1729 and
 Aprealle the 6 day goin to
 Pencatllen for wagen whealls and
4 days that week 2/1 cutten them
 May the 19 day goien to Cllarkintun[100]
 and cuten wagen whealls ther and
 at hom
5 days that week
 May 25 cuten whealls at hom
3 days

---

[98] Clerkington, near Haddington, East Lothian.
[99] belonging.
[100] Clerkington, near Haddington, East Lothian.

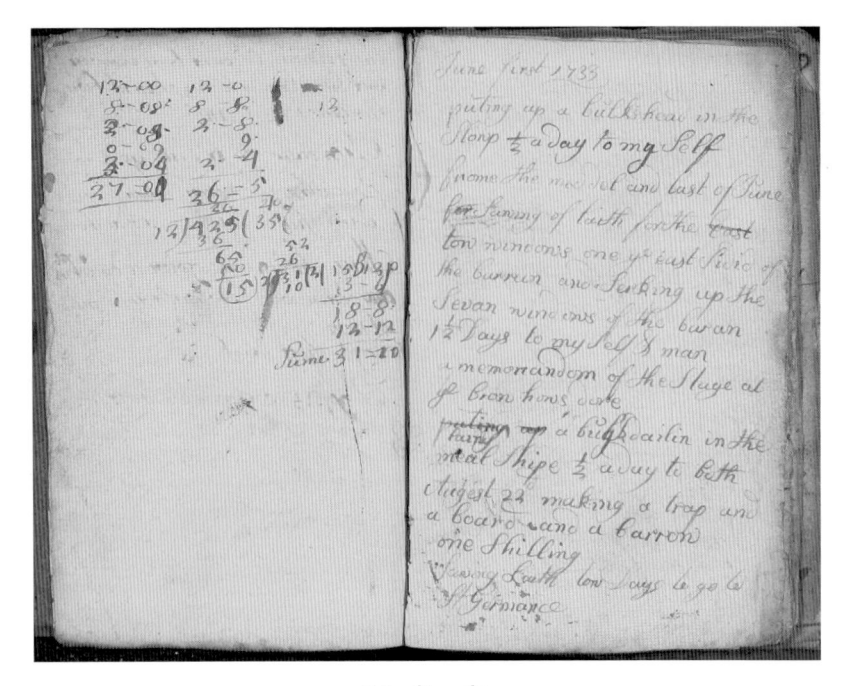

B2, f4v, f5r

[B2, f4v][101]

  12 - 00 12 - 0
   8 - 08   8 - 8   12
  5̶2 - 08   2 - 8
   0 - 09   9
  5̶2 - 04   2 - 4

---

[101] This page of rough working is rendered as closely as possible to the original. Note that the figures, which are clearly based on 1 shilling equalling 12 pence, are not always correct. He did catch his errors on the first of the sums, though the mistakes in the division below (eg: 2 x 12 = 36) seem to have been left. Perhaps there was further information not jotted down in this rough working.

$$27 = 01 \quad 26 = 5^{102}$$

$$\underline{20} \quad 2|0$$

12)425(35(
          36
          ―
          65   52
          50   26
         (15)   2|6)31|2| 15s| 2p
                   10   3 - 6
                                18 - 8
                                12 - 12
                  Sume   31 = 20

[B2, f5r]

June first <u>1733</u>

puting up a bulkshead in the
sloup 1/2 a day to my self
frome the middel and last of June
for sawing of laith for the ~~East~~
two[103] windows one the east sidid of
the barran and serking up the
sevan windows of the baran
1 1/2 Days to my self & man
a memoriandom of the stage at
the brow hous dore
~~puting up~~ a bugkdailin in the
meal shipe 1/2 a day to both
Augest 22 making a trap and
a board and a barrow

---

[102] Shillings and pence. Note that the right-hand sum is a correction of the work on the left-hand side. He started again after writing various numbers over the previous figures and discovering that his arithmetic was incorrect.

[103] In the manuscript, Dickson transposed the w and o in 'two' as 'tow'.

one shilling
sawing Laith two Days to go to
St Germance

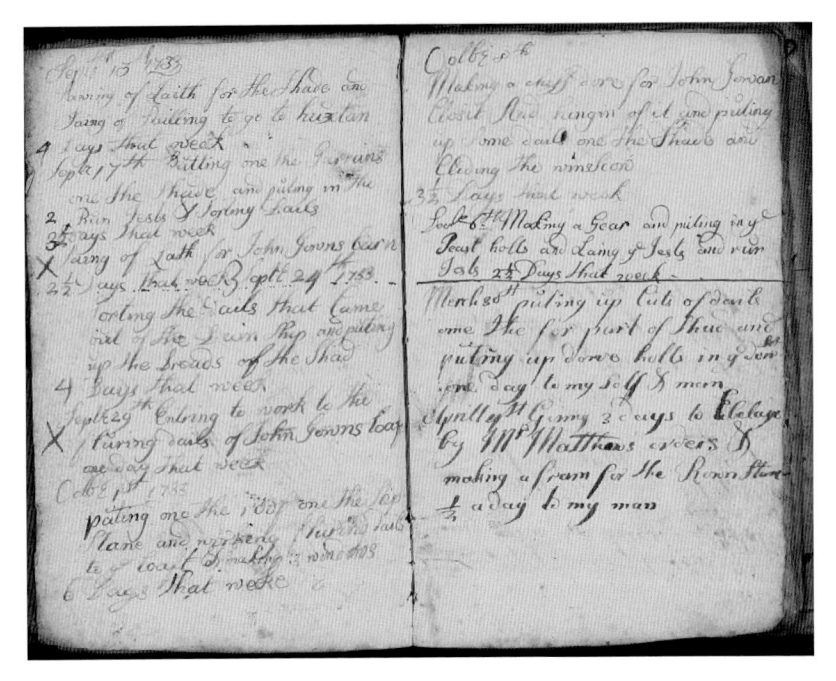

B2, f5v, f6r

[B2, f5v]

    September 13th <u>1733</u>
    sawing of Laith for the shade and
    Laing of Dailling to go to Huxtan
4 Days that week
    September 17th Putting one the Garrans
       one the shade and puting in the
2   Run Jests & sorting Dails
3 1/2 days that week

   X   Laing of Lath for John Gowns barn
2 1/2 Days that week } [104] September 24th 1733
        sorting the dails that Came
        out of the Dain ship and puting
        up the broads of the shad
4 Days that week
    September 29th Entring to work to the
   X   fluring dails of John Gowns loaf[t]
    one day that week
    October 1st 1733
        puting one the roof one the step
        stane and working fluring dails
        to the loaft & making 3 windows
    6 Days that weeke

[B2, f6r]

    October 8th
    Making a chelf dore for John Gowan
    Closit And hingin of it and puting
        up some dails one the shade and
        Cliding the winsscow[105]
3 1/2 Days that week
    December 6th Making a Gear and puting in the
        Jeast holls and Laing the Jests and run
        Jests 2 1/2 Days that week
    Merch 30th puting up Cuts of dails
        one the for part of shad and

---

[104] It would appear that the following date was added afterwards, and corresponds to the entry relating to the Danish ship. Dickson used a dividing bracket, which looks most like the '}' symbol, to allow space to add the September date.

[105] Windskew? See Glen L. Pride, *Dictionary of Scottish Building* (Edinburgh: Rutland Press, 1996), 84.

puting up dowe holls in the dowset[106]
one day to my self & man
Aprill 7th Going 3 days to Ebelaye
by Mr Matthows[107] orders &
making a fram for the Rown stare
1/2 a day to my man

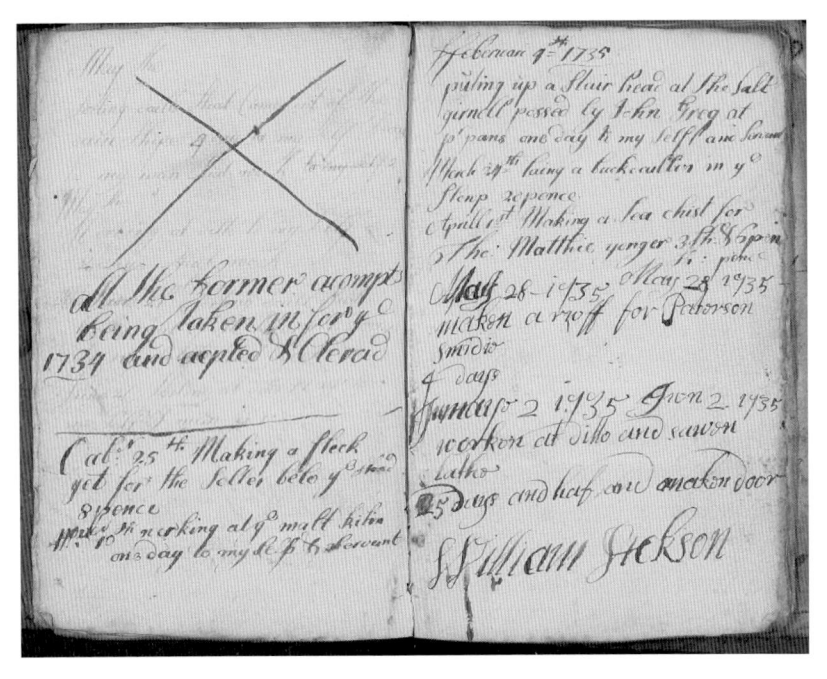

B2, f6v, f7r

[B2, f6v]

May the [blank]
sorting daills that Came out of the
Dain shipe 4 day to my self & 3 day

---

[106] dovecote.
[107] See appendices.

~~to my man that week to my self 2~~
~~May the~~ [blank]
~~Working at ditto to my sellf~~
~~2 days that week~~
all the former acompts
being taken in for ye
1734 and acpted & Clerad[108]

June 27 sorting at ditto 1 day to
my self & man

October 25th Making a fleck
yet for the seller belo the shead
8 pence
November 10th working at the malt kilin
one day to my self & servant

[B2, f7r]

Feberwari 4th 1735
puting up a stair head at the salt
girnell possed by John Greg at
Prestonpans one day to my self and servant
Merch 24th laing a buckdaillin in ye
sloup 20 pence
Aprill 1st Making a sea chist for
Thomas Matthie yonger 3 sh: & 6 pen[ce]
                           sh: pence
May 28-1735   May 28 1735
maken a ruff for Paterson
smidie

---

[108] The passage beginning 'all the former...' and ending with '...& Clerad' was written over part of the passage which was crossed out above it. He seems to have left the final section, beginning with 'June 27 sorting...', so we have included it here.

4 days
Junaye 2 1735   Jun 2 1735
   worken at ditto and sawen
   lathe
2̶ 5 days and haf and maken door

William Dickson

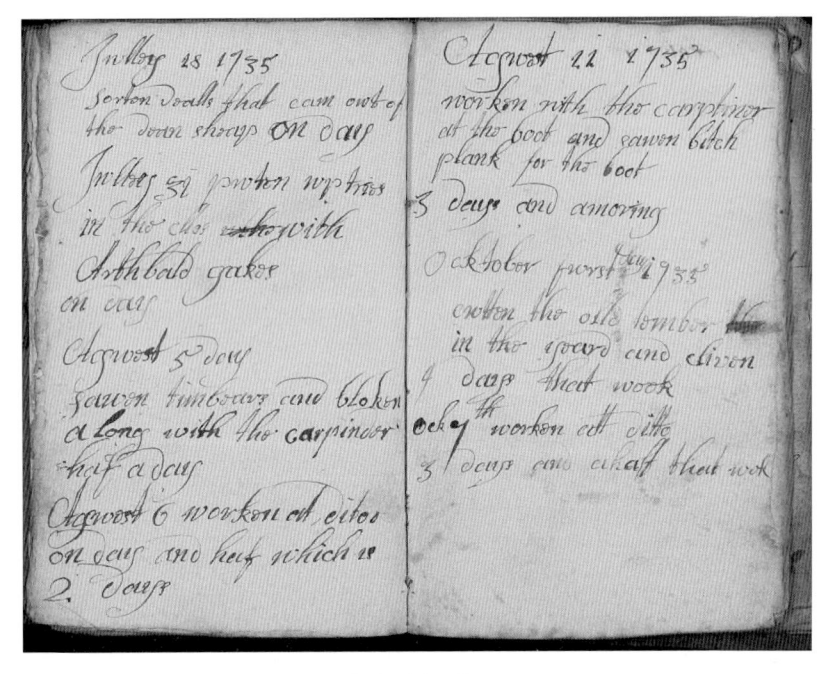

B2, f7v, f8r

[B2, f7v]

Julley 18 1735
   sorten dealls that cam out of
   the Dean sheap on day
Julley 31 puten up tries

in the cllos ~~wthe~~ with
Arthbald Gakes
on day
Aguest 5 day
sawen timbears and bloken
along with the carpinder
haf a day
Aguest 6 worken at ditoe
on day and haf which is
2 days

[B2, f8r]

Aguest 11 1735
worken with the carptiner
at the boot and sawen bitch
plank for the boot
3 days and a morning
Ocktober furst day 1735
cutten the olld tember
in the yeard and cliven
4 days that week
Ocktober 7th worken att ditto
3 days and a haff that week

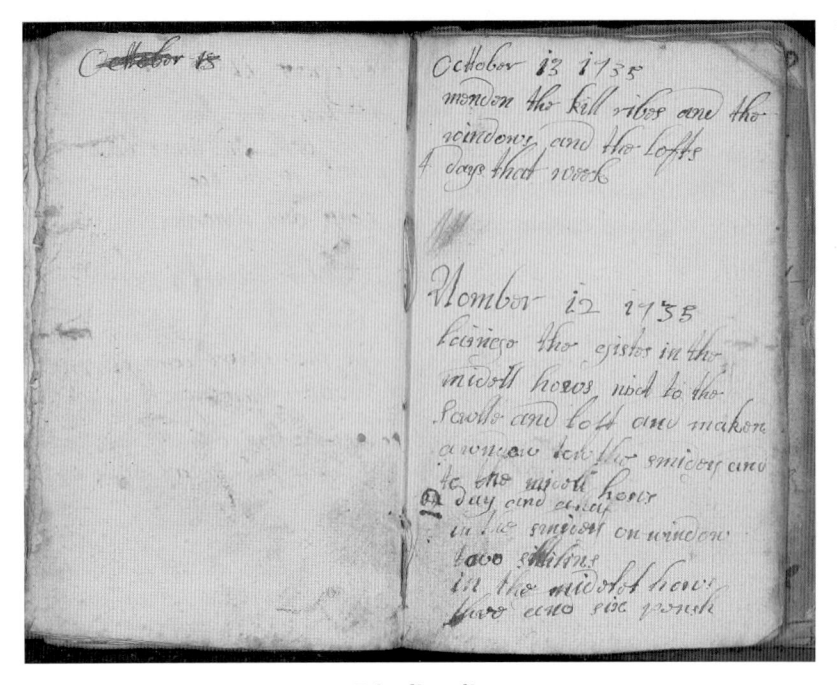

[B2, f8v]

~~Octtober 13~~

[B2, f9r]

Octtober 13 1735
    menden the kill ribes and the
    windows and the Lofts
4 days that week

November 12 1735
    lainge the gistes in the
    midell hous nixt to the
    sculle and loft and maken
    a window tow the smidey and

to the midell hous
2 day and a haf
in the smiddey on window
two shilins
in the midelel hous
thre and six pensh

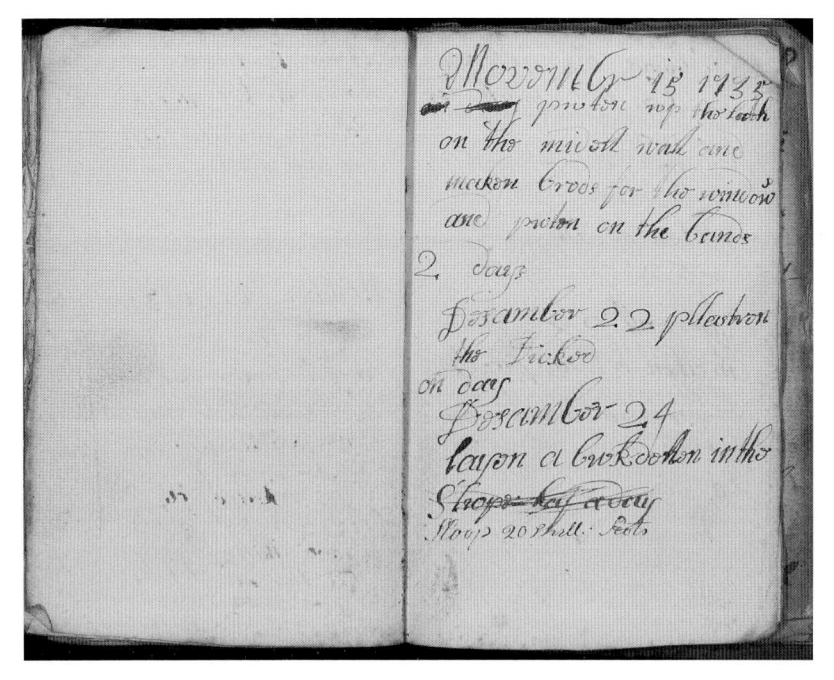

B2, f9v, f10r

[B2, f9v] [Blank]

[B2, f10r]
November[109] 15 1735

---

[109] Dickson wrote 'Movembr', but as he clearly meant 'November', we have rendered it accordingly.

~~on day~~ puten up the lath
on the midell wall and
maken brods for the windows
and puten on the bands
2 days
Desamber 22 pllastren
the Duked
on day
Desamber 24
layen a bukdellen in the
~~slupe haf a day~~
sloop 20 shillings Scots[110]

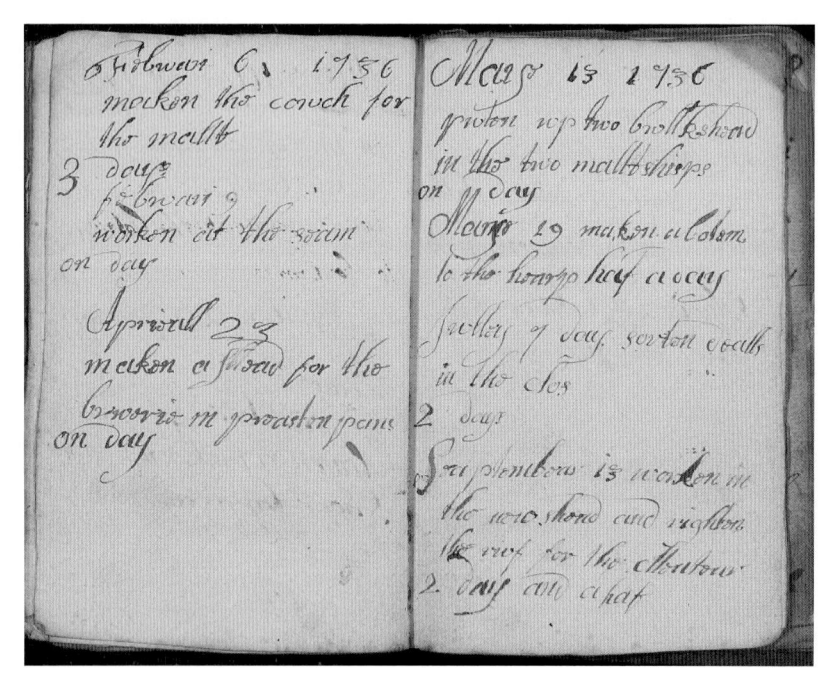

B2, f10v, f11r

---

[110] Note that the correction and the value in shillings is in a different hand.

[B2, f10v]

    Febrewari 6 1736
    maken the couch for
    the mallt
3 days
    Febrewari 9
    worken at the seam
on day
    Aprieall 23
    maken a sllead for the
    brewerie in Preastenpans
on day

[B2, f11r]

Maye 13 1736
    puten up two bullkshead
    in the two malltshisps
on day
    Maye 19 maken a botem
    to the hearp haf a day
Julley 7 day sorten dealls
    in the clos
2 days
Seaptembear 13 worken in
    the new shead and righten
    the ruf for the clleatear
2 day and a haf

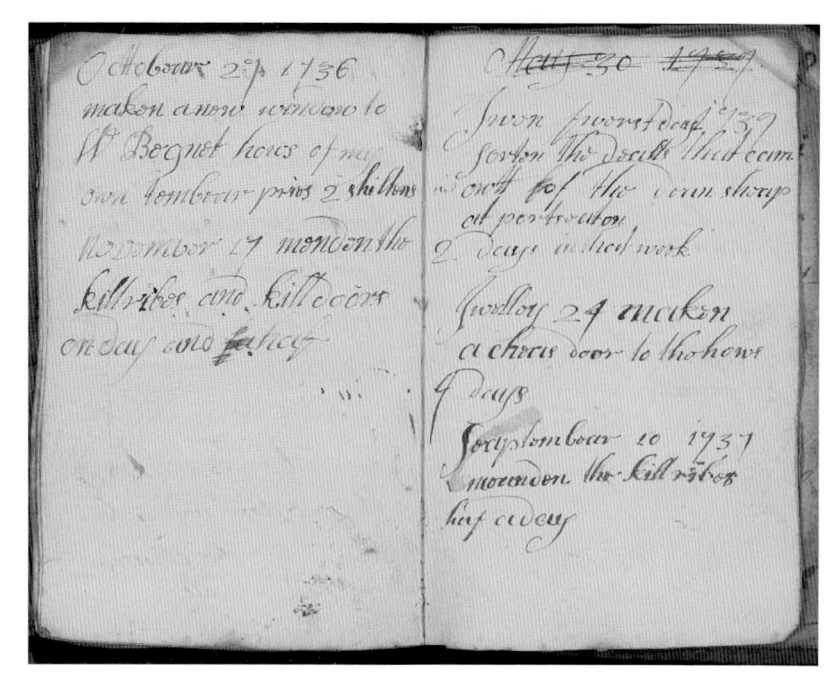

B2, f11v, f12r

[B2, f11v]

    Octtobear 27 1736
    maken a new window to
    W Begnet hous of my
    own tembear pries 2 shillens
    November 17 menden the
    kill ribes and kill doors
on day and ~~fa~~ haf

[B2, f12r]

    ~~May 30 1737~~
    Juen fuerst day 1737
    sorten the dealls that cam

    outt of the Dean sheap
    at Port Seaton
2 days in that week
    Juelley 24 maken
    a cheas door to the hous
4 days
    Seaptembear 10 1737
    meanden the kill ribes
    haf a day

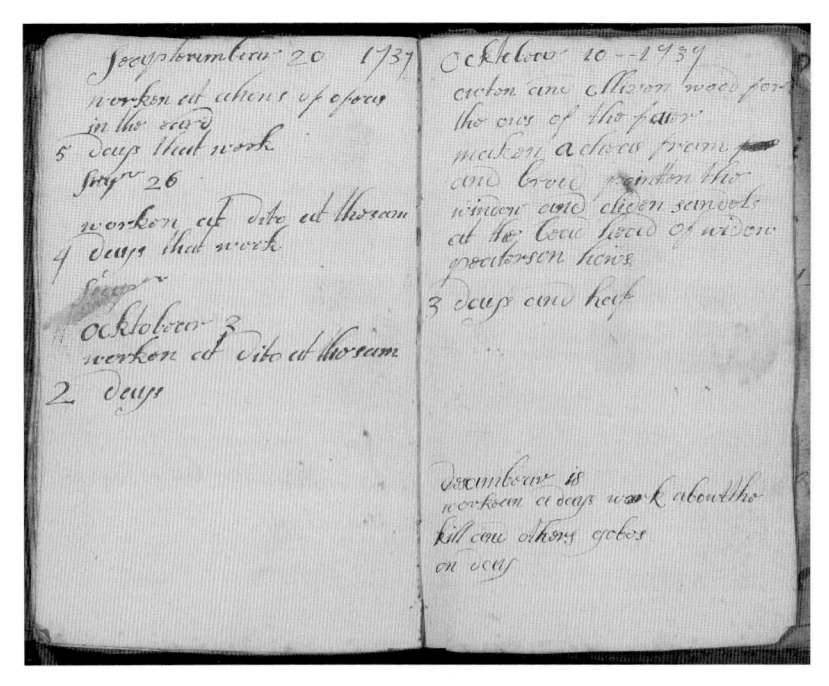

B2, f12v, f13r

[B2, f12v]

    Seapteambear 20 1737
    worken at a hous of ofeas

   in the eard
5 days that week
   September 26
   worken at dito at the sam
4 days that week
   Ocktobear 3
   worken at dito at the sam
2 days

[B2, f13r]

Ocktobear 10 - - 1737
   cuten and clliven wood for
   the ows of the faier
   maken a cheas fram ~~for~~
   and brood pointten the
   window and cliden sandels
   at the bead head of Widow
   Peaterson hous
3 days and haf

Desambear 18
workean a days wark about the
kill and others gobes
on day

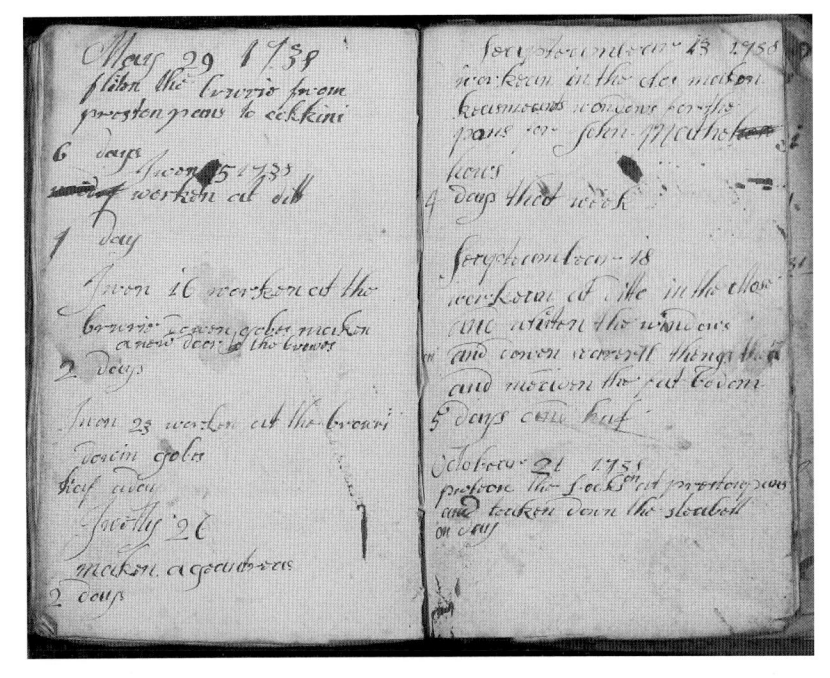

[B2, f13v]

> May 29 1738
> fliten the brewerie from
> Prestonpans to Cokkini

6 days

> Juen 5 1738
> worken at ditto[111]

1 day

> Juen 16 worken at the
> brewerie dowen gobes maken
> a new door to the browes

---

[111] At the beginning of the line is a word which was scored out so heavily it can no longer be read.

2 days
Juen 23 worken at the browri
   dowin gobes
haf a day
   Juelly 26
   maken a geantreas
2 days

[Note: It appears a folio has been removed here.[112]]

[B2, f14r]

   Seapteambear 13 1738
   worken in the clos maken
   keasmeants wondows for the
   pans for John Mathe ~~hose~~
   hous
4 days that week

   Seapteambear 18
   workean at ditto in the cllose
   and whiten the windows
[on] and dowen seaverll thengs thear
   and meaden[113] the fat bodom
5 days and haf

Octobear 21 1738
puteon the Locks on at Prestonpans
and teaken down the steabell
on day

---

[112] In the gutter are the letters '-on', suggesting that a word which had once been written on a now-missing folio had been carried over onto f14r. As we cannot be sure, foliation has not been changed.

[113] Making. See DSL/DOST: 'Mak'.

B2, f14v, f15r

[B2, f14v]

~~Januar the 22 day 1730~~
~~James Curhre eantr to work with mye seallf~~
~~at the hearbour~~
~~3 days that week~~
~~Munday the 26~~
~~3 days that week at ditto~~
    Robeart Kinlle at ditto - - - 2 days
    Octobear 30 1738
        worken in the clos puten upe
    plastear Lathe
3 days that week

Novembear 6 1738
puten up plastear Lathe in
the clos in the broows[114] and menden
the kiell riebs and maken a fuenell
for the mallt Loeafst and dowen
other gobeas aboutes the hous
4 days and two haef days
which is 5 days

[B2, f15r]

William

Novembear 14 1738
worken in the clos puten
a shead up at the bruhous
door and dowen seavreal
things about the close
3 days that week
sorten the dealls in the cloes
that cam out of Mastear
Forkear sheap
3 days
~~Juelley worken in the Begexty~~
Juelley 16 worken in the close
on day and haf
Juelley 23 worken in the clos
3 days

---

[114] brewhouse.

B2, f15v, f16r

[B2, f15v]

    June 1730
Recaved from John Gowns
19 tean fut dealls and two cutts
    Jully bien about the midell of
    the munth Rescaved from John Gown
18 ten futs comen dealls
on dubeall trei
on singeall trie
3 ten futs two inshs thik bien att wan tim
5 ten futs in Agust
    Novembear the 11 day
    Recaved from John Gown
ten shillenshe

Januarie the 2 day 1731
Recaved from John Gown
twenteie shilleanshe

[B2, f16r][115]
a not of tries sawen at the hearbour
befor Friday biean the tweallt day
of Desambear 26}
14}
100   fut

Mesrean - - - -		500 - - 50	
Dito mesran - - -		200 - - 63	
Dito mesran - - -		200 - - 66	
Dito mesran - - -		300 - - 54	
	31		
Dito mesran -	20	200 - - 56	
	620		
Dito mesran - - -		100 - - 14	
2745	3127	500 - - 47	460
382	620	200 - - 32	
3127	2507	2200	382
382		382	3127
11010		2582	
2745110	3127	25000	
110210	10		
2745	3117		

---

[115] Note: This page was used as rough working, so it is not always clear which numbers correspond with which equations. Where numbers have been overwritten, the topmost (where discernible) has been given here.

```
300          3127
 10           310
310          2817
```

The whole Acoount of plank that
was sawn at the harbour by
William Dickson 25 00 63

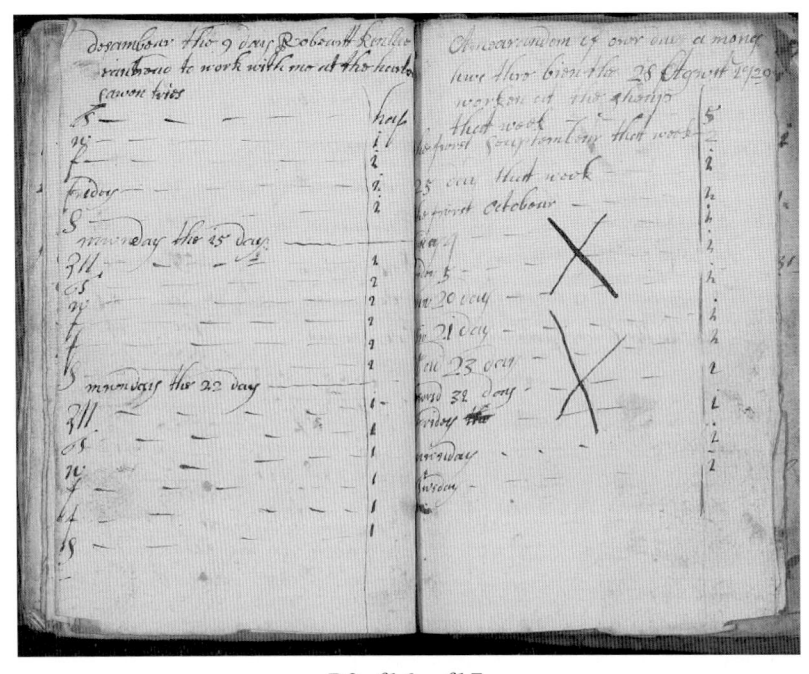

```
              310
              310
3075          620
```

B2, f16v, f17r

[B2, f16v]

>Desambear the 9 day Robeartt Kinllie
>eantread to work with me at the harbour
>sawen tries

T - - - - - - - - - - - - - - -	- - - - - - - -	haf
W - - - - - - - - - - - - - -	- - - - - - - -	1
F - - - - - - - - - - - - - - -	- - - - - - - -	1
Friday - - - - - - - - - - -	- - - - - - - -	1
S - - - - - - - - - - - - - - -	- - - - - - - -	1

    Munday the 15 day

M - - - - - - - - - - - - - -	- - - - - - - -	1
T - - - - - - - - - - - - - - -	- - - - - - - -	1
W - - - - - - - - - - - - - -	- - - - - - - -	1
F - - - - - - - - - - - - - - -	- - - - - - - -	1
F - - - - - - - - - - - - - - -	- - - - - - - -	1
S - - - - - - - - - - - - - - -	- - - - - - - -	1

    Munday the 22 day

M - - - - - - - - - - - - - -	- - - - - - - -	1
T - - - - - - - - - - - - - - -	- - - - - - - -	1
W - - - - - - - - - - - - - -	- - - - - - - -	1
F - - - - - - - - - - - - - - -	- - - - - - - -	1
F - - - - - - - - - - - - - - -	- - - - - - - -	1
S - - - - - - - - - - - - - - -	- - - - - - - -	1

[B2, f17r]

    A mearandom of our days a mong
    hus thre bien the 28 Agust 1729
    worken at the sheap

that week - - - - - - - - - - - - - - -	5
the furst Seaptembear that week	2
25 day that week - - - - - - - - - - - -	1
the furst Octobear - - - - - - - - - -	1
~~Thursday 4~~	~~1~~
~~Fridey 5~~	~~1~~
~~Mun 20 day~~	~~1~~
~~Tu 21 day~~	~~1~~
~~Wad 23 day~~	~~1~~

~~Fursd 31 day~~ ----------------	1
~~Friday the~~ ----------------	1
Munday -------------------	1
Tusday -------------------	1

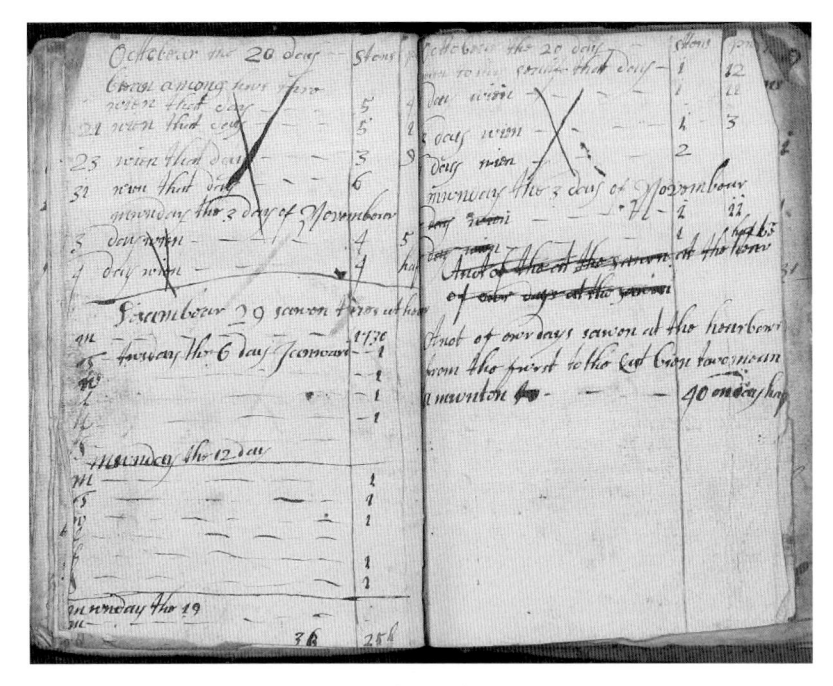

B2, f17v, f18r

[B2, f17v]

	Stons	punds[116]
Octtobear the 20 day ------		
~~biean among hus thre~~		
~~wien that day~~ ----------------	5	4
~~21 wien that day~~ ----------------	5	1
~~23 wien that day~~ ----------------	3	9

---

[116] Note that Dickson put the totals at the bottom of this folio in the wrong columns: 36 stones; 25 pounds.

~~31 wien that day ------~~	~~6~~	
~~Munday the 3 day of~~		
~~Novembear~~		
~~3 day wien ------~~	~~4~~	~~5~~
~~4 day wien ------~~	~~4~~	~~Haf~~
Desambear 29 sawen		
tries at hearbor	in	1730
T Tusday the 6 day Januari - - -	- - 1	
W -	- - 1	
F -	- 1	
F -	- 1	
S -		
Munday the 12 day		
M -	1	
T -	1	
W - - - - - - - - - - - - - - - - - - -	1	
F -		
F -	1	
S -	1	
Munday the 19		
M -		
	36	25$^{li[bra]}$

[B2, f18r]

Octtobear the 20 day - - - - - - - -	Sttons	punds
wien to my seallf that day - - - -	1	12
~~21 day wien------~~	~~1~~	~~11~~
~~23 day wien------~~	~~1~~	~~3~~
~~31 day wien------~~	~~2~~	
~~Munday the 3 day of~~		
~~Novembear~~		

[ ] day wien	1	11[117]
[ ] day wien	1	
A not of the at the sawen		
at the henr heaber of our		
days at the sawen		

A not of our days sawen at the hearbour from the furst to the Last bien two mean amunten to - - - - - - - - - - - - -	40 on day haf

B2, f18v, f19r

---

[117] Note that the dates at the beginning of these lines are sewn into the binding.

[B2, f18v]

   1729
   Aguest the 28 day taken of
   aren[118] and wien of bowts
   4 ston and heallf
   ditto 29 day wien of bowts and
   nealls
6 ston and 6 pound
   ditto the 30 day inclluden the wholl
   wien amongs hus
4 stton and haf
   Seaptembear the furst wien
3 ston and nien pund
   2 day wien
3 ston and 6 punde
   the 25 day wiean arean that day
   wiean that day - - - - - - - - S^{S}6 P 12[119]
   Octtobear the furst
   that day wiean - - - - - - - - - 6   6
   Fursday the 4 day wien - - - 4   14
   Friday the 5 day wien - - - - 5   10

[B2, f19r]

the 8 day of Feabruarie
                1789[120]
Reseaved from M^s Robeson
wan pound 6 shellens six pens
Marth the 24 day
four pund from Janet Dasen

---

[118] Iron.
[119] Table in stones and pounds, as on the folios above.
[120] Clearly a mistake.

for a dead cofean
_____ Agust the 28 day 1729 _____
Meamrandom for our days
worken at the sheap hus thre that week
days
Seapteamber the furst that week
days to thre
the 25 day worken at the sheape
day that week
Octtobear the furst on day
on Fursday the 4 day
on Fridey the 5 day

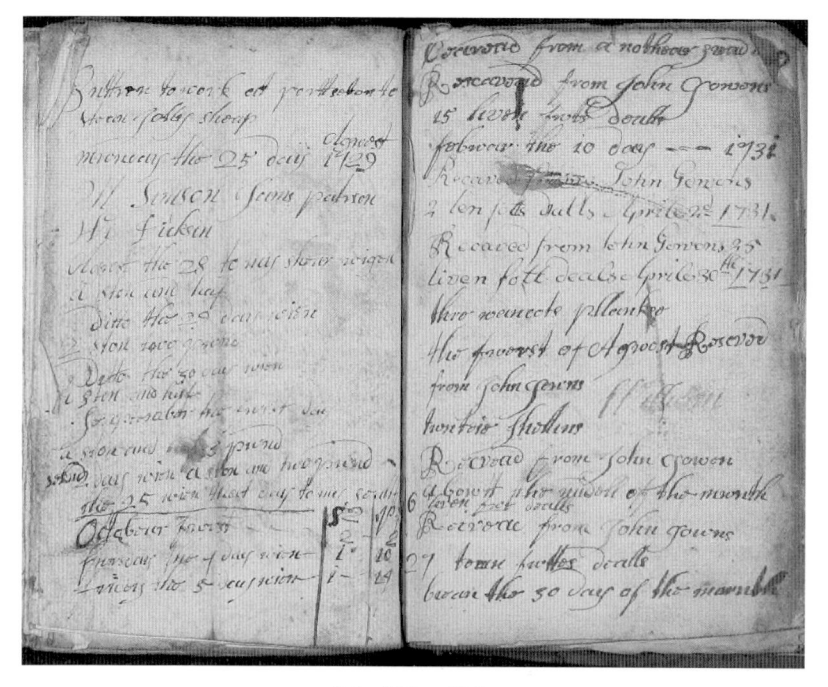

B2, f19v, f20r

[B2, f19v]
Enttren to work at Portt Seton to
   Stephan Jolly sheap
   Munday the 25 day Aguest 1729
   M Simson James Paterson
   Wi Dickson
   Agust the 28 to my shear wigen
   a ston and haf
     ditto the 29 day wien
   2 ston two pund
   2 ditto the 30 day wien
   a ston and haf
     Seaptember the furst day
   a ston and 3 pund
seknd 2 day wien a ston and two pund
   the 25 wien that day to my seallf

	S	p [ ][121]
- - - - - - - - - - - - - - - - - - - -	2	
Octobear furst - - - - - - - - - -	2 -	2
Fursday the 4 day wien - - - -	1	10
Fridey the 5 day wien - - - - -	1 -	14

[B2, f20r]
Cearead from a nothear siead heir
Rescavead from John Gowens
    15 eliven futs dealls
    Febrewarie the 10 day - - - 1731
    Recaved frome John Gowens
    2 ten fotts dialls Aprile 2^{d} <u>1731</u>
    Recaved from John Gowens 25
    eliven fott deals Aprile 30th <u>1731</u>
    thre wancots pllankse
    the fuerst of Aguest Resceved

---

[121] Page damaged. Units in stones and pounds as above.

from John Gowns   William[122]
twenteie shellins
Recevead from John Gowen
aboutt the midell of the munth
6 eleven fut dealls
Recevead from John Gowns
27 tean futtes dealls
biean the 30 day of the munth

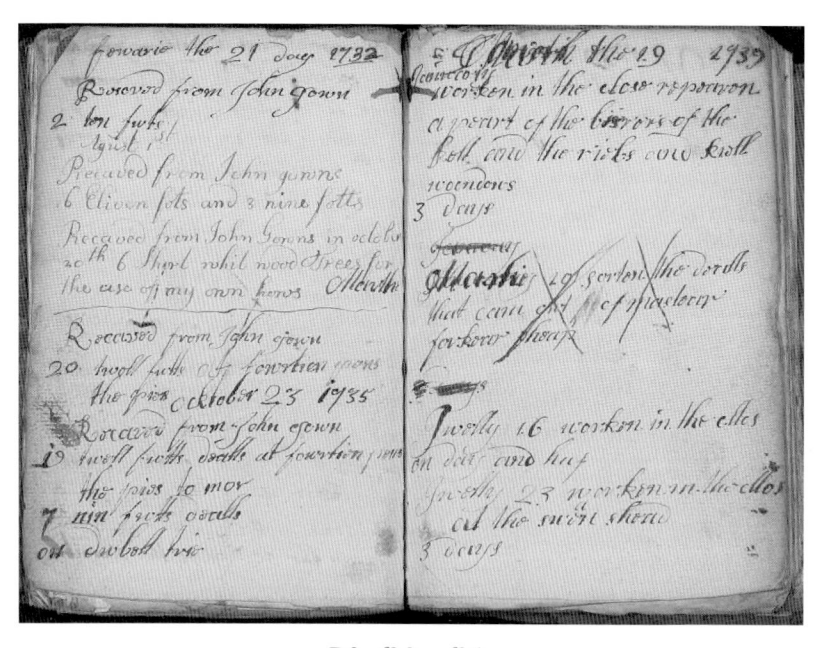

B2, f20v, f21r

[B2, f20v]

Febrewarie the 21 day <u>1732</u>
Resceved from John Gown
2 ten futs

---

[122] Signature practice, unrelated to text.

Agust 1ˢᵗ
Recaved from John Gowns
6 Eliven fots and 3 nine fotts
Recaved from John Gowns in October
20ᵗʰ 6 short whit wood Trees for
the use of my own hous
Recaved from John Gown
20 twell futts at fouertien pens
    the pies
        Ocktober 23 1735
Recaved from John Gown
19 twell futts dealls at fourtien pens
   the pies to mor
7 nin futts dealls
on dubell trie

[B2, f21r]

Januariy the 19 1739
   worken in the close repearen
   a peart of the bisrers of the
   kell and the riebs and kiell
   woondows
3 days
  ~~January~~
  ~~Martie 19 sorten the dealls~~
  ~~that cam out of Mastear~~
  ~~Forkear sheap~~
~~3 days~~
Juelly 16 worken in the cllos
on day and haf
Juelly 23 worken in the cllos
   at the sawen shead
3 days

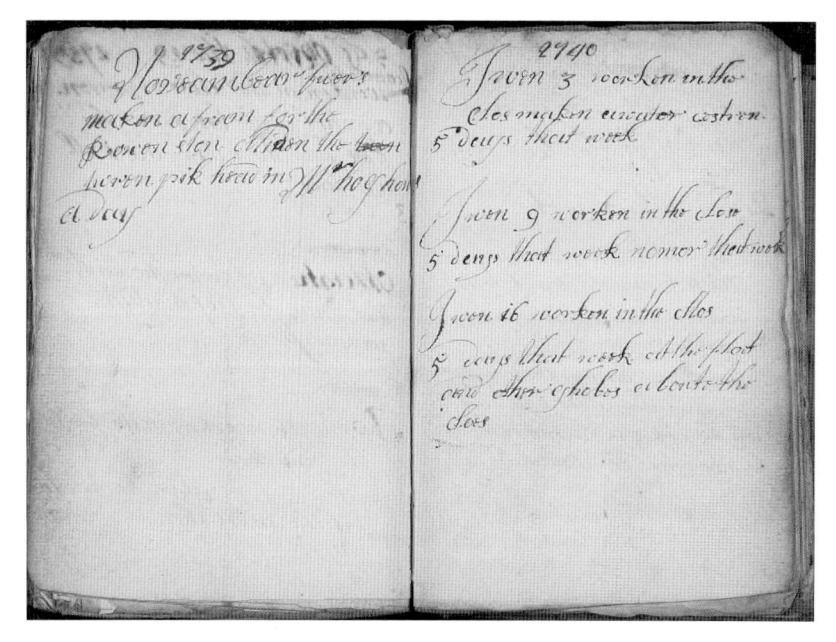

B2, f21v, f22r

[B2, f21v]

   1739
  Noveambear fuers
 maken a fram for the
 Rowen ston clliden the ~~twen~~
 turenpik head in Mr Hog hous
a day

[B2, f22r]

   1740
 Juen 3 worken in the
  clos maken a water cestren
5 days that week

Juen 9 worken in the close
5 days that week no mor that week

Juen 16 worken in the cllos
5 days that week at the floet
   and other ghobes aboute the
   cloes

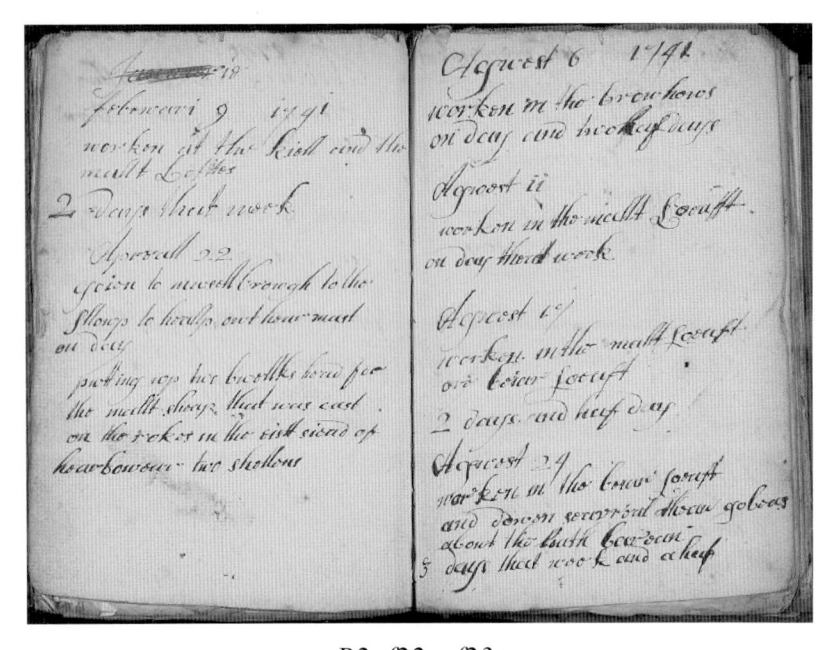

B2, f22v, f23r

[B2, f22v]

   ~~Januarie~~
   Febrewari 9 1741
   worken at the kiell and the
     mallt Lofttes
2 days that week

Apreall 22
goien to Musellbrough to the
slloup to heallp out hearbour mastear
on day
putting up two buellkshead for
the mallt sheap that was cast
on the rokes in the eistt siead of
hearbouear two shellens

[B2, f23r]

Aguest 6 1741
worken in the browhous
on day and two haf days
Aguest 11
worken in the mallt Loeafft
on day theat week

Aguest 17
worken in the mallt Loeaft
ore beiar[123] Loeaft
2 days and haf day
Aguest 24
worken in the beiar Loeaft
and dowen seavreal othear gobeas
about the [ath][124] barean
3 days that week and a haf

---

[123] Bere, or barley.
[124] Whilst the '-ath' is clear, the first part is indecipherable. It possibly begins with an 'L' – Lath barean?

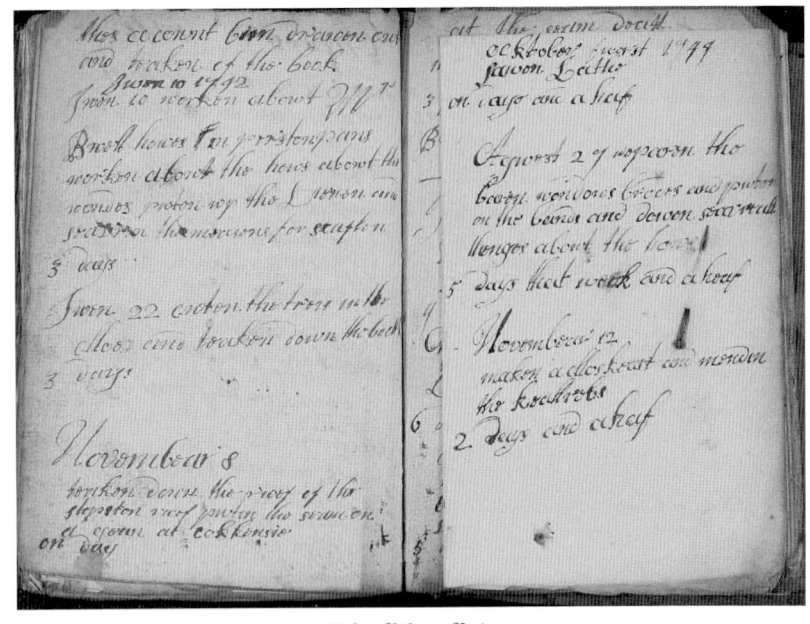

B2, f23v, f24r

[B2, f23v]

    thes acount bien drawen out
    and teaken of the book
        Juen 10 1742
    Juen 10 worken about M^r
    Bwell houes in Perstonpans
    worken about the hous about the
    wondes puten up the Lienen and
    seavren[125] the measens for scaften
3 days
Juen 22 cuten the treis in the
    clloes and teaken down the bootth[126]
3 days

---

[125] Serving the masons for scaffolding.
[126] Booth.

Novembear 8
    teaken down the ruef of the
    stipston ruef putin the seam on
    a gean at Cokkensie
on day

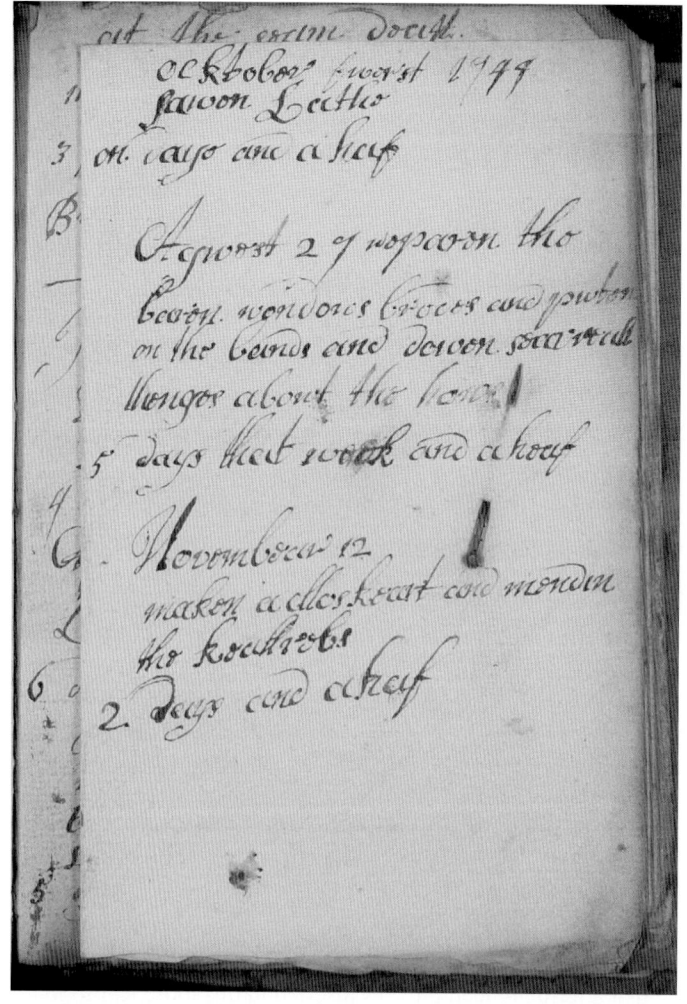

B2, loose leaf pinned between f23v and f24r

[B2, loose leaf pinned between f23v and f24r][127]

 Ocktober fuerst 1744
 sawen Lathe
on daye and a haf

 Aguest 27 reparen the
 baren wondows brodes and puten
 on the bands and dowen seavreall
 thenges about the hous
5 days that week and a heaf

 Novembear 12
 maken a clloskeart and mendin
 the keallrebs
2 days and a haf

---

[127] Note that a ferrous-metal pin was inserted in this loose leaf folio to attach it to the book.

at the same docth
maken 3 sashwondows and
3 pear of kasment wondows for
Bredls hous in the pens

Janueri 16 1744
Repearen the koetsribs
caben tres and lepen the sam
4 days this acount Gen greuen
 ent contruken of the book
Apriel 13 reparen the brower
Lonems for the treumstows
Octtobeer twenti on vear 1744
6 days   seven letter on vear and half
Augest 29 repearen the cown
wondows troets and yonten in the
bardes on the wondows and doues
severoll thongs about the hous
5 days and a half
 0

[B2, f24r]

    at the seam deatt
  maken 3 sase wondows and
3 pear of keasmeant wondows for
Bwells[128] hous in the pans

Januari 16 1744
    Repearen the kiell ribs
  sawen tries and Layen the sam
4 days} thes acount bien drawen
        out and teaken of the book
    Aprieall 15 repearen the breowen
  Lowems for the browen hous
        Ockteobear fuerst on day 1744
6 days sawen Lathe on day and haf
    Aguest 29 repearen the baren
  wondows brodes and puten on the
  bandes on the windows and dowen
  seavrell thenges about the hous
5 days and a haff
        O[ctober]

---

[128] See above: B2, f23v.

B2, f24v, f25r

[B2, f24v]

October Last day 1743
sawen oc[129] tember for realls to
M[r] Greant and Boorows[130]
5 days that week

November 7
worken at ditto
6 days that week

---

[129] Oak.

[130] This passage probably refers to the Captain William Burrows and Sir Archibald Grant who were sent to Scotland to further the interests of the York Buildings Company, circa 1727. For example, they were mentioned in a 1730 letter in relation to a lease from Lord Hopetoun. See David Murray, *The York Buildings Company, A Chapter in Scotch History Read Before the Institutes of Bankers and Chartered Accountants, Glasgow 19th February 1883* (Glasgow: James Maclehose & Sons, 1883), 72.

November 14
    worken at ditto
6 days that week

November 21
6 days that week

[B2, f25r]

    November 28   W
    worken at ditto   W
6 days that week

    Desambear 5
    worken at ditto
6 days that week

    Desambear 12
    worken at ditto
6 days that week

    Desambear 19
    cutin a plan trie at Seaton for
    wagen whealls and sawen in
    cheop
6 days that week

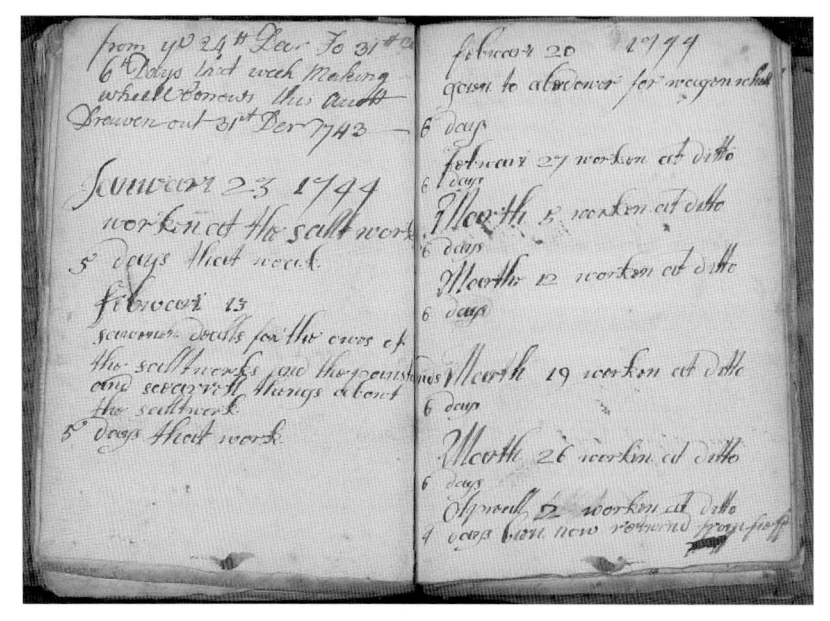

B2, f25v, f26r

[B2, f25v]

    from the 24th December To 31st December
    6 Days that week making
    wheellborrows this accountt
Drawen out 31st December 1743 -

Januari 23 1744
    worken at the salltworks
5 days that weak
    Febrewari 13
    sawenen dealls for the owes[131] of
    the salltworks and the panstands
    and sceavrell thengs about

---

[131] use.

the salltwork
5 days that work

[B2, 26r]

Febrewari 20 1744
goien to Abedouer for wagen whell
6 days
Febrewari 27 worken at ditto
6 days
Marth 5 worken at ditto
6 days
Marthe 12 worken at ditto
6 days

Marth 19 worken at ditto
6 days
Marth 26 worken at ditto
6 days
Apreall 2 worken at ditto
4 days bien now returned from Fieff

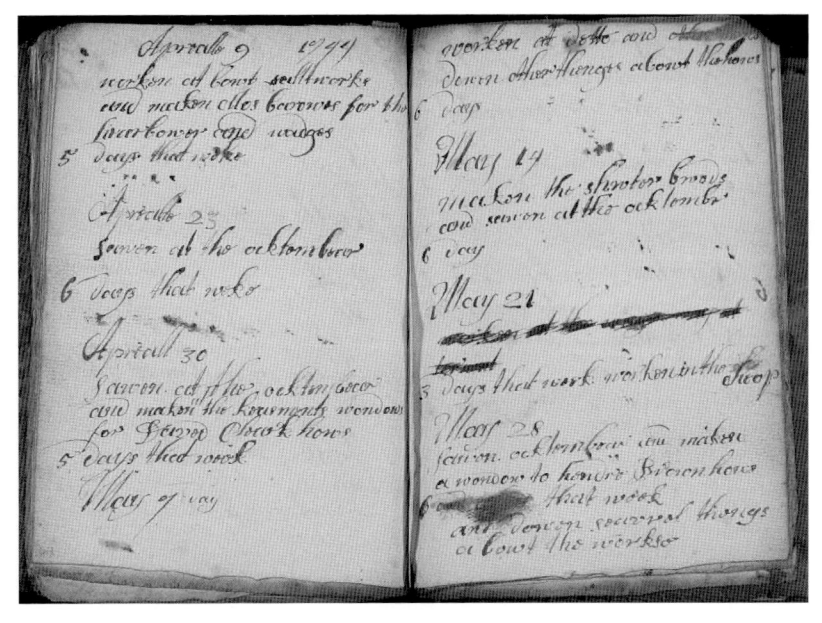

B2, f26v, f27r

[B2, f26v]

    Aprealle 9 1744
worken at bout salltworks
and maken cllos barowes for the
hearbouer and wadges
5 days that weke

    Aprealle 23
sawen at the ock tembear
6 days that weke

    Apreall 30
sawen at the ock tembear
and maken at the keasments wondows
for Daved Cleark hous

5 days that week
    May 7 day

[B2, f27r]

    worken at detto and ~~other thens~~
    dowen other thenges about the hous
6 days

    May 14
    maken the shuter brods
    and sawen at the ock tember
6 day

    May 21
    ~~worken at the wagen way at~~
    ~~Ternent~~
3 days that week worken in the cheop

    May 28
    sawen ock tembear and maken
    a wondow to Hendre Brown hous
6 that week[132]
        and dowen seavrel thengs
        about the workse

---

[132] Note that two words were scribbled out after '6', but are now illegible: '6 ~~and [ ]~~ that week'.

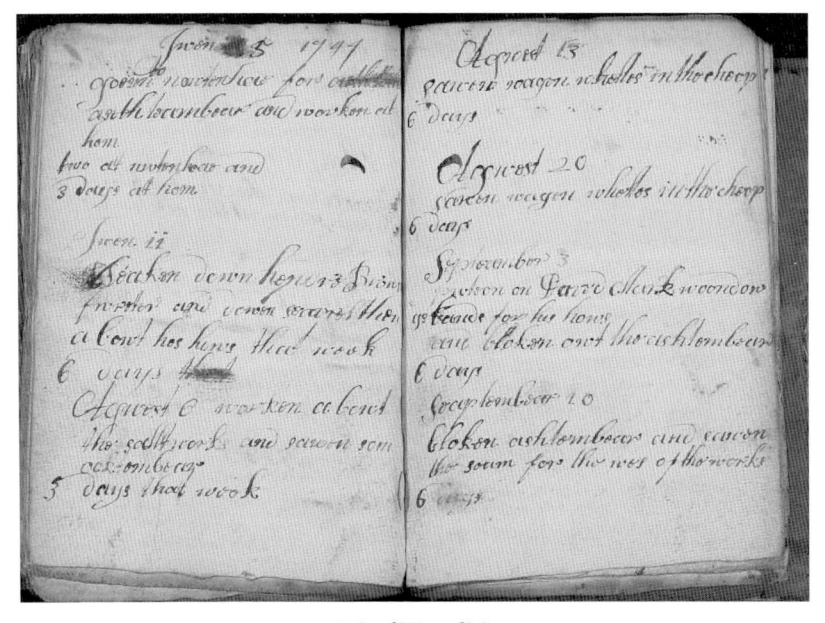

B2, f27v, f28r

[B2, f27v]

    Juen 5 1744
goeien to Nowtenhae[133] for
aseth teambear and worken at
hom
two at Nowtenhae and
3 days at hom

    Juen 11
Teaken down Hendre Brown
fwreter[134] and dowen seavrell thengs

---

[133] Newton Hall, Yester Parish, East Lothian.
[134] Meaning unclear – possibly a 'feretour', or a bier. See DSL/DOST: 'Feretour' and 'Ferter'.

about hes hous that week
6 days ~~that~~
   Aguest 6 worken about
   the salltworks and sawen som
   ock tembear
3 days that week

[B2, f28r]

    Aguest 13
   sawen wagen whelles in the cheop
6 days

   Aguest 20
   sawen wagen whelles in the cheop
6 days
   Septeamber 3
   puteon on Daved Cllark woondow
   bands for his hous
   and bloken out the ash tembear
6 days
   Seaptembear 10
   bloken[135] ash tembear and sawen
   the seam for the ues[136] of the works
6 days

---

[135] See DSL/DOST: 'Bloking, Blocking' – Bargaining, trading.
[136] use.

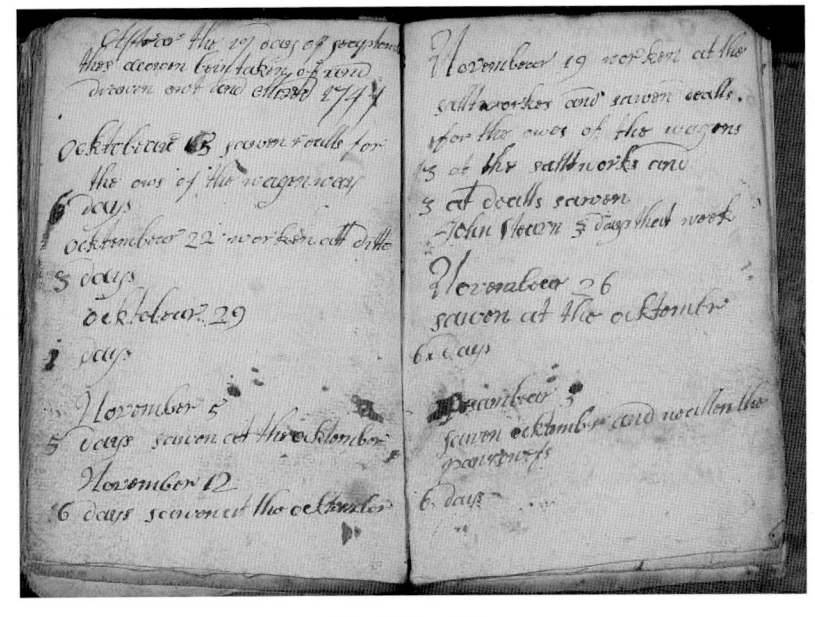

[B2, f28v]

 Aftear the 17 day of Seaptember
thes acouen bein taken of and
drawen out and cllired 1744

Ocktobear 15 sawen realls for
 the ows[137] of the wagenway
6 days
 Ocktembear 22 worken att ditto
3 days
 Ocktobear 29
1 days

---

[137] use.

November 5
5 days sawen at the ock tember
November 12
6 days sawen at the ock tember

[B2, f29r]

Novembear 19 worken at the
salltworkes and sawen dealls
for the oues of the wagens
3 at the salltworks and
3 at dealls sawen
John Steavn 3 days that week
Novembear 26
sawen at the ock tembr
6x days

Desambear 3
sawen ock tembr and neallen the
panrowefs
6x days

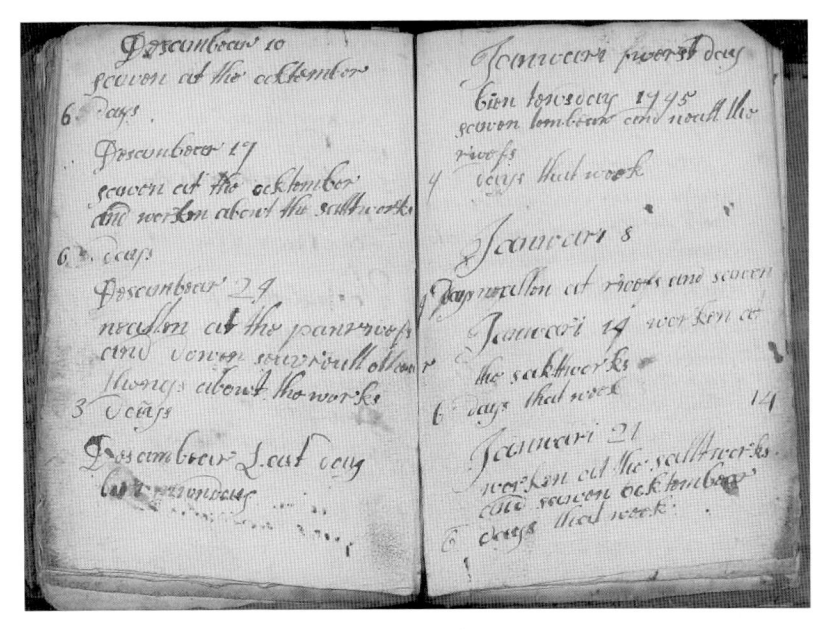

B2, f29v, f30r

[B2, f29v]

    Desambear 10
  sawen at the ock tember
6 days

    Desambear 17
  sawen at the ock tember
  and worken about the salltworks
6 days
    Desambear 24
  neallen at the panruefs
  and dowen seavreall othear
  thengs about the works

3 days
    Desambear Last day
    bein Munday

[B2, f30r]

      Januari fuerst day
      bien Teusday 1745
    sawen tembear and neall the
    ruefs
4 days that week

    Januari 8
4 days neallen at ruefs and sawen
    Januari 14 worken at
    the sakltworks[138]
6 days that week

                  14

    Januari 21
    worken at the salltworks
    and sawen ock tembear
6 days that week

---

[138] Read 'salltworks'.

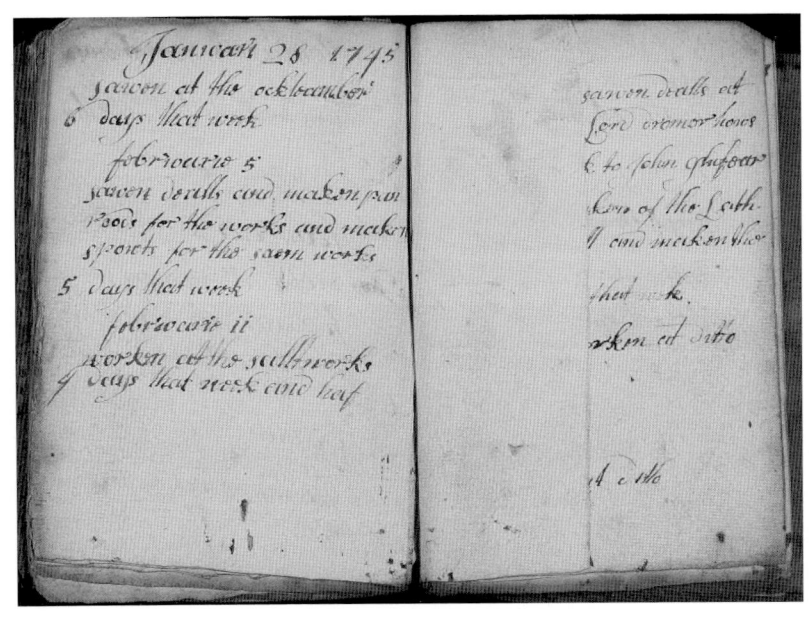

[B2, f30v]

  Januari 28 1745
 sawen at the ock teamber
6 days that week
  Febrewarie 5
 sawen dealls and maken pan
roods for the works and maken
spouts for the saem works
5 days that week
  Febrewarie 11
 worken at the salltworks
4 days that week and haf

[B2, f31r] [Blank page, cut in half from top to bottom]

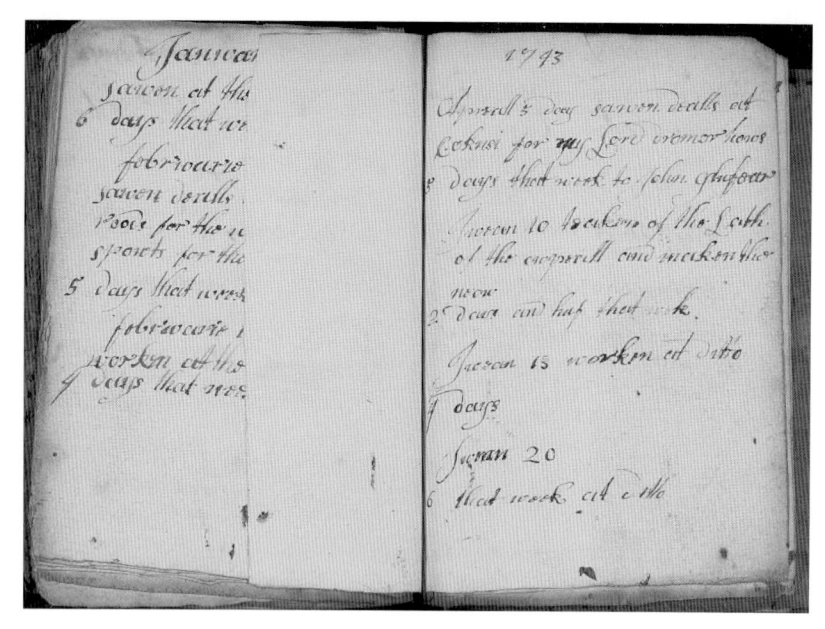

B2, f31v, f32r

[B2, f31v] [Blank page, cut in half from top to bottom]

[B2, f32r]

    1743
Apreall 5 day sawen dealls at
Coknsi for my Lord Dromor[139] hous[140]
5 days that week to John Ghifear
    Juean 10 teaken of the Lath
    of the cupeall and maken the

---

[139] Sir Hew Dalrymple, Lord Drummore (1690-1755)

[140] Presumably the predecessor to Drummore House, to the southwest of Musselburgh, which M'Neill tells us was not built until 1753. He apparently built a smaller house on the property before the existing house was built. Peter M'Neill, *Prestonpans and Vicinity: Historical, Ecclesiastical, and Traditional* (Tranent: P. M'Neill, 1902), 250-1.

neow
2 days and haf that wek

 Juean 13 worken at ditto
4 days

 Juean 20
6 that week at ditto

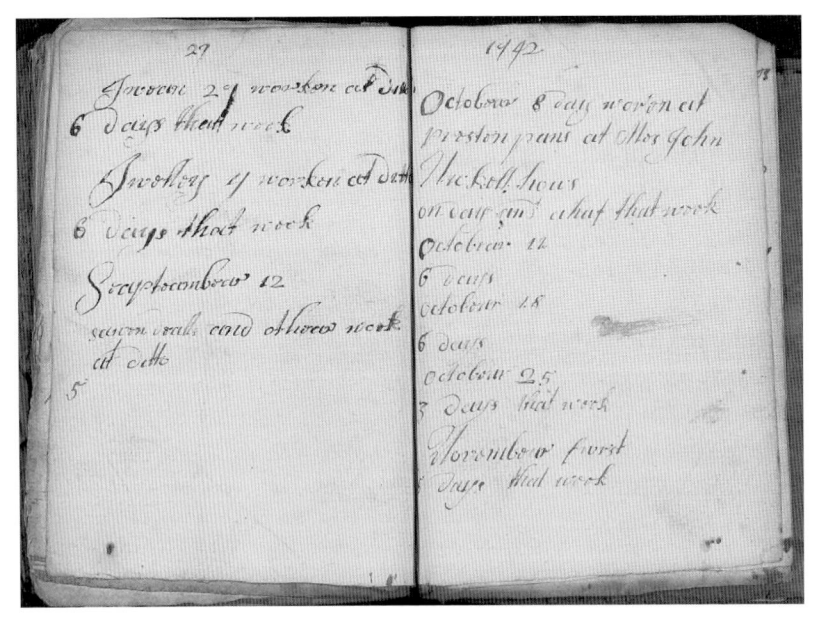

B2, f32v, f33r

[B2, f32v]

  27
 Juean 27 worken at ditto
6 days that week

Juelley 4 worken at ditto
6 days that week

Seapteambear 12
sawen dealls and othear work
at ditto
5

[B2, f33r]

    1742
Octobear 8 day worken at
Prestenpans at Mes[ter] John
Nuckell hous
on day and a haf that week
Octobear 11
6 days
Octobear 18
6 days
Octobear 25
3 days that week
Novembear furst
5 days that week

[B2, f33v]

Novembear 8 1742
  worken att ditto
6 days that week

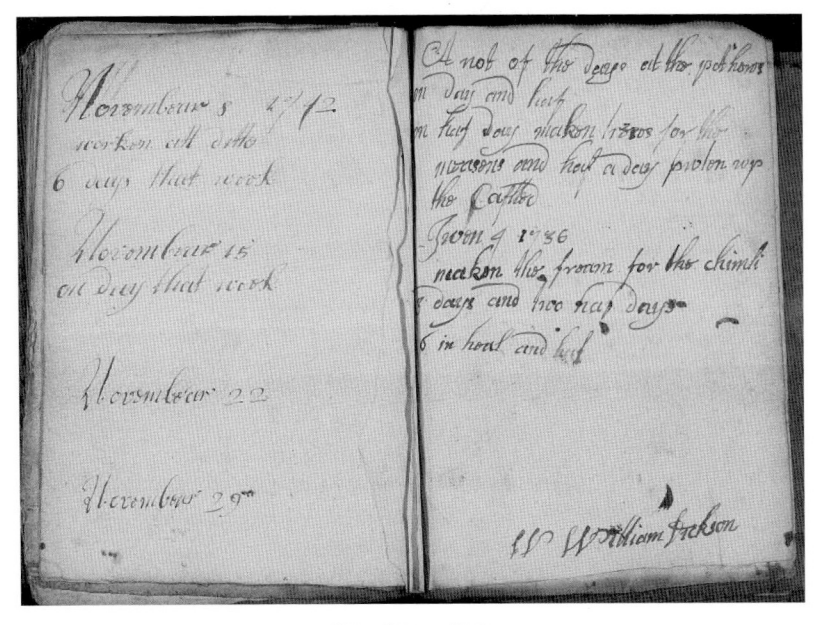

  Novembear 15
on day that week

Novembear 22

Novembear 29

[B2, f34r-f40v] [These seven folios were all torn out]

[B2, f41r]

   A not of the days at the pot hous
on day and haf
on haf day maken treses for the
    measens and haf a day puten up
    the Caflled
    Juen 4 1736
    maken the fream for the chimli
3 days and two haf days
6 in heal and haf

                W William Dickson

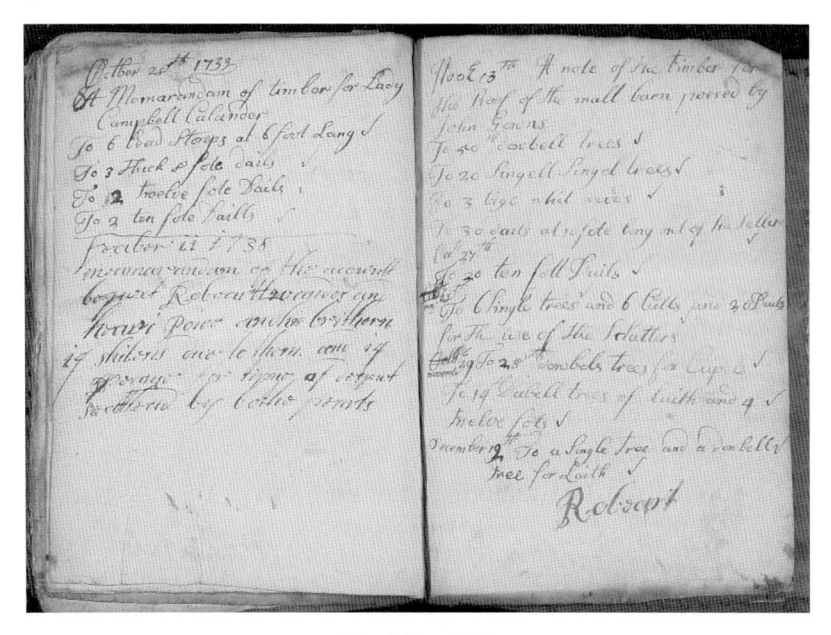

B2, f41v, f42r

[B2, f41v]

October 28th 1733
A Memarandam of timber for Lady
  Campbell Calander
To 6 bead stowps at 6 foot Lang √
To 3 thick 8 fote dails   √
To 2 twelve fote Dails   √
To 2 ten fote Daills   √

Feaberuary 11 1738
meamarandam of the acountt
bewixt Robeartt Wandes and
Heari Powe and his brithern

14 shilens due to them and 14
  peanse for tipne of desput
  seattlead by bothe pearts

[B2, f42r]

  November 13th A note of the timber for
  the Roof of the malt barn possed by
    John Gowns
  To 50[ ][141] doubell trees ✓
  To 20 singell singel trees ✓
  To 3 bige whit woods ✓
  To 30 dails at 10 fote long out of the seller
October 27th ✓
  To 20 ten fott Dails ✓
~~October~~
November 28th ✓
  To 6 single trees and 6 Cutts and 20 Dails
  for the use of the sclatters ✓
~~October~~ November 29 To 28[ ][142] doubels trees for Cupels ✓
  To 14[ ][143] Dubell trees of Laith and 4   ✓
    twelve fots ✓
December 12th To a single tree and a doubell ✓
      tree for Laith   ✓
        Robeart

---

[141] Dickson uses a glyph here which is similar to the superscript 'th' on the dates, but does not have the downstroke at the end of the 'h'. Perhaps it is a 'ft' for 'foot'? As it is unclear we have left all three instances of it (all on this folio) blank.

[142] Ibid.

[143] Ibid.

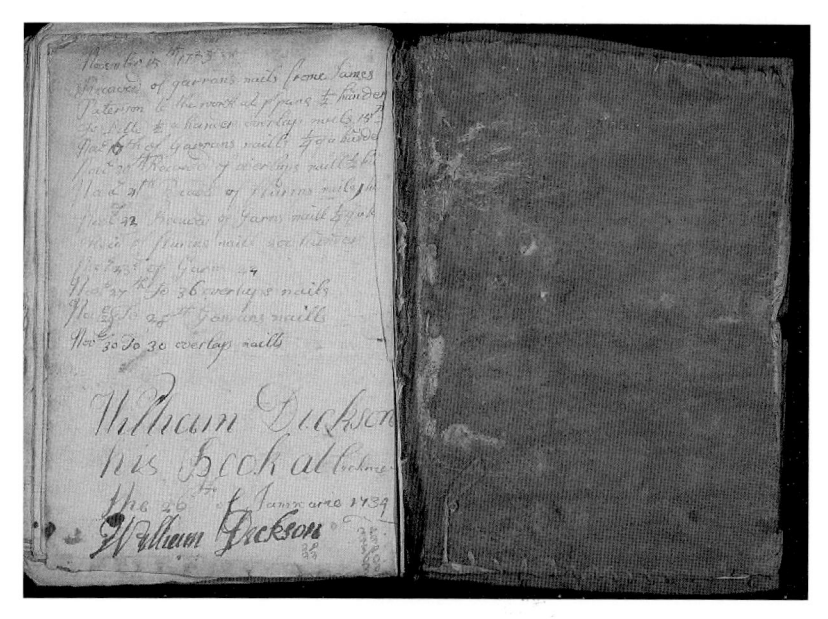

B2, f42v

[B2, f42v]

November 15th 1733
Recaved of garrans nails frome James
Paterson to the work at Prestonpans 1/2 hunder
To Ditto 1/2 a hunder overlap nails 15th
November 16th of Garrans naills 1/4 of a hunder
November 20th Recaved of overlaps naill 1/2 hunder
November 21th Recaved of flurins nails 1 hunder
November 22 Recaved of Garns naill 1/4 of a hunder
Recaved of flurins naill 200 hunder
November 23^{d} of Garns 22
November 27th To 36 overlaps nails
November 29 To 28th Garrans naills
November 30 To 30 overlap naills

William Dickson
his Book at Cocknesi
the 26th of Janiuarie <u>1734</u>
William Dickson   28
                    28   22
                    22   30
                          60
                          30

[B2, f43r-f45v] [These three folios were all torn out]

[B2, Back endpapers][144]

---

[144] Sewn into the back endpaper are a series of at least five folios of scrap paper, apparently intended to stiffen the binding so that it keeps its shape. The sewing is coming apart, and one can just see the edges of pages of writing practice, biblical quotes from the Psalms, and other unknown writings. Unfortunately they cannot be accessed to transcribe at the present time.

APPENDICES

Appendix 1

Articles of Roup of the Coal and Saltworks of Tranent and Cockenzie, 1736

The document below is from a bundle of papers relating to the tack of the coal and salt works at Tranent and Cockenzie.[145] It is a 'representation and articles of roup' for a forthcoming auction of the works, dealing specifically with the mine 'sittings' and the waggonway.[146] As such, important details are given about the industrial context in which Dickson worked. For example, opportunities are afforded to see the workings of an eighteenth-century coal mine. Use of specialist jargon, such as pillars, wastes and dyke metals, give insights into mining techniques and problems.[147] Greedy removal of too much coal at the cost of the (coal) pillars holding up the ceiling would put the entire mine at risk of collapse, so stipulations were put in place to ensure future tacksmen would abide by the rules. Similarly, care was taken to ensure three elements of the waggonway system were maintained: the waggonway itself, the waggons, and the 'trunks

---

[145] 'Representation for the York Building Company Annuitants, 1736', in NRS, CS133/421, 'Archibald Robertson, Tacksman of Coal and Salt Works of Cockenzie and Tranent vs Coal and Salt Works of Cockenzie and Tranent: Decreet of Tack of Coal and Salt Works, 28 September 1736'.

[146] For more on the context of this sale by roup, including the financial difficulties of the estate, see Jill Turnbull, *The Scottish Glass Industry, 1610-1750: 'To Serve the Whole Nation with Glass'* (Edinburgh: Society of Antiquaries of Scotland, 2001), 238-65, especially 264-5.

[147] For more on 'Room and Stoop Working', where linear rooms are cut from the coal seam, leaving pillars, or 'stoops', to hold up the ceiling, see Baron F. Duckham, *A History of the Scottish Coal Industry, Vol. I 1700-1815: A Social and Industrial History* (Newton Abbot: David & Charles, 1970), 59-60.

at the pans'.[148] *Specifications were given that oak timber was to be used, and that the 'earthen road' on both sides of the waggonway was to be kept in good order. Such articles of roup were important as they would have provided guidelines for the wrights, such as Dickson, who kept the industrial system working.*

[Appendix 1 (A1), f1r]

7 September 1736 Unto the right Honourable the Lord Justice Clerk
    The Representation of
     The York Building Company Annuitants and their factor

Humbly sheweth

  That your Lordship by warrand and remitt from the Lords in presence has lately upon the [blank] day of August last adjusted certain articles of roup of the Coal and Saltworks of Tranent and Cockenzie To be sett in tack for five years after Michaelmass nixt Which roup has been duly published in terms of your Lordships ordinance; and the roup comes on before the ordinary on the bills the 9th current

  As it must be supposed wee are very great strangers to the nature of such works and of all the articles that may be necessary for such a roup wherein wee can only act by the information of others skilled in such affairs, which in every particular Coalyiary admitts of variations, and requires different conditions, according to the circumstances and Situation of the Coal Wee have it now to trouble your Lordship with That three most

---

[148] Trunk: either a form of 'trunk-staithe' or 'trunk-spout' (a device originating in Newcastle-upon-Tyne for depositing coal from a tipped waggon down a wooden chute to a lower level), or a short siding linking to the main Waggonway.

materiall articles as wee are advised have been omitted concerning the carrying on and finishing of a Levell already begun and which if neglected would ruin the Coal forever: And concerning the pillars in the wasts already wrought and the keeping up of the waggon ways which at first view we hope your Lordship will think reasonable And upon that account we have presumed to annex hereto The said articles drawn out at length

[A1, f1v]

May it therefore please your Lordship to consider the forsaid articles annexed and to ordain the same to be added to these formerly adjusted and the roup to proceed accordingly According to Justice &c:

Follows the additionall articles

I^{mo} [149] That for preventing the hazard of the Main Coals being lost to the proprietors And that the Coal may be wrought in a regular manner The purchaser or Tacksman shall be obliged to carry on the Levell after mentioned in a regular manner to the said Main Coal on his own proper charges and expence As it is already begun by William Adam[150] the present tacksman And whereof one hundred fathoms or thereabouts is already wrought and carried on by the said William Adam at his charge and expence Which Levell was begun a Litle below an old open Coal pitt on the post road a Litle above the head of the heugh of Tranent And which Level face stands about one hundered fathom to the north of the present going

---

[149] '[Pri]mo', or first.
[150] The document next to this one in the bundle refers to him as 'William Adam Architeck Tacksman'. 'Execution at Crosses of Edinburgh and Haddingtoun – 27th and 28th August 1736', in NRS, CS133/421.

pitts commonly called the South Cro:well:-:pitt, And the bottom of said Levell about two fathoms perpendicular below the pavement of the Splinty Coal: And because the tack is only to be sett for five years And that by the neglect of carrying on the Level, the working of the Coal may become impracticable Therefor the Tacksman shall be obliged to run and compleat at least Two hundered fathoms of said Levell Each year of

[A1, f2r]

his tack untill the same shall hitt the Great Seam, that so the same may be carried on regularly for the future by succeeding tacksmen And that the Company or others who shall be intitled by Law to uplift the tack duty their factors or doers May from time to time cause view the said Level or Mine, that it may be regularly carried on according to their direction

2do [151] That the Tacksman shall not cutt any thing off nor impair the present pillars of the Coal, And that he shall be obliged to leave pillars in the Coal, where he shall happen to work, of at least as large dimensions as any of the pillars now in the coal, And in case of any Dyke mettalls appearing in the wal, which may endanger the Sitting[152] thereof at that place, In that case he shall be obliged to leave such a body of coal as shall be necessary to prevent the sitting thereof And that at the sight of such

---

[151] '[Secun]do', or second.
[152] See DSL/DOST: 'Setting, *vbl. n.*' – 2. a. Founding or erecting (a construction, etc.); 11. *Setting down*, b. Sinking (a coalmine); and 'Set, *v.*' – 68. *To set doun,* f. *specifically* To sink (a coalmine).

persons as shall be appointed by the person or persons haveing right to uplift the rents of the Companys estates

3^{tio} [153] That whatever method is taken for carrying down the coals from the Coal pitts to the Salt works The Tacksman oblige himself to leave the waggon way waggons and Trunks at the pans in as good condition at the end of the tack as they are at his entry thereto with no less quantity of oak timber than is now contained in them And particularly that he be obliged to keep and leave Not only the timber of the waggon way but also the breadth of the earthen road on both sides of the way which supports the timber Sleepers and raills And at the narrowest place to keep and leave them two foot of well rammed earth on each outside of the raills of the said waggon road

[A1, f2v]

Haveing considered this representation and Articles of roup within mentioned consisting of three articles Approves of the same And Ordains them to be added to these formerly adjusted and the roup to proceed accordingly

And^r Fletcher[154]

---

[153] '[Ter]tio', or third.

[154] Andrew Fletcher of Saltoun, Lord Milton, who became a Lord of Session in 1724. A. J. G. Cummings, 'The York Buildings Company: A Case Study in Eighteenth Century Corporation Mismanagement', Vol. 2 (Unpublished PhD Thesis, University of Strathclyde, 1980), 296, and A. Murdoch, 'Andrew Fletcher, Scotland and London in the Eighteenth Century' (University of Edinburgh Working Paper: School of History, Classics and Archaeology Website, 2013), 1-2.

signed 9th September 1736

[Endorsement on outside of document when folded:]

Representation
for
The York Building Company
Annuitants

1736

Appendix 2

Sale of Cockenzie House: *Caledonian Mercury*, Thursday 4th February 1748

The advertisement below for the sale of Cockenzie House by public roup (auction) was published in the Edinburgh newspaper, the Caledonian Mercury, *on Thursday, 4th February 1748. Included are details of the historic house as it existed three years after the last entry in Dickson's work journals. Several of the rooms mentioned in the advertisement appear to correspond with entries, such as the office-houses (B2, f12v), the maltings and brewery (B2, f13v and f23r), or the kitchen (B1, f22v and f27v), offering further detail of the work of William Dickson. As 'the hous' survives today,[155] there are rich opportunities afforded by the extant fabric and historical documentation, despite the fact that the building has been much altered by subsequent generations. Indeed, these alterations make the advertisement reproduced below all the more significant as it helps us to make clearer sense of Dickson's work journals.*

---

[155] Canmore ID: 53644.

By ADJOURNMENT.

To be SOLD by publick voluntary Roup in John's Coffee-house, Edinburgh, on Wednesday the 10th of February inst. betwixt the Hours of 3 and 4 Afternoon, the following Subjects,

The large DWELLING-HOUSE, Malting, Brewery, and other office-houses, lying on the South side of Cockenzie, 6 Miles East from Edinburgh, in the Shire of Haddington and Lordship of Winton, viz. The Dwelling-house, consisting of a Kitchen and 13 Fire rooms, with Closets and Cellars, all well finished, fronting South to a Garden, Bowling and Washing-greens, with a Washing-house, fine Washing-water, all within the Garden-walls; as also, The large Malting Granaries, Brewery, and a convenient Place for a large Distillery, all calculated for an extensive Corn or Victual Trade in any shape, having the Harbour of Preston[156] just at hand for shipping, being well watered, as the same comes in by Lead-pipes to the Kitchen, Malting and Brewery; the Water good and plenty, and goes off by a Conduit to the Sea. There is also a very good Draw-well within the Court, with Stables, Byres, and large Hay-lofts above them, with two large Under-houses below the Granaries, well adapted for a large Linnen Manufactory, all lying on the West, North and East-sides of the said Dwelling-house, Court-ways, inclosed with Stone and Lime-walls; and the whole shut up by two large Gates, at which Carriages of all kinds can enter into the Court. The Progress of Writs and Conditions of Roup are to be seen in the Hands of John Flockhart Writer in Edinburgh. – Any Person that wants to see the above Subjects, or inclines to make a private Purchase, may call at the said John Flockhart, or

---

[156] Note that the proprietor does not mention Cockenzie's or Port Seton's harbours here. From 1680 a new customs precinct was established at Prestonpans, so perhaps exports like grain or victuals were required to go through a port with a customer. Hustwick, *The George of Port Seton*, 52-3.

Thomas Mathie the Proprietor at Cockenzie, any Time before the Roup. – There are likewise to be sold the same Day, some Dwelling-houses, lying upon the East side of and adjacent to the above Subjects in the Town of Cockenzie.

    N.B. The Subjects first above-mentioned are to be set up at 700 l[ibra]. Sterling.[157]

Appendix 3

Notice of the Glass House at Port Seton, *Caledonian Mercury*, 1730

The following notice was published in the Edinburgh newspaper, the Caledonian Mercury, *on Monday, 9th February 1730. Included are details of the products, sales arrangements and sources of raw materials for the Glass House, or the 'Pavillion' as it was also known. This is included here, as Dickson both worked on the building (B1, f30v-f31r) and made crates for transporting the made glass (B1, f29v), from May of 1728 to April of 1729. As such, the newspaper notice below gives important details of one of the local industries which provided work for Cockenzie tradesmen like Dickson.*[158]

    That at the GLASS-HOUSE[159] at Port-Seton, there is to be Sold, Window-Glass of several Sorts, viz. Crown, Common or Broad Glass, either in whole or Half-cases, or Peins of

---

[157] BL, *Caledonian Mercury* (Edinburgh: Thomas Ruddiman and Company, 4th February 1748).

[158] For more on the glass industry in the area, see Turnbull, *Scottish Glass Industry*, 238-65, and Jill Turnbull, 'Venetian Glassmakers in the Prestonpans Area in the Seventeenth Century', in *Scottish Archives*, 23 (2017), 103-13.

[159] Also called the 'Pavillion' or the 'Ink Bottle' due to the shape of the structure (Canmore ID: 368962). See B1, f30v.

different Dimensions, ready cut, or to be cut, as shall be commissioned; Also all Sorts of Flint or Cristal-Glass, consisting of Drinking-glasses of all Sorts, Decanters, Lamps, Gellie-glasses, Mustard-boxes, Salvers and Vials, &c. Glasses for Alchimists, Bell-Glasses for Gardens, &c. All at very reasonable and fix'd Rates. THAT broken Glass or Cullet, of all Sorts, will be bought at reasonable Prices, either at the Works, or the Shop of William Turnbull, Merchant near the Cross of Edinburgh, or the House of Mr. John Stevens, Merchant at Leith: To whom, or to John Ramsay at the Glass-works at Port-Seton, Commissions may be directed.[160]

Appendix 4

Caledonian Mercury **Excerpts Relating to Thomas Mathie, 1730 and 1737**

The two excerpts below are from the Edinburgh newspaper, the Caledonian Mercury, *dating to 1730 and 1737 respectively. Both related to Thomas Mathie, merchant in Cockenzie, who often employed William Dickson.[161] They have been included for the detail they give to the malting and other business ventures taking place in the wider community in which Dickson lived and worked.*

Excerpt A:

Superfine pale BARLEY MALT, made and sold at Cockenzie, at *L.* 08 12 00 per Boll, or delivered at Edinburgh, or

---

[160] BL, *Caledonian Mercury* (Edinburgh: Thomas and Walter Ruddiman, 9th February 1730)

[161] For more on the Mathies' standing and place names associated with the family, see M'Neill, *Prestonpans and Vicinity*, 155 and 162 ('Mathie's Rock'), and NLS, OS, 25 Inch, Haddingtonshire IX.1, 1892.

any Place within 6 Miles, at *L.* 9 Scots per Boll, ready Money. Any who want the same, may direct to THOMAS MATTHIE Merchant in Cockenzie. One Boll and an half being an Horse-load, is the least Quantity that can be sent six Miles off.[162]

Excerpt B:

ADVERTISEMENTS.
At PRESTON-PANS,
There is to be Sett at Whitsunday next, a convenient DWELLING HOUSE, with *Cellars, Warehouses, Stables,* and other Officehouses, with a large *Timber yard, Shades* for holding Timber, with Variety of other Accommodations, well adapted for Merchant business, all inclosed with good and sufficient Stone Walls, lying on the North, or Sea side of said Town of Preston-pans, at the foot of the Lane leading to the Customhouse; lately possess'd by the deceast Mrs. Matthie senior. Any who want to take the same, may call at Mr. William Watson Writer to the Signet his Chamber, the 4th Storey of Gavin Loch's Land, Edinburgh; or at Thomas Matthie Merchant in Cockenzie.[163]

Appendix 5

Testament of John Mathie, Skipper in Prestonpans, 1733

The document below is the testament dative and inventory of the Prestonpans skipper, John Mathie, who died intestate on 12th December 1732. Mathie was the father of Thomas Mathie, who was appointed his executor. Both father and son feature in Dickson's journals, so it is hoped that this testament will shed

---

[162] BL, *Caledonian Mercury* (Edinburgh: Printed For and By Mrs. Thomas and Walter Ruddimans, 29th January 1730).
[163] BL, *Caledonian Mercury* (Edinburgh: s.n., 15th February 1737)

further light on the wider business community which Dickson served. The conventions used for the rest of the volume have also been followed here, though indentation has also been added for the sake of clarity.

[Margin: '28 March 1733 John Mathie~']

The Testament Dative and Inventory of the Debt and sume of money pertaining & addebted to umquhill John Mathie skipper in Prestounpans the time of his decease who deceased in the moneth of March Jaj vij^c & Twenty six years Faithfully made and given up by Thomas Mathie merchant in Prestounpanns Eldest Lawfull son to the said umquhill John Mathie only Executor Dative decerned as nearest in kin to him and that by Decreet of the Commissaries of Edinburgh as the samen of date the Twelth day of December Jaj vij^c thirty two years In it selfe at more Length proports

In the First the said umquhill John Mathie had addebted and Resting owing to him the time of his decease foresaid the debt and sume of money aftermentioned To witt by the now deceast William Elliot of Arkletoun designed[164] in the bond after mentioned second Lawfull son to Walter Elliot of Arkletoun the sume of Lxxviij lib xvj s viij d Scots money remaning of the sume of j^c vj lib mony foresaid principale and annualrents thereof at the fourth day of September Jaj vij^c and Eleven years Togither with a proportionall part of xxx lib money foresaid of penalty Conform to bond granted be the said deceast Walter Elliot To the Defunct of date the third day of February Jaj vij^c and Two years Item the sume of Lx lib iij s iiij d of annualrent for the said Remaning sume from the said fourth day of September Jaj vij^c and Eleven years To the time foresaid of the said Defunct his decease

---

[164] See DSL/DOST: 'Design' – Scots law: to assign something (to a person); to bestow, grant.

Summa of the debt owing to the dead j^c xxxix ^{lib}
Masters Andrew Marjoribanks etc Make Constitute ordane and Confirm the said Thomas Mathie In only Executor Dative Quha nearest in kin to the said umquhill John Mathie his father and maid to the debt and sume of money abovewritten with full power etc Cautioner John Gowan merchant in Prestounpans~[165]

---

[165] NRS, CC8/8/95, Edinburgh Commissary Court, 1733 Testament of John Mathie, 208-9.

GLOSSARY

Unless otherwise stated, the glossary is based on DSL/DOST and Glen L. Pride, *Dictionary of Scottish Building* (Edinburgh: Rutland Press, 1996).

Aeis	ash, a type of tree. See also 'aseth'
Aren	iron
Arenworke	ironwork
Ark	a part of the curved waterway (in stone or wood and concave in form) which carries off the water from a breast-mill wheel; sometimes refers to the entire waterway from the end of a mill-lad to the tailrace (Pride, *DSB*, 12)
Aseth	ash, ashen, as in made of ash wood
Bands	iron straps; a part of door hinges which sit on the 'cruks'
Båren, barran	a barn
Bark	a barque, which was a type of ship
Bate	as used in a shipbuilding context, this may be an abbreviation for 'batten'. According to Steffy, a batten was, 'A thin plank or strip of wood used to determine hull curvatures or to temporarily connect timbers during construction'[1]
Bead	a bed. In some contexts, Dickson was clearly referring to a piece of furniture for sleeping, though it was also used to refer to a surface or a platform, just as 'bed' is used today

---

[1] J. Richard Steffy, 'Illustrated Glossary of Ship and Boat Terms', in Ben Ford, Donny L. Hamilton, and Alexis Catsambis (eds), *The Oxford Handbook of Maritime Archaeology* (Oxford: Oxford University Press, 2013), 'batten'.

Bead stide	bed stead
Beiar	bere, or barley
Bitch	beech, a type of tree
Bocks, bockess	box, boxes
Bodem	bottom
Bordren	bordering
Bowns	a 'boan'; a small outhouse or lean-to
Bowts	bolts
Bread, breadh, breath	breadth
Broods	'brods', or boards
Brooen	brewing
Browrie	brewery
Bucket patt	a bucket pot; a rock cut pond near at saltpan house for obtaining the sea water needed to make salt. Several survive near Cockenzie Harbour
Bugkdailin, bukdellen, bukdeallan, buckdelen, etc.	buk-denning, or a plank-lining in the hold of a vessel
Bunker	a bench or storage box with an opening lid
Busk	to make ready or prepare
Buste	a 'buist', or box. In relation to a kiln, it was the kiln box
Caeart	cart
Caflod	scaffolding
Cappear, capper	a copper; a brewing kettle made of copper or copper alloy
Catband	a bar used to hold a gate closed
Cheas, ches windows	sash windows
Cheallf, chellef	shelf or shelves

Cheop	a 'chop', or a shop
Chiest	chest
Chimlihead	chimney head
Chop	shop
Cleater	cleated, scaffolding with cleats to hold the planks in position
Cllired	cleared
Cllos, clos, closs	1. a close, as in a vennel or sidestreet, usually with a lockable gate; 2. clothes, or clothing; 3. close, as in held close, or held tightly
Closit	closet, cupboard
Cofean	Coffin
Coines	possibly a phonetic spelling of 'quoins'. See 'quoines'
Cokkini, Cokkeani	Cockenzie, East Lothian, which was formerly known as a variant of 'Cockenʒy' or 'Cockenni'. The letter 'z' was later used for the letter 'yogh'. There was no intention to change the sound, but in some cases 'sight' pronunciation has, like a cuckoo, pushed out the 'correct' pronunciation.
Collbaket	coal bucket
Collcorf	a box or basket in which coal is drawn out of a mine. They were described in mine regulations of the 1740s for Loanhead, Woolmet and Gilmerton as: 'a case of timber measuring 24 inches square and the same in depth'. Duckham noted

	corfes having specific capacities ranging from 2·5 to 6 hundredweight[2]
Collheal	coal hill
Collmeat	coal-mett, or a coal measure
Coren chest	a corn (grain) chest
Cowme	1. arch or vault, or the frame for making it; 2. coom, sloping part of an attic or ceiling
Creabe, crebb	crib
Cruks	the part of an iron hinge mounted in the wall. On it sits the bands attached to the door
Cueller, culler, coller	cooler; the cooling tray for a brewery
Cuppil	couple, a pair of sloping rafters
Deal, deall, dail, dale	plank
Deans	Danes, as in Danish
Deato	ditto
Dighten	'dighting' or 'dichting', meaning to dress
Dowe	dove, pigeon
Dowhear, dowghtear	daughter
Dram	timber, especially deals, from Drammen in Norway[3]
Duked	doocot, or a dove cot

---

[2] B. F. Duckham, *A History of the Scottish Coal Industry, Vol. I 1700-1815: A Social and Industrial History* (Newton Abbot: David & Charles, 1970), 369.

[3] S. Kjærheim, 'Norwegian Timber Exports in the 18th Century: A Comparison of Port Books and Private Accounts', in *Scandinavian Economic History Review*, 5:2 (1957), 190, and H. Louw and R. Crayford, 'A Constructional History of the Sash-Window, c.1670-c.1725 (Part 2)', in *Architectural History*, 42 (1999), 191.

Eall	ale
Eans	ends
Eansh	inch, as in measurement
Falles	false
Fase bodam	false bottom; a filtration system for brewing
Fatt	vat, used in brewing
Fisherae	Fisherrow, across the River Esk from Musselburgh, East Lothian
Flleak, fleck	a 'flake', or a hurdle or framework of crossed slats; portable fencing
Fllwer, flwer, flwor	floor
Floar	floor
Fut	foot, as in measurement
Fwersday	Thursday
Gabeart	a gabbart, sailing barge
Gang	a gangway, or ramp; scaffolding
Garrat	a garret
Geantreas	gantry, or a wooden frame for holding casks
Gearden	the cooperage process of fastening, or 'girding', with hoops
Geats	gates. See also 'yeats'
Geasts	joists
Ghean, ghene	coal gin; a mechanical device for lifting coal and men out of mine pits
Ghobes	jobs
Girden	the cooperage process of fastening, or 'girding', with hoops
Gistes	joists
Gobes	jobs
Gllearis	glaziers

Hanspeak	a 'handspike', which was one of the wooden levers used by sailors to turn a capstan for hauling in ropes, chains, etc
Heaght	height
Hearp	a 'harp', or a sieve for cleaning grain
Heough	heugh; a ravine, pit or quarry, often related to coal mining
Hus	house
Hwerd	hoard, as in a gathering of materials
Hwrelbarow	wheelbarrow
Keaben	cabin, as on a boat or ship
Kellrebs, keallrebs, kiell ribs	keel ribs or kiln ribs, apparently depending on context (see 'kiel'). Such 'ribs' were timbers making up a framework to give shape to the structure
Keasmeat, keasment	casement windows
Kiel	either 'kiln' or 'keel', depending on context. See 'kill' and 'kellrebs' also
Kill, kiell, kilin	kiln
Kitsin, kittsin	kitchen
Lathe	lathboards, as those used in roofing
Lead	a 'brew leid', or a leaden brewing vessel; a kettle
Leather	a 'ledder', or ladder
Leatrean	latrine, privy
Liead	a mill lade, or a channel for diverting water to power a mill's water wheel
Limber	relating to a drainage system in the bottom of a ship[4]
Loeaft	loft

---

[4] Steffy, 'Illustrated Glossary of Ship and Boat Terms', 'Limber'.

Lowem	'lumes', or tools (eg: a Weaver's loom)
Lowm	lum, a chimney
Marth	March
Masstrothers	a 'mask-ruther', or an implement used in brewing for stirring the malt in a mash tub
Mat	possibly a kind or coarse fabric used in shipbuilding[5]
Measen	a stonemason
Muor	moor or muir
Nauth	beneath, below
Neain	nine
Neascear	necessary
Newtenhae	Newton Hall, Yester Parish, East Lothian[6]
Oc, ock	oak
Ofeas	office
Ows, owes	use
Pall	a post or beam[7]
Pan house	a building housing a salt pan
Pan rouf, pannruf	the roof on the pan house containing the salt pan
Panstand	the supports holding a salt pan within a pan house
Panwand	long pole for raising water with a bucket from a bucket pot
Panwood	the smaller pieces of dross coal which are less marketable, and therefore used to

---

[5] See DSL/DOST: 'Mat, *n.*[1]', 2.a.
[6] Canmore ID: 56109.
[7] See DSL/DOST: 'Pall', 1 and 2.

	make salt; aka 'pan coal' or 'magwood'[8]
Pavellen	the 'Pavilion', which was one of the names used for the Glassworks at Port Seton. *See* Introduction, Figure 2
Peallen	'pealling', or fencing; as in the expression, 'beyond the pale'
Pearten	parting, or splitting
Peartisen, pearttisean	partition
Pillar	a column of coal or rock left in a mine to support the ceiling
Pleatt forem	platform
Pomp	pump
Preas	a press
Preantic	apprentice
Quarter	a part of a ship; as in the term 'quarter deck'
Quoins	wedges used to elevate cannon or to separate casks[9]
Reb	rib
Renges	rings; iron hoops to stop wood from splitting
Rightean	righting, as in correcting or repairing
Roup	auction
Rwem	room
Sarking	a covering of boards, whether on a roof or on something else
Scaften	scaffolding. See also 'caflod'

---

[8] C. A. Whatley, 'A Saltwork and the Community: The Case of Winton, 1716-1719', in *TELAFNS*, 18 (1984), 46 and 52.

[9] I. C. B. Dear and P. Kemp (eds), *The Oxford Companion to Ships and the Sea* (Oxford: Oxford University Press, 2005), 'quoin'.

Sculle	school
Seallor	cellar
Seam	same
Searken, searknet	see 'sarking'
Serking	see 'sarking'
Shade, shad	shed
Sheaf	a 'schefe', or a quantity of timber used as a temporary support
Shot hole	an opening for a 'shot window'
Shot window	small opening in a wall, often with a wooden shutter
Shuen	the act of shoeing a wheel
Siead	side
Skeaper	skipper
Sleoup, sleuop, slloup, sllup, sloup	sloop; a small trading vessel or warship
Speaks	spokes, presumably of wood
Spoute	a channel, pipe or trough (often wooden). Some were for moving sea water from the bucket pot to the salt pan; others for loading coal on ships[10]
Standart	a wooden upright
Starlens	pounds sterling, as opposed to pounds Scots, which continued in use for several decades after the Union of 1707
Stealllen, sttellen	possibly a 'stealer', or a type of planking on boats and ships[11]

---

[10] Whatley, 'A Saltwork and the Community', 49; B1, f27v
[11] Steffy, 'Illustrated Glossary of Ship and Boat Terms', 'stealer' and 'strake'.

Stipston	a 'steepston', or 'steeping stone'; a stone vat for soaking barley during the brewing process
Stoke	stock; cross beam of an anchor
Swipes, swipse	'soups'; planks or strips of wood
Tack	a lease or tenancy
Tacksman	one who holds a tack, or lease; a lessee
Talk	take
Teabl	table
Terles	trellis
Terneant	Tranent, East Lothian
Thwart	a transverse plank on a boat or ship which is used as seating, to support a mast, or to strengthen the structure[12]
Triefish	a 'triffice', or a stall or box in a stable
Trinealls	treenails or trennals: wooden pegs or pins, such as those used to secure mortise and tenon joints, or in shipbuilding
Tris	trees
Trunk	a 'trunk' may refer to: 1. a 'trunk-staithe' or 'trunk-spout', which was a device originating in Newcastle-upon-Tyne, used for depositing coal from a tipped waggon down a wooden chute to a lower level, either at a coastal or inland setting; 2. a short siding linking such a device to the main waggonway[13]
Tune	a tun cask
Tweall	twelve

---

[12] Steffy, 'Illustrated Glossary of Ship and Boat Terms', 'thwart'.
[13] We are grateful to Dr Anthony L. Dawson for his expert advice on possible definitions for this term.

Wadge	to wedge; to repair by filling a gap with materials
Wallpleit, waplleats	a 'wall plate', or a spar of timber attached to either the vertical face of a wall, as a support, or the top of a wall as a fixing point for rafters and joists
Wanscot	wainscot, to line walls with boards generally of oak
Wear hous	warehouse
Wiek	week
Wiring	'wairin', or straps of wood nailed to the ribs of a boat on the inside underneath the gunwales, on which rest the 'thwarts'
Wrack	wreck, as in a shipwreck
Yeat, yet	a 'yett', or a gate. See also 'geats'

INDEX OF PERSONS

Adam, William (architect, grieve and tacksman)	xvii-xviii, xxii, 229
Balvaird (Beveard), Peter (salter)	57, 85, 91
Balvaird (Beweard), R	131
Barclay (Barklley), John (in Seton)	121
Beal, James (ship)	12, 16, 21, 24, 25, 28, 102, 113, 139, 146
Begbie, James	116
Begnet, W	178
Bredwod, James	141
Brotherston, George	139, 141
Brown, James (salter)	78
Brown, Henry	210, 211, 212
Brown, Isobel	82
Buell (Bwell), Mr (in Prestonpans)	200, 201, 204
Burnet, Adam (sawer)	10
Burrows (Boorows), Captain William	205
Cairns (Carens), John	144
Campbell Calander, Lady	223, 224
Ceallen (Cellen), Mr	19, 21
Chaplin (Cheapllean), Sepkaar (ship)	99
Clark (Cleark, Cllark), David	209, 212
Cubey, Barbri (in Prestonpans)	101
Curie, T	28
Currie (Curreth, Curhre, Cwrchre), James	129, 130, 141, 183, 184
Dawson (Dasen), Janet	192, 193
Dickson, Cibilla (Sibllie) (Dickson's daughter)	xxxviii, 122
Dickson, Elizabeth (Dickson's daughter)	xxxviii
Dickson, Jean (Dickson's daughter)	xxxviii
Dickson, Robert (Dickson's father)	xxxviii
Donaldson (Donellson), unnamed salter	73, 75
Donaldson (Donellson), John (salter)	87

Donaldson (Donellson), Robert (salter)　54, 88, 131
Drummore, Sir Hew Dalrymple Lord　218, 219
Farquhar (Forkear), Master (ship)　184, 196
Fletcher of Milton (West Saltoun)　231
Fleuker, C　131
Flockhart, John (writer in Edinburgh)　233
Gakes, Archibald　See Jacks, Archibald
Geallee, Stephan　See Jolly
Ghifear, John　218, 219
Golly, Stephan　See Jolly
Gowan (Gowen, Gown, Gowns), John (timber and malt merchant)　27, 34, 69, 122, 169, 185, 186, 194, 195, 196, 224, 238
Graham (Grame, Gream), Duncan　51, 81
Grant, Adam　70
Grant (Greant), Mr (Sir Archibald Grant)　xviii, 205
Grieg (Greg, Greag), John (salter)　57, 171, 172
Grieg (Grage), W[idow?]　61
Henderson (Heandresen), Sibilla (Seblle) (Dickson's late mother)　xii, xxxviii, 148, 149
Hogg, Mr　197
Hunter (Huntear), Widow (Wid[ow]e) (salter)　161
Hunter (Huntear), Mr (ship)　102
Hutton (Huten), John (ship)　111
Jacks (Gakes), Archibald　172, 173
Jamieson (Jameson, Jamison, Jamson), John　82, 88, 94, 138, 142
Johnston (Jonson), James　54, 82, 127, 128
Jolly (Jollee, Jollie, Jolye, Jolley, Geallee, Golly), Stephan (Stean) (ship)　6, 9, 18, 25, 48, 51, 63, 76, 81, 87, 194
Kinnlie, Robert　xii, 183, 187, 224
McDougall (Mackduckell), Master (ship)　73

Index of Persons

Maknis, George	121
Mathie Family	xviii, xxii, xxvii, xxix, xxxvi, xxxix-xl; *see also* the Mathies listed individually
Mathie, James	21; *see also* Matthews
Mathie, John (ship)	9, 19, 21, 52, 60, 76, 79, 96, 99, 114, 119, 141, 142, 144, 151, 182, 236-8; *see also* Matthews
Mathie, Mr (ship)	111, 149; *see also* Matthews
Mathie, Mrs, senior	236; *see also* Matthew
Mathie, Thomas (Merchant)	28, 152, 234-8; *see also* Matthews
Mathie, Thomas, Younger[1]	171
Mathieson, Alexander (Sanders)	87, 90
Mathieson (Mathisin), (unnamed salter)	55, 61
Matthew, Betty	111; *see also* Mathie
Matthews (Matthow), John	113; *see also* Mathie
Matthews (Matthows), Mr	170; *see also* Mathie
Mealler, Mr (ship)	22
Miller, Patrick	119
Munro (Menro, Menroe), George	142, 147
Nicoll (Nuckell), John, of Prestonpans	220
Paterson, James (blacksmith)	xl, 171, 172, 194, 225
Paterson, James (blacksmith's son, killed on Waggonway in 1762)	xl
Peaterson, Widow	180
Pillan (Pllan), James (Pencaitland)	147
Powe, Harry (Heari)	223, 224
Robert, Thomas	124; *see also* Robertson, Thomas

---

[1] Note: this may be the same man as 'Thomas Mathie, Merchant' who is listed above.

Robertson (Robertsoun, Roberttown), Thomas (Tommy)	127, 128, 134; *see also* Robert, Thomas
Robeson, Ms	192
Sead (Siead), Stephan (ship)	21, 25
Simson, M	194
Smith (Smethe), John	130
Steven (Steavn), John	214
Steven (Steaven), George	164, 165
Thomson (Tomson), Alexander (ship)	60
Tintoo, John	52
Turnbull, William (Merchant in Edinburgh)	235
Wandes, Robert	223, 224
Watson, James (salter)	82
Watson, Nicol (salter)	30, 128
Watson, (unnamed child of Nicol Watson)	128
Watson, William, Writer to the Signet	236
White (Whieitt), Master (ship)	9
Winton, Earls of	xv-xvii, xxxvi
Young, Alexander (sloop)	98
Young (Yonge), Andrew (ship)	12, 18
Young, George (in Fisherrow)	142
Young (Yong), John (ship)	4, 16, 31, 45, 55, 63

INDEX OF PLACES

Aberdour (Abedouer)	208
Aberlady (Ebelaye)	170
Clerkington (Cllarkintun, Cllearkinten)	165
Coalhill, the (Collheal)	72, 73, 75, 85
Coalfald, the (Colfald, Collfald)	xxxvii, 31, 33, 42, 66, 70, 122, 130
Cockenzie (Cokkensie, Cocknesi, Coknsi, Cokkini, Cokkeani, Cokkni)	Introduction, 121, 142, 161, 181, 201, 218, 226, 227-8, 232-6
Close, the (Closs, Cllos)	15, 16, 19, 21, 28, 54, 58, 78, 94, 102, 104, 105, 107, 113, 114, 119, 172, 173, 177, 182, 183, 184, 196, 197, 198, 200
Coalfald (Colfald, Collfald)	xxxvii, 31, 33, 42, 66, 70, 122, 130
Saltgirnell	52
Sawing Shed	196
Wright Workhouse	58, 67
Cockenzie House (the House)	xxxi, xxxvi-xxxvii, 4, 16, 27, 30, 34, 43, 45, 46, 52, 58, 64, 69, 76, 78, 79, 82, 84, 104, 111, 113, 119, 124, 127, 179, 184, 202, 210, 232-4
Bowling green	232-4
Brewery	232-4
Byres	232-4
Court yard	232-4
Gardens	232-4
Garret	6, 43, 94, 104, 116
Green Room	82, 84

Hay loft	232-4
Kitchen	69, 84, 232-4
Maltings	232-4
Nursery	57, 58, 66, 79, 81
Stables	232-4
Washing green and house	232-4
Well	232-4
Dalkeith (Dullkith)	161
Drummohr (Dromor, Drummore) House, near Musselburgh, East Lothian	xxxvi, 218
Edinburgh	108, 232-8
John's Coffee House	233
Fife (Fieff)	51, 208
Fisherrow (Fisherae)	142
Gilmerton (Gellmerten)	144
Humbie Wood	164
Huxton (Huxtan, Huxstone, Hukston)	102, 108, 168
John's Coffee House, Edinburgh	233
Milton (Millton) (near West Saltoun, East Lothian)	48
Musselburgh (Musellbrough)	199; *see also* Fisherrow
Newton Hall (Nowtenhae) (Yester Parish, East Lothian)	211
Pencaitland (Pencatlen, Pencatllen)	147, 165
Pickletillum, near Kirkcaldy	51
Port Seton	88, 90, 91, 179, 194, 234-5
Pot House, the	222
Prestonpans (Perstonpans, the pans)[2]	Introduction, 101, 104, 105, 108, 110, 111, 128, 131, 134, 171, 177, 181, 182, 200,

---

[2] While 'the pans' is used frequently, only on B1, f24r, p73, can we be certain that it refers to Prestonpans, as it notes an individual's house as being in 'the pans'.

INDEX OF PLACES

	204 ('the pans'), 220, 225, 233, 236-8
Customs House	233, 236
Saltgirnell	171
St Germains	168
Seton	10, 79, 121, 206
Seton Park	79
Seaameowr House	119
Tranent (Terneant, Ternent)	Introduction, 28, 136, 142, 210, 227-9
Heugh, the (Heough, Howgh)	xv-xvii, xxxiv, 28, 34, 229-30
Tranent Moor	10

INDEX OF SUBJECTS

Accounts	xi-xiii, 12, 27, 42, 49, 61, 78, 85, 94, 98, 161, 165, 200, 204, 207, 223, 224
Clearing of	xii-xiii; 27, 98, 165, 204, 213
Ale	121
Anchor stock	116, 117
Apprentices (preantes, preantic, preants)	xxxix, 31, 33
Ash	*See* timber
Bands	30, 34, 37, 39, 46, 58, 130, 176, 200, 202, 204, 212; *see also* catbands
Barns (baren)	xxx, xxxvii, 6, 34, 66, 70, 125, 167, 169, 199, 202, 204, 224
Coalfald barn	66, 70
Malt (John Gowns' malt barn)	xxx, 169, 224; *see also* girnels
Barque	*See* ships and shipbuilding
Beds (bead)	4, 7, 15, 39, 57, 58, 81, 96, 111, 125, 138, 180, 223
Bed doors	125
Bed stead	81
Bed stoup (post)	223
Beech wood	*See* timber
Bere (barley)	*See* grain and malt
Boan (bown) (outhouse or lean-to)	96
Malt boans	96
Boards	*See* timber
Bolts (bowts)	192
Bowling green	233
Boxes (bocks, boks, buste)	7, 9, 12, 25, 27, 39, 88, 124, 125, 127, 133, 134, 234-5
Buist	133

For glass	88
For sash windows	39
Harp box	9, 124, 134
Hearth box	7
Of glass	234-5
Spout box	125, 127
Brewing and breweries (browari)	xxix-xxxi, xxxvii, 19, 46, 82, 107, 110, 111, 124, 134, 167, 177, 181, 182, 184, 199, 204, 232-3
Brew house	19, 46, 82, 107, 124, 134, 167, 181, 182, 184, 199, 204
Brew lumes (breowen lowems)	204
Cooler (cueller, culler, coller)	104, 107, 110
Copper	46, 48, 108
Crib (creabe, crebb) (for holding a brewing copper)	46, 108
False bottom (falls bodem, fase bodam)	28, 46
Mashing vat (fatt)	28, 45, 46, 48, 182
Mask-ruther (masstrothers) (for stirring the mash)	22
Prestonpans	110, 111, 177, 181, 182
Sled	177
Steeping stones (stipston, step stane)	125, 133, 169, 201
Trellis	19
	See also kiln, malt
Bucket pots	88
Bukdellen	*See* timber
Bunkers	3, 12, 28
Butter	119
Calender	*See* fabric, cloth
Carts (caeart, ceartt, keart)	4, 9, 21, 28, 45, 49, 58, 124, 134, 165, 202

Axle tree	4, 9, 21, 45, 124, 134
Close carts	28, 58, 124, 134, 202
Long cart	49
Salt carts	49, 165

See also sleds, waggons, wheelbarrows, wheels and wheelwrights

Catbands	91, 130
Chamomile seat	28
Chest of drawers	28
Chests (chiest)	28, 55, 171
Chimneys and chimney head (chimlihead), lum	28, 30, 49, 78, 222
Closes (closs, cllos)	15, 16, 19, 21, 28, 54, 58, 78, 94, 102, 104, 105, 107, 113, 114, 119, 172, 173, 177, 182, 183, 184, 196, 197, 198, 200
Closet (clloset)	25, 28, 52, 169, 233
Cloth	*See* calender, fabric, cloth
Coal (coll)	xiv-xxi, xxxiv, xxxvii, 84, 227-31
Coal bucket (collbaket)	46, 49, 55, 57, 85, 130
Coal corf (collcorf)	70, 73, 76
Coalfald (colfald, collfald, collfolld)	xxxvii, 31, 33, 42, 66, 70, 91, 122, 130
Coal hill (collheal)	72, 73, 75, 85
Coal-mett (collmeat)	46, 130
Spouts for loading coal on ships	84

See also heugh, mines and mining, panwood, pillars

Coffins	xxxi, 192, 193; *see also* undertaking
Coom, cowme	4, 90, 91, 124
Coopering and cooperage	
Girding (with hoops)	46, 108
Tun	108
Coppersmith	108
Corn chest	55; *see also* grain

Index of Subjects

Cornice	39
Couples (roofing)	31, 52, 66, 75, 85, 90, 110, 218, 219, 224
Crib (creabe, crebb) (for holding a brewing copper)	46, 108
Cudell (meaning uncertain)	99
Danes, Danish (Deans, Dain)	xxvii, xxxii, 22, 52, 58, 88, 169, 170, 171, 172, 178, 179
Doors (dor, dorr, dore)	39, 72, 101, 116, 125, 133, 167, 169, 172, 178, 179, 181, 182, 184
Bed doors	125
Lifting doors in kiln floors	125, 133, 178
Sash doors	179
Waggon doors	72
Dove (dowe)	169, 170
Dovecot, doocot (dukit, duked, dowset)	34, 169, 170, 176
Dyke metals (mining)	230
Fabric, cloth	21, 117
Calender	12
Dyed	117
Matting	21
Plaiding	117
Serge	117
Fair, the Cockenzie	xxxiii, 134, 180
Flakes (flleak, fleck)	125, 127, 171
Flooring (floar, fluring, fllwer, flwer, flwor)	15, 51, 75, 116, 125, 133, 169, 225
Gantries (Geantreas)	21, 182
Gardens	233, 235
Garrets	6, 43, 94, 104, 116
Gates (geats, yeats, yett)	31, 34, 84, 90, 91, 93, 125, 127, 130, 131, 133, 171, 233

Flake gates	125, 127, 171
Gin (mechanism) (ghean, ghene)	xvii, xxxiv, xxxix, 10; see also Burnet, Adam
Girnells	See salt
Glass (glleas)	xxv-xxvi, 88, 234-5
Glasshouse (gleashous, glleashous, glleshous)	xv, xxv-xxvi, 93, 94, 234-5
Glaziers	88
	See also Pavilion
Grain	
Bere (barley)	199
Corn	55, 233
	See also corn chest, harp, malt, meal
Handspike (hanspeak)	7; see also ships
Harbour (herbour, hearbour, hearbre, hearbur, hearbrie)	xv-xvi, xix, xxviii, xxxiii-xxxiv, xxxvii, xl, 7, 18, 27, 28, 33, 43, 46, 49, 52, 57, 58, 60, 69, 73, 84, 85, 93, 94, 99, 111, 160, 183, 186, 187, 188, 189, 190, 191, 199, 209, 233
Spouts for loading coal on ships	84
Harp (hearp)	9, 85, 124, 134, 177
Harp box	9
Hay	233
Heughs (heough, howgh)	xv-xvii, xxxiv, 28, 34, 229-30
Iron (aren)	34, 72, 192
Jacobite Uprising, 1715	xvii, xxxvi,
Joists (geasts, gistes)	73, 75, 90, 174, 175
Keel	See ships
Kielriebs, kiell ribs[3]	98, 202

---

[3] The meaning of these instances is unclear, so they have been separated out from the ship-related 'Keel' and malt-related 'Kiln' entries, which use the same spelling.

Index of Subjects

Kiln (kill, kiell, kilin, kell, keell, keal)	xxx-xxxi, 4, 6, 18, 19, 22, 27, 113, 125, 133, 171, 174, 178, 179, 180, 184, 196, 198, 204
Kiln ribs (kiell riebs, kellrebs, kill ribs)	125, 133, 174, 178, 179, 184, 196, 204
Lifting doors in kiln floors	125, 133, 178
	See also grain, malt and maltings
Kitchen (kitsin kittsin)	69, 84, 232-3
Ladders (leather)	19, 63
Lath (laith)	34, 66, 82, 110, 125, 127, 128, 133, 167, 168, 169, 172, 176, 183, 184, 199, 202, 218, 219, 224; *see also* plaster
Latrines (leatrean)	22, 24, 34, 37
Locks	27, 40, 182
Lofts (loeaft)	9, 19, 54, 57, 98, 101, 110, 141, 174, 184, 198, 199, 233
Bere (barley)	199
Hay	233
Malt	98, 110, 184, 198, 199
Meal	9
Wright (lofte)	57
	See also grain, malt and maltings
Looms, lumes (lowem)	204
Lum	*See* chimney
Malt and maltings	xxvii, xxix-xxxi, xxxvii, 96, 98, 99, 110, 169, 171, 177, 184, 198, 199, 224, 232-3, 235-6
Malt barn	169, 224
Malt kiln	*See* kiln
Malt loft	98, 110, 184, 198, 199

Malt ship	177, 199
	See also boan, grain, kiln, lofts
Manger	45; see also stables, triffice
Masons (stonemasons) (measen)	6, 28, 36, 49, 73, 90, 91, 93, 200, 222
Coom, cowme	4, 90, 91, 124
Traces (templates) (treases)	28, 73, 90
Measurement	
Fathoms	229-30
Feet, foot (fott, fote, fut)	3, 117, 119, 121, 131, 136, 142; 149, 160, 185, 186, 187, 194, 195, 196, 223, 224, 231
Inches (ensh, eansh)	3, 117, 131, 136, 149, 160
Meal	9, 87, 167
Mills: ark; lade	45
Mines and mining	xiv-xix, 227-32
Pillars	227-9
Pit, pithead (pithied)	xv-xvi, xvii, xix, xxxiv, 130, 229-31
	See also coal, gin, heughs (heough, howgh)
Model	96
Muir, moor (muor)	10
Newspapers	
Caledonian Mercury	232-6
Oak	See timber
Paling (peallen)	79, 98, 111
Panwood	See salt
Parting (pearten) (splitting)	xxxiii, 28, 31, 79
Partition (peartisen, pearttisean, peartision)	15, 57, 70, 84, 99, 124
Pavilion, the (Pavillion, Pavellen)	xv, xxv-xxvi, 93, 234-5; see also glasshouse
Plaster	125, 133, 183, 184; see also lath
Pot house	222

Index of Subjects

Press (preas) (cupboard)	25, 40, 66, 94
Proclamation week	147
Pumps	
For ships	12, 114
For salt pans	88
Tap tree, trie	88
Rings (renges)	116
Roofs	82, 88, 93, 169, 201, 215, 216, 224
Couples (cupels, cupels, cupealls)	31, 52, 66, 75, 85, 90, 218, 219, 224
Roup	227-34
Salt	xiv-xxv, xl-xlii
Bucket pots	88
Panstands	30, 31, 45, 51, 61, 84, 85, 87, 207
Panwands	88
Panwood	xvi, 42
Pickletillum pan, near Kirkcaldy	51
Pump	88
Salt carts	49, 165
Salt girnells	52, 171
Saltpans (salt pans)	xvi-xvii, xxiv-xxv, xxxiv, xl, 42, 43, 51, 55, 75, 78, 138
Saltworks	xvi-xviii, xxi, xxiv-xxv, 57, 70, 72, 73, 75, 78, 82, 85, 87, 90, 91, 131, 161, 162, 163, 165, 207, 208, 209, 212, 214, 215, 216, 217, 227-8
Spout (spoute)	30, 51, 54, 55, 84, 104, 217
Tap tree	88
See also Cockenzie, Pickletillum and Prestonpans	
Sarking (serking, searken, searknet)	52, 128, 167
Sawing (sawen)	xx-xxi, xxxiii-xxxiv, xxxvi, 7, 10, 15, 18, 27, 34, 36,

	42, 48, 52, 57, 60, 61, 63, 64, 66, 67, 69, 82, 107, 122, 124, 127, 128, 130, 139, 142, 147, 162, 163, 164, 165, 167, 168, 172, 173, 186, 187, 190, 191, 196, 200, 202, 204, 205, 206, 207, 209, 210, 212, 213, 214, 215, 216, 217, 218, 220
Sawing shed	196
Scaffolding (scafellt, scafelld, scaften, caffolden, caflod, cafflod)	6, 48, 49, 73, 82, 93, 200, 222
Cleated	82
Gangway	46, 60, 73, 84, 90, 136
School (sculle)	174
Sheds (shade, shad, shead)	42, 105, 134, 168, 169, 171, 177, 184, 196, 236
Sawing shed	196
Swine shed	105
Shelves (cheallf, chellef)	39, 142, 169
Ships and shipbuilding (shep, sheap, sheep)	xxvii–xxix, xxxii, xxxix, xl, 3, 4, 7, 9, 12, 18, 21, 22, 48, 51, 52, 57, 60, 61, 63, 76, 79, 84, 87, 88, 96, 99, 102, 111, 113, 114, 138, 141, 142, 144, 146, 151, 152, 167, 169, 170, 171, 172, 177, 179, 184, 188, 193, 194, 196, 199
Anchors	116, 117
Barque (bark)	4, 7, 27
Beatte, the (sloop)	57
Cabins (caben, keaben)	3, 18, 19, 138, 139

Danish (Deans, Dain)	xxvii, xxxii, 22, 52, 58, 88, 169, 170, 172, 179
Gabert (gabearts)	78
Handspike (hanspeak)	7
Hold (howelld, howld)	4, 144
Keels (kiel)	4, 7, 9, 16, 98, 99
Keel ribs (kiellriebs,[4] kellrebs)	9, 98, 99
Knights	116
Malt ship	177, 199
Pawl (pall)	116
Pumps, pump walls	12, 114
Quarter	7, 114
Quoins (coines)	113
Skipper (skeaper)	6, 111, 236-7
Sloop (slupe, slloup, sllup, sloup, slupe, sleoup, sleuop)	57, 69, 98, 99, 113, 114, 116, 167, 171, 176, 199
Stealers (stealllen, sttellen)	12, 21, 99, 102, 111, 144
Windlass	116
Wairin (wiring)	114
Ship wrecks	xxviii, xxxi-xxxii, 136, 199
Shoes (shues)	121
Shop (cheop, chop)	162, 206, 210, 212, 235
Shovels (shoells)	39
Sleds (slead)	127, 177
Sloop	*See* ships and shipbuilding
Smithy (blacksmith's shop and forge) (smidie, smidey, smiddey)	xxxvii, xl, 171, 174, 175
Stables (stabel, steabel)	54, 104, 182, 233, 236
	See also manger, triffice
Sterling (pounds)	128, 234
Steeping stones (stipston, step stane)	125, 133, 169, 201
Table (teabl, teabell, tabell)	22, 27, 40, 138
Winged table	22

---

[4] The spelling 'kiel' is also used for kiln ribs, but these ones are clearly ship-related. See 'Kiellriebs' for instances where the type is unclear.

Tack and tacksman	xxi-xxii, 227-31
Timber	xxxi-xxxiv, *passim*
Ash (aseth, aeis)	28, 211, 212
Beech (bitch)	173
Boards (brods, broods)	4, 6, 34, 78, 113, 125, 133, 167, 169, 176, 180, 202, 204, 210
Buk-denning (bugkdailin, bukdellen, bukdeallan, buckdellen, bukdllen, buk dellen)	3, 9, 25, 43, 48, 55, 57, 60, 61, 69, 73, 87, 98, 99, 142, 144, 152, 167, 171, 176
Deals (deall, dail)	6, 15, 19, 21, 22, 25, 27, 28, 30, 31, 34, 36, 42, 45, 51, 52, 57, 58, 61, 63, 64, 66, 67, 69, 76, 78, 79, 81, 88, 94, 96, 102, 107, 108, 113, 114, 119, 121, 124, 131, 133, 134, 135, 136, 139, 142, 147, 168, 169, 170, 172, 177, 178, 184, 185, 194, 195, 196, 207, 214, 217, 218, 220, 223, 224
Dram deals	135, 136
Lath (laith)	34, 66, 82, 110, 125, 127, 128, 133, 167, 168, 169, 172, 176, 183, 184, 199, 202, 204, 218, 224; *see also* plaster
Oak (oc, ock)	205, 209, 210, 212, 214, 215, 216, 217, 231
Plane	206
Planks	136, 173, 187
Schefe (sheaf)	138
Soups (swipse, swipes)	128
Standards (standert)	21

Stockhollen deals	135, 136
Treenails (trinealls)	141
Trees (treais, tries, tris)	xxxii-xxxiv, 9, 15, 52, 58, 79, 119, 131, 160, 172, 185, 186, 187, 190, 196, 204, 206, 224
Wainscot (wanscot, wancot)	136, 194
White (whit) wood	196, 224
Wreck (reclaimed timber from shipwrecks)	xxxi-xxxii, 136
	See also parting, sawing
Trellis	19
Triffice (triefish)	45; *see also* manger, stables
Trunks	31, 42, 227-8, 231
Undertaking	xxxi, 192, 193; *see also* coffins
Waggons (wagens, wagon)	xx, 34, 48, 58, 61, 66, 67, 69, 72, 162, 164, 165, 206, 208, 212, 214, 227-9, 231
Waggon doors	72
Waggon wheels	48, 162, 164, 165, 206, 208, 212
Wagonway (wagenway, wagen way)	Introduction, 24, 33, 60, 61, 63, 64, 66, 67, 69, 70, 72, 130, 163, 164, 210, 213, 227-9, 231
Wall plate (wallpleit, waplleats)	6, 19
Warehouse (wear hous, wearhous)	24, 87, 236
Washing green	233
Water cistern (water cestren)	197
Wheelbarrows (wheall barows, whell barows, whillbarows, hwrelbarow, hwerll barrows, close barrows)	4, 31, 33, 49, 51, 58, 72, 87, 153, 161, 167, 207, 209

Wheels and wheelwrighting (wheall, whell)	12, 48, 49, 124, 134, 162, 163, 164, 165, 206, 208, 212
Cart wheels	124, 134
Salt-cart wheels	49
Shoeing (showen, shuen)	124, 134
Waggon wheels	48, 162, 164, 165, 206, 208, 212
See also carts, waggons, waggonway, wheelbarrows	
Widows	61, 161, 180
Windows (wondow, wendow)	6, 30, 34, 36, 39, 43, 67, 69, 81, 84, 93, 101, 113, 117, 119, 125, 133, 138, 149, 167, 169, 174, 175, 176, 178, 180, 182, 200, 202, 204, 209, 210, 234
Casement (keasmeat, keasment)	30, 104, 117, 119, 182, 204, 209
Garret	6, 43
Sash (sase, cheas, ches)	39, 93, 119, 179, 180, 204
Shot hole	34
Storm	67
Workhouse (warkhouse)	58, 67
Yetts	*See* gates
York Buildings Company	xiv, xvi-xvii, xx, 205, 227-8, 232

Cuttle

Flint M.

Morrisons Haven
Rocks
Mill
Pottery
Bathing house
Pottery
Prefton Grange
Lady Hy

Ravens Haugh
Pofs
Mile Stone
Coal Waste
Barn
Clinking gate

West Pans
Road
Drummore Capt Findlay
Upp. Toll
Dolphingst

inks
Mile Stone
Beggars bush
Goshan
Pinky Burn
Dolphingston Loch

House
Hope
urgh
Pinky Mains
Dolphingston Mains

Walkford Findlay Esq.

Road from Dalkieth
Mains
Fountain head

St Clements Wells Distillery